DATE			

COPING WITH CAPITALISM:

THE ECONOMIC TRANSFORMATION OF THE UNITED STATES, 1776-1980

Roger L. Ransom
University of California–Riverside

PRENTICE-HALL, INC., Englewood Cliffs, New Jersey 07632

Library of Congress Cataloging in Publication Data

RANSOM, ROGER L   (date)
  Coping with capitalism.

  Bibliography: p.
  Includes index.
  1. United States—Economic conditions. I. Title.
HC103.R32   330.973   80-21310
ISBN 0-13-172288-3

to my father,
whose enthusiasm and entrepreneurial spirit
enabled him to cope so effectively with the
changes of the last 50 years

to my mother,
who, in addition to everything else,
coped with my father

© 1981 by Prentice-Hall, Inc., Englewood Cliffs, N.J. 07632

Printed in the United States of America

10 9 8 7 6 5 4 3 2 1

Editorial/production supervision
and interior design by Lori E. Wieseneck
Cover design by Infield/D'Astolfo Associates
Manufacturing buyer: Gordon Osbourne

Prentice-Hall International, Inc., London
Prentice-Hall of Australia Pty. Limited, Sydney
Prentice-Hall of Canada, Ltd., Toronto
Prentice-Hall of India Private Limited, New Delhi
Prentice-Hall of Japan, Inc., Tokyo
Prentice-Hall of Southeast Asia Pte. Ltd., Singapore
Whitehall Books Limited, Wellington, New Zealand

CONTENTS

PREFACE

The ideas and themes that are outlined in this book are the product of twenty years of trying to explain the economic process of American society to students in introductory courses in economics and economic history. As a teacher of both economics and history, I have always been dismayed by the degree to which the two disciplines are separated. Economists tend to be too preoccupied with their theories to devote enough attention to history, and historians seem similarly reluctant to devote enough attention to the economic theory that might assist in explaining the historical development of our economic system.

Since I am myself an economist by training (that is, I pursued my graduate studies in a department of economics), I will not presume to assess the magnitude of the losses that this gulf between economics and history imposes on students of history. I can, however, attest to the void that is created by the paucity of history in the study of economics. It is my contention that we are entering a period when, more than ever before, it is imperative to understand the historical roots of the institutional setting that governs our economic activity. The past fifty years have been ones of unprecedented change. If we are to make sense of our current economic problems, we must gain a better understanding of the economic and social changes that have swept over our economic system since the outset of the Great Depression. For better or for worse, American capitalism today is not the same economic system that existed in 1933 when Franklin Roosevelt launched his "New Deal." It is not even the same system that existed when John Kennedy called for a "New Frontier" in 1960. Yet the events and decisions that occurred during the administrations of Roosevelt and Kennedy helped shape the situation we have today.

The process of economic change in the United States is the focus of this book. Because that process has not always proceeded at a steady pace, we will concentrate our attention on certain periods in which significant reforms were introduced—though not always accepted—into the economic system. The methodology I employ is that of an economic historian who wishes to illustrate how blending economics and history can shed light on the ways in which economic activity both shapes, and is shaped by, the institutional framework of our society.

Since I was trained as an economist, and since economists (as I note in chapter one, the introduction to this book) have a singular preoccupation with "models" of behavior, the temptation to construct such a model of economic change was overpowering. Hence arose chapter two. But that dream, as the reader will quickly see, proved illusory, and what emerged instead was a discussion of the process of economic change and some of the more obvious economic relationships it involves. Since I was concerned with melding economics and history, I chose to examine several periods of American development with regard to that change. Hence arose chapters three, four, and five, which touch upon four periods when the pressures for change in the institutional framework of our economy were particularly severe. Finally, since I was concerned with the implications of all this on contemporary economic problems, I could not resist making some comments on those problems, viewed from an historical perspective. Hence arose chapters six and seven.

In any work of this sort, the whole is equal to much less than the sum of the parts. I have liberally drawn on the ideas of others throughout this book. Though I have indicated those cases in which I used some specific work of an author, I am indebted to many people who are not adequately recognized in the notes or text of the book.

Foremost among these are my students. For two decades now they have, with their questions and responses to my questions, forced me to rethink ideas, made me search for better ways to express my thoughts, and insisted that I place my narrow economic ideas in some broader framework. Most of them were probably not even aware that they were doing this; they were simply trying to find some way to get through the final (or comprehensive) exams. I thank them all.

I also have accumulated some more specific debts in preparing this manuscript. Professors Michael Moore of Bowling Green State University and Robert Craig West of Drake University each provided detailed and insightful criticisms which (I hope) substantially improved the manuscript. My erstwhile colleague at the University of California at Riverside, E. Kay Hunt, provided an exchange of ideas over many years which helped me to develop the themes expressed in the book. I benefited from the suggestions offered by Howard Sherman and Nai Pew Ong, who read early drafts of the manuscript. Finally, it has been my good fortune over the past decade to work closely with Richard Sutch of the University of California at Berkeley. Though he had very little to do directly with the writing of this book, Richard's influence surfaces in many places and in many ways. It was our work together on the postbellum South that first shaped many of the thoughts on institutional change which appear in this volume.

I have two very personal thanks to extend: to my brother, David, who constructed the "word processing machine" on which my manuscript was written; and to my wife, Connie, who never lost faith that my "BIP" (Book In Progress) would someday progress to the point of publication.

I will close this preface with a word to the reader about the style of the book. In its initial version, the text of the book was drafted from lecture notes. In an effort to retain the flow of ideas presented in those lectures, I have suppressed the urge to reproduce the many charts, tables, and graphs which are the staple diet of economists and economic historians alike. I hope the result will be a more readable book, a book which both economists and lay people can enjoy.

Roger L. Ransom

INTRODUCTION

There appears to be an increasing interest in the "dismal science" of economics lately. That is not surprising; a significant part of our lives is taken up by economic matters. Every day, Americans are bombarded with economic analyses in the morning papers, in the evening newscasts, in the weekly magazines. National economic policy, which has been front page news for years, has been joined—and often even pushed aside—by state and local economic news. The inside pages are filled with advice on how consumers and investors can best cope with the economic situation in our complex modern society. Even the sports pages have become filled with discussions involving the economics of tax shelters, deferred bonuses, and the capital improvements required to ensure the continued presence of the local football or baseball franchise.

Whether we like it or not, the economic system determines most of the choices available to us. It would be nice to understand a system that so permeates our day-to-day existence. Ironically, at the very moment when people are eager to hear what economists have to say, economists themselves are becoming less and less certain about what to say. This has not led them to say less. It has, however, created a situation in which both the producers and the consumers of economic theory are becoming more and more dissatisfied (or at least increasingly uncomfortable) with the existing explanations of our contemporary economic problems.

Economics as an academic discipline is almost exactly two hundred years old. During that period, economists have struggled—with mixed success—to provide insights into contemporary economic and social problems. The cumulative effect of these efforts has been to develop several analytical approaches to the study of economic institutions in our society today. Each of the major paradigms which currently are part of the science of economics is constructed around a logical framework which the economists call a "model." The assumptions built into these models are intended to reflect the salient features of the economic system in a manner calculated to demonstrate how the system works.

These economic models are, for the most part, deductive in nature. That is, they begin with some highly simplified assumptions about the nature of economic institutions and the behavior of people within that institutional framework, and then proceed to infer some logical consequences of those assumptions. If the economist is so inclined, he may then go back to the "facts" (or "data") to see if the conclusions of the model seem consistent with the results produced by the economic system itself. This testing of the economic model reassures the economist that the theory does (or does not) provide results that are a close enough approximation to the real world.

This approach has proven fruitful in producing insights into how various economies—particularly market economies—function. Working from a very abstract picture of the institutional framework and the way people behave, economists have been able to explain how the market system allocates resources and distributes income. They have also developed some important implications of how market behavior will affect not only the economic system, but other aspects of our society as well.

Unfortunately, the world is not a simple, abstract concept. It is possible to imagine an almost infinite variety of economic "models" which reflect "reality" as viewed by different economists. And the views of reality which economists have incorporated into their models have been varied indeed! This variety in approaches may, in part, account for why economists put forward so many divergent views on just about every subject. Economic models differ in the assumptions they make, the scope they establish for the analysis, and the style in which they present the analysis. To illustrate this variety, we need consider only a few of the possible ways in which economic models differ. Some models focus their attention on decisions made by individual groups (these are called "microeconomic models"); others concern themselves primarily with the outcome of many decisions on an aggregate level (these are called "macroeconomic models"). Some models are presented in a descriptive (or narrative) form; others employ sophisticated mathematical techniques for their exposition. Some models are primarily concerned with establishing the validity of empirical measurements of effects; others look for properties of the economic system which do not lend themselves to empirical measurement. Small wonder that lay persons are convinced that economists are confused. As George Bernard Shaw once noted: "If you laid all the economists in the world end to end, they would not reach a conclusion."

In view of the combinations and permutations of economic models available to explain what is supposedly a single set of problems, even the professional economist is at times hard pressed to recommend one model as "best." Yet amid all this variety there is at least one common thread. Virtually all the economic models built since Adam Smith started all this in 1776 have been formulated with a fixed set of postulates which define the institutional setting and the way people behave. And once this institutional setting is fixed, it is not allowed to change substantially as the story unfolds. As the group of economists who currently represent the dominant view put it, economic analysis is conducted subject to the caveat of *ceteris paribus,* or "other things equal."

Of course, other things do not remain equal over time. Indeed, the very process of economic activity, which is the focus of the economist's model, brings about significant changes in the structure of the economy and of society itself. In other words, change is not something external to the economic system; it is an integral part of the economic system. It is this feedback between the process of economic activity in one period and the institutional arrangements which govern that activity in subsequent periods that confounds the economic "models" predicated on a static institutional framework, making them of limited value in explaining events in an ever-changing world.

This is not to say that economic theory is of no use and should be abandoned altogether. Whatever their shortcomings, contemporary models of the marketplace have proven to be extremely valuable in examining the problem they purport to address: the allocation of scarce resources in a market society. We would be foolish to ignore this usefulness and not incorporate economic theory into our analysis of economic change.

In fact, to a considerable extent, people do behave as the economist presumes: They take their institutional setting as given, and not subject to drastic or sudden changes. However, whether or not they are always aware of it, people are also constantly working to change their institutional environment. New forms of activity, changes in the legal structure, and a myriad of other factors work to gradually alter the economic structure. That change is a *historical* process, a process which, with very rare exception, builds on the existing economic structure. Understanding the institutional environment at any point in time—and the direction of forces working to change that environment—requires a view that incorporates not only economic theory, but historical perspective as well. That is the aim of this book: to examine the process of economic change in the United States, utilizing both economic theory and perspective provided by the historical record. In doing so, I hope to present more than just the cold analysis of how economic forces or historical laws operate. I have tried to capture, at least in a small degree, the frustrations and successes of those who have had to cope with our economic system for the past two hundred years.

2

THE
PROCESS
of ECONOMIC
CHANGE

Among the many challenges which confront every society, none is more pressing than the need to overcome scarcity. Conquering the "economic problem" (as economists have ingeniously labeled it) is vital to the smooth functioning of any social system. Somehow the scarce resources must be mobilized and employed in a manner which produces enough food, clothing, shelter, together with all the other goods and services desired by people. Through most of written history (and undoubtedly through all of unwritten history) there was a pronounced tendency for societies, once they developed a feasible solution to the problem of scarcity, simply to stick with the proven method. As long as it continued to prove a successful way to produce enough output and distribute that output among the members of society, the "traditional" method was likely to experience very little revision over successive generations. Indeed, there was likely to be strong resistance to even the suggestion of change.

This conservatism had a practical basis. Early societies were able to provide for themselves only by the barest of margins—margins which at times disappeared entirely. As a result, there was little room for the errors (and potential losses) that might accompany the trial period in which some new technique was first introduced. The consequences (whether good or bad) from any major "experiments" would affect not only the innovators, but others as well. Not surprisingly, individuals in "primitive" societies were seldom encouraged in any quest for new solutions, and when novel ideas did emerge, they typically consisted merely of revisions in the techniques already in use. Change was rare and seldom very "radical" when it did occur. Nevertheless, even very small changes can eventually produce significant alterations in the institutional arrangements and technology of a society. Towards the end of what we call the "Middle Ages," the economies of Northern Europe had progressed to the point where, in any given year, there was likely to be at least a small surplus which could provide a margin for experimentation.

As the fifteenth century drew to a close, this slow pace of economic growth was suddenly accelerated by the discovery of "new worlds." The potential for experimentation (and possible increases in the surplus available) was greatly expanded by the discovery of new routes to the Orient and the acquisition of territory in Africa and the Americas. The vast, uncharted areas of these new continents promised to free European economies from a dependence on the limited land of their own countries, offering new opportunities to their crowded populations. New resources meant that economic activity could expand, and expand it did. Great colonial empires were carved from virgin lands, or, where a desirable area was already occupied, by wresting land from its former owners by force.

The utilization of these new resources posed problems at the same time as they brought benefits. Europeans discovered that the rapid increase in economic activity which accompanied the development of colonial territories produced strong pressures for economic change. Traditional arrangements, with their reliance on replicating past situations, could not keep pace with the complex pressures that arose from the need to cope with the rapidly changing colonial activities of the sixteenth, seventeenth, and eighteenth centuries.

THE CHANGING ECONOMIC PROBLEM

By the end of the eighteenth century, the economic systems of several Northern European nations had been reorganized into a combination of individual property ownership and a system of market exchange which has come to be called *market capitalism*. In this institutional arrangement, the economic problem is solved through the actions of individual producers and consumers exchanging their products in impersonal marketplaces. Traditional methods of production could only survive if they were able to compete successfully with new alternatives introduced by entrepreneurs who hoped to gain an advantage in the marketplace.

Gradually, it became clear that successful invention brought rewards, rather than the threat of punishment, to those who discovered and introduced them. As a growing share of economic activity came under the influence of these market forces, the pressure for competitive behavior throughout society increased. The three centuries following the discovery of America saw a persistent increase in production and exchange among countries such as Great Britain and her colonies, the Low Countries, and a few other enclaves on the European mainland. These areas developed economies which depended upon the use of money and employed a capitalistic method of production. By the end of the eighteenth century, these economies had reached the threshold of the Industrial Age.

The changes which have occurred in the two hundred years since the American Revolution make the progress of the previous three centuries seem agonizingly slow. The European living in 1500 would have found much that was familiar had he been transported to the Europe of 1775. By contrast, an American of 1775 who was moved forward to the present would feel totally lost. Even if he were able to understand the miracles of present day technical developments, he would still be astounded at the social changes which 200 years of economic change had produced. One of the ironies he might notice would be the extent to which the process that freed people from the uncertainties of eking out a subsistence living with only a few crude tools has left us today entirely dependent upon an impersonal economic system which most of us do not understand and which we seem unable to control. A visitor from two centuries past might ask whether or not increases in economic security had kept pace with increases in physical comforts.

This increased importance of markets for both labor and the fruits of its production has created an interdependence among groups (and individuals) which has necessitated a complete restructuring of social as well as economic institutions. Whether we call it the Industrial Revolution or refer to it as a case of rapid industrial evolution, the transformation of America from the rural, agrarian society of the 1770s to the urban, industrial society of the 1980s involved enormous changes. Just how complete the transformation was can be seen by comparing the situation of the typical American family in 1775 with that of a family of today.

In the late eighteenth century, most families lived on farms which, by modern standards, were quite small. Social contact between families was, for the most part, confined to rather infrequent meetings with people who lived within a vicinity of only a few square miles. A trip of more than twenty miles over the "roads" of that time was a fairly strenuous undertaking for even a single person and horse; any significant baggage or freight greatly impeded the journey. Contact between persons and families did take place, of course. There were occasional community gatherings at church, and town meetings. From time to time some significant social event—a marriage, a funeral, or some special holiday—provided an occasion when news which had been gleaned from various visitors passing through the area could be exchanged, along with the usual local gossip.

The isolation of this life was evident in the economic situation of the family. Apart from the all-important role of the weather, the income of a colonial family depended primarily upon the size of their farm, the quality of their land, and the labor available from the family members living on the farm. The diet was monotonous, consisting of cereal, corn, and whatever fresh vegetables could be grown on the farm. The limited supplies of meat from animals slaughtered in the fall or spring might be supplemented from time to time by wild game or fish caught nearby, but, as areas became more settled, such opportunities became increasingly limited. Most of the utensils in the house and around the farm were made on the premises, as were all but the fanciest of clothes. Life on a colonial farm—and nine out of ten colonists lived on farms—was largely free from influences other than the forces of nature. In a normal year the bulk of the family's labor effort would go simply to maintain their modest material comforts. In a good year there would be a greater abundance of food and an opportunity to improve their situation; in a bad year the meals were smaller and more monotonous, clothes would be worn for an extra season, and any thoughts of luxuries had to be put aside.

Small though it was, the surplus wrung from the farm was important. It provided the family with the means to trade for those items which had to be purchased rather than made on the farm. Some of these were necessities such as salt, spices, gunpowder, and a few metal utensils; others were luxuries such as fine-spun cloth, tailored clothes or shoes, books, tobacco, and jewelry. Shopping trips more often involved a visit to the farm by some itinerant peddler selling his wares than a trip to the nearest village store by the farmer or his family. Still, the gains from trade were evident enough that most farmers were induced to expand production in the hope of increasing the surplus for the next year. Rudimentary though they were in colonial times, markets for farm products offered a strong enticement not only to increase production generally, but to concentrate on the most marketable crops. From the earliest years of settlement to the present, the American farmer had an eye on the market prices of his farm produce. The small surpluses of colonial times were the forerunners of the huge cash crops harvested on farms today.

The bleak existence of rural life in colonial America should not obscure the fact that, compared to most people in the eighteenth century, American colonists were extremely well-off. Our typical family enjoyed a diet and material comforts shared by very few in the world at that time. Yet, judged by conditions in contemporary America, their standard of living seems almost primitive. In terms of our present concept of income, it is doubtful that the average colonial family received more than $1,500, and it was denied such modern necessities as indoor plumbing and electricity. Commonplace luxuries of today, such as automobiles and television, were not even imagined back in 1775.

Obviously, any comparison of income which spans 200 years will reveal little more than an order of magnitude of the differences between the two eras. Colonial farm output, valued at prices of the time, was probably not much more than $75 per capita, so a farm family of five would have produced about $375 in cash output. To this must be added the value of any home production of items, and the rent of the farmhouse(s). Prices since 1775 have risen considerably for those few items (food, clothing, and shelter) that still comprise a common basis for comparison in both periods. But, of course, both the quality and range of items available to people have also vastly increased. Hence my "guestimate" that a colonial living would be equivalent to about $1,500 today is only a very rough approximation of the change in economic well-being between 1775 and the present. Notwithstanding these difficulties, the order of magnitude revealed by my calculation indicates an enormous increase in economic welfare. By this accounting, a family in the United States today receives about ten times as much income on the average as did our colonial stereotype.

That, of course, is only the most obvious change in the situation of the typical American family. In 1975 the median family income in the United States was just under $14,000. In contrast to the colonists, only one out of four families today live in what can be termed a rural setting. (Colonists might have trouble understanding our definition, since a town of 5,000 inhabitants was an urban environment to them.) The colonist would be even more dumbfounded to discover that eight out of ten families today reside in a city of at least 50,000 people—or about twice the population of New York during the late colonial period. In contrast to earlier times, the modern family depends on an income earned as wages for their support. Shopping trips today are hardly a luxury; Americans purchase all of their needs—luxuries as well as necessities—at the local shopping center. The variety of goods offered there, and the means with which to purchase these goods and services, would stagger the imagination of any colonist. Furthermore, this increase in material well-being—vast though it is—still pales in comparison to the total increase in general welfare. Improvements in diet and medicine have greatly extended the life expectancy of the average American.

But to focus on this well-known result of economic progress is to miss a major portion of the entire picture. Not all of the changes that have occurred have proven favorable to individual welfare. In the world of colonial America, with farms scattered over the landscape, the actions of one family seldom affected others. But in contemporary society, as people press closer and closer together in cities (which in turn seem to be pressing closer to one another as the suburbs of one city run into those of another nearby), it becomes more and more the case that one person's actions directly affect his neighbors. Life is not as simple as it used to be.

Market systems create other interdependencies as well. Individuals are confronted with some very direct economic relationships which cause us to depend on one another in an impersonal way. Virtually everyone who lives in America today relies on the smooth operation of markets to provide their income and to make available the goods and services that income will purchase. A sudden (and, from the standpoint of a single person, wholly uncontrollable) shift in the demand for labor can cut off a family's income and wipe out much of its wealth. Consumers are, to be sure, free to shop around for the best buy in most transactions. Yet, for the vast bulk of purchases made by individual consumers, the desires of a single purchaser have little or no effect on the price offered by the seller. The same is true for people seeking jobs; they accept or reject the wage offered. It may be true that (as economists constantly remind us) individual decisions on whether or not to work for the wage offered, or whether or not to buy the product at the quoted price, will eventually produce cumulative effects on wages and prices. But such effects are seldom obvious to the person whose job has been terminated because of a deterioration of the economic situation, or to a consumer who insists that the price of meat is too high. Unemployment and inflation are such frustrating problems in our modern society precisely because individuals can, at best, only react to a situation over which they have no control. Our material well-being (and perhaps our peace of mind as well) is governed by the need to cope with *market forces.*

When things are moving smoothly, our dependence on markets does not trouble us; indeed, we welcome the chance to pass on to others those tasks which we are either unable (or unwilling) to perform ourselves. But when things are not moving smoothly, the extent of our dependence on outside forces is brought home with particular force. While modern Americans enjoy the enormous advantages afforded by specialization and the market system, they have lost a large measure of the economic independence their ancestors enjoyed.

Perhaps that is a trade-off most of us would freely choose even if we thought about it. The "good old days" always seem good partly because they are old. But there is still another way in which industrial society affects our freedom to determine our own fortunes. The process of industrialization acts to greatly concentrate economic power in the hands of those who direct the process of production. There is little assurance that this economic power will necessarily be wielded for the good of society rather than for private gain. When the power to control production is concentrated, the competitive pressures which are supposed to check abuse of economic power are greately diminished. Markets can be manipulated to the advantage of the controlling group, and such a group is likely to accrue these gains at the expense of others. Nor is the issue simply one of monopoly distortion through pricing; economic power can be employed in more subtle ways to obtain or enlarge market advantages which favor a single group of producers.

As long as economic power was diffused, markets worked well. But the market institutions which proved so successful in continuously expanding industrial production have been less successful in dealing with the consequences of the revolution they set in motion. Just as there is more to life than simply earning a living, so are there challenges to society besides just overcoming the problem of scarcity. The success of market organization in generating an improved level of material welfare at a time when the burden of simply making ends meet was the overriding concern of society helps to explain why those institutions that deal with the economic problem have played such a dominant role in fashioning change in our society. That success has also been an important force pressing for control of market forces since late in the nineteenth century.

It is important to note at this point that much of the change we are discussing was the result, not of a few large and sudden disturbances, but of small changes whose effects cumulated over a period of years. As our comparison of the way of life in 1775 and 1975 showed, the effects of even a small annual rate of increase can be enormous over a long period of time. If, for example, aggregate production grew by a modest 3 percent each year, what we call the gross national product would double every quarter of a century. As long as the annual increase in production is relatively small, the impact of growth in any given year can be absorbed rather easily by the system. Even those changes that involve some dislocation or readjustment because of new processes of production, new products, or changes in consumer tastes will represent a small enough change in the aggregate levels of employment and production that the disturbance is hardly noticed. Viewed in this fashion, the problem of growth is one of seeing that the economic system is able to maintain a small but steady addition to total output each year. Society can handle the market adjustments created by such growth readily enough. It is the larger effects, which may only become evident over a long period of time, that pose problems for the structure and performance of the economic system.

In fact, one might argue that the process of economic growth and change is going to create inevitable instabilities within the political structure. The market system is constantly adjusting to changes in taste, technology, unexpected events, and the like. In doing so, the economic system will impose costs on some and benefits on others. At any point in time, therefore, one might expect to find both "losers" (those who must bear the costs of adjustment) and "winners" (those who reap the gains from market change). Since these groups change over time, the political structure is pressured to adjust to the economic changes. The political process is caught, in this case, between those who seek institutional change to mitigate the effects of the market, and those who seek to pursue the market opportunities with even greater vigor.[1]

Americans have always been ready to turn to the government as a means of mitigating hardships caused by market forces, or of shaping market forces to their own advantage. But the past four decades have witnessed an unprecedented expansion of the role of government in the American economy. While there are relatively few areas in which government decisions have completely replaced the marktplace, the impact of government policy can be seen in virtually *all* market transactions. Government activity accounts, directly or indirectly, for at least a third of, the total spending in our economy, and regulates in some fashion or another most market activity. The United States has become a "mixed economy," where government decisions and individual choices are mixed together, and we are still in the process of determining what the proper mix of government and private economic activity should be.[2]

This is not the first point in our history when Americans have pondered the question of rearranging those institutions that govern our economy. Both social and economic change have been integral parts of American development, and those changes have occurred both with and without governmental assistance. Nor have the changes always proceeded smoothly. Twice within the first hundred years of their country's existence, Americans waged war to secure major alterations in the institutional framework. The American Revolution established the United States as an independent nation, and the Civil War eighty-five years later struck down the legal basis for slavery in our society. While both of these conflicts involved much more than economic issues, the forces of economic change played a significant role in causing the frictions that led to conflict, and in shaping the reorganization that followed the end of fighting.

Since the Civil War, we have had no further restructuring of society involving internal conflict on the scale of these military episodes. However, the need to adjust to economic forces did not disappear. The problem of economic power being concentrated in the hands of industrial capitalists elicited a response on the part of people who sought to change the power structure which had been formed by the emergence of industrial

---

[1] This is a problem which will require a great deal of our attention later in this study. A very concise statement of the difficulties discussed in the text can be found in Douglass North, "A Framework for Analyzing the State in Economic History," *Explorations in Economic History*, 16 (July 1979), 255–59.

[2] There is a considerable body of literature dealing with the role of government both today and in the past. On the willingness of Americans to accept government intervention and the changing role of government throughout the history of our nation, see J.R.T. Hughes, *The Governmental Habit: Governmental Control from Colonial Times to the Present* (New York: Basic Books, 1977).

capitalism. The economic reforms put forward at the end of the nineteenth century and in the first decades of the twentieth century tried to spread out the concentration of economic power and mitigate the impact of adjustments to industrialization in a market society. As we shall see, the reforms fell short of their goals and may have had only a minor impact on either the course of economic development or the redistribution of economic power. Still, these efforts reveal insights into the process of economic change. In the 1930s, the collapse of the American economy known as the "Great Depression" spurred new pressure for change, and this time the efforts at reform were more successful. Franklin Roosevelt's "New Deal" ushered in a new view of the economic system, and began a process of reform which fundamentally altered the economic relationships within the United States.

ECONOMIC THEORIES
AND ECONOMIC CHANGE

The changes that grew out of the development of capitalism and the expanding economic activity of the past two centuries brought drastic alterations in the thoughts of men as well as in their institutional surroundings. The development of economics as a social science has reflected the changes which have taken place. In the same year in which a band of American colonists proposed a revolutionary doctrine so that they might legitimately sever their bonds with Great Britain, a Scottish professor of moral philosophy named Adam Smith published in London a treatise called *The Wealth of Nations*.[3] Smith's book presented a very careful explanation of the manner in which markets offered great advantages for the organization (and, when necessary, the reorganization) of production and consumption patterns in a society. The logic of *The Wealth of Nations* remains the theoretical foundation for the analysis of markets today.

The work has also had a much broader impact on intellectual development since 1776. Smith intended his work to be more than a text which explained how markets worked: he wrote it as a spirited attack on the existing system of government regulations and interferences, commonly referred to as *mercantilism*. To Smith's way of thinking, these interferences by government were not only unnecessary, they were counterproductive. Left to its own devices, the marketplace would—through what Smith termed an "invisible hand"—produce that mixture of goods and services which would best satisfy the desires of the people.

---

[3] *The Wealth of Nations* has been reprinted many times. The most commonly cited edition is the one edited by Edward Cannan: Adam Smith, *The Wealth of Nations* (New York: Modern Library Edition, 1937).

Adam Smith is generally regarded as the founder of the modern discipline of economics. The group of economists who enlarged on Smith's framework in the first half of the nineteenth century—particularly men such as Thomas Malthus, David Ricardo, and other members of the Political Economy Club in London—are usually referred to as the *classical* economists. Toward the end of the nineteenth century a new group of scholars refined the analytical tools of the classical economists and created what is now termed the *neoclassical* school of economics. The leading figure in this school was the English economist Alfred Marshall, whose *Principles of Economics* was first published in 1890 and subsequently went through eight editions (at a time when new editions were far less fashionable than they are today). Neoclassical economics remains the foundation of modern analysis of how markets work.[4]

The argument presented in *The Wealth of Nations* formed one of the intellectual cornerstones of the liberal movement which came to dominate the nineteenth century. The classical economists, and the paradigm of economics which they constructed, provided a philosophical defense for the industrial capitalism which emerged in the middle of the 1800s. That defense insisted that the government refrain from any interference in the operation of the market system. *Laissez faire* (French for "let it be") became the trademark of nineteenth century economics.

The theoretical arguments which so convincingly demonstrated the efficacy of allocating resources according to markets were reinforced by the economic growth that the American market system experienced after 1790. Because it offers the most obvious promise of material improvement for a population, economic growth has always been a primary concern of economists, and we shall begin our brief examination of the "economics of change" with some thoughts on economic growth.

For the classical economists of Smith's time, as well as for the neoclassical economists who followed later, expansion of output would be encouraged by two main forces: specialization and the accumulation of capital. The possibilities for improving efficiency (and thereby increasing output) through a greater degree of specialization and division of labor seemed almost endless. Indeed, Smith was confident that the natural propensity of people to "truck, barter, and trade" would encourage everyone to continually seek ways to take advantage of the gains that division of labor offered. These gains seemed self-evident. By organizing production so that each laborer concentrated on tasks which he or she could do best, the total product would be its greatest, and therefore the productivity of

---

4 Daniel Fusfeld provides an excellent synopsis of the development of economic thought in his book, *The Age of the Economist*, 3rd ed., (Glenview, Ill.: Scott, Foresman, 1977). For an interesting picture of the personalities behind the analysis, see Robert Heilbroner, *The Worldly Philosophers*, 3rd ed., (New York: Simon & Schuster, 1967).

labor would also be greatest. The only limit to the gains possible from such a division of labor was the size of the producer's market.

The second—and, in the eyes of later economists, more important— way to achieve economic growth was through the accumulation of capital. Increased capital meant additional inputs and greater efficiency of labor. Capital accumulation was the product of *investment:* the diversion of a portion of current effort towards the production of capital goods. The community that saved for the future would have more capital, and hence a greater productive capacity available. Like other facets of economic life, the process of saving and investment would be handled by the all-encompassing influence of the market. People would save because it was prudent (and rewarding) to do so; people would invest in capital goods because it was a remunerative way to use their (or someone else's) savings. Left to their own devices, an industrious population would tend to accumulate capital over time, and this investment would provide an impetus for economic growth.

Although they examined the sources of economic *growth* in some detail, the classical and neoclassical approaches to the economic problem did not devote much attention to the problem of economic *change.* Recently, there has been an effort to extend the economic logic of neoclassical thinkers beyond the confines of the marketplace. This *new political economy* has developed an analysis of the political process which treats political decisions the same way economists treat economic decisions. According to this approach, the question of whether or not any revisions to the existing system will be made depends on a comparison of the perceived benefits of any action and the costs associated with that action.[5] While the efforts of economists have been directed primarily toward analyses of contemporary issues of political economy, the analytical framework of the new political economy has been applied to the question of institutional change in a historical context by Lance Davis and Douglass North.[6] Institutional change, according to Davis and North, is the outcome of decisions reached by individuals who assess their own self-interest as it relates to the proposed change. As they rather succinctly state their thesis:

> An institutional arrangement will be innovated if the expected net gains exceed the expected costs. Only when this condition is met would we

---

[5] Two of the early statements of this "new political economy" are James Buchanan and Gordon Tullock, *The Calculus of Consent* (Ann Arbor: University of Michigan Press, 1962), and Mancur Olson, *The Logic of Collective Action* (Cambridge, Mass.: Harvard University Press, 1964). Richard McKenzie and Gordon Tullock use the new approach to explore a variety of economic issues in *The New World of Economics,* rev. ed. (Homewood, Ill.: Richard D. Irwin, 1978).

[6] Lance Davis and Douglass North, *Institutional Change and American Economic Growth* (New York: Cambridge University Press, 1971).

expect to find attempts being made to alter the existing structure of institutional and property rights within a society.[7]

If people see net benefits to a proposed change, they will presumably join the group pressing for reform. This analysis has the useful feature that the investigator need not be concerned with the exact reasons why each person joined the group. People with diverse motives may band together as long as they feel that the objective of the group is one which will benefit them. As one would expect in an analytical framework patterned after an economic model which stresses the virtues of freedom of individual actions, the emphasis is on individual behavior. And, consistent with the neoclassical economic model, the Davis-North analysis of institutional change is pictured as a process of bargaining toward some equilibrium. Change, in this context, is seen typically as a gradual process, the result of continuous pressures from groups that seek to effect changes in the institutional arrangements.

As we shall see in subsequent chapters, the Davis-North approach provides valuable insights into certain types of proposed reforms of the economic system. It is somewhat less valuable as an analysis of institutional change outside the economic system. The narrow focus on economic motives as the basis for group action makes the analysis best suited for situations in which gains and losses can be readily measured by each individual and then translated into some meaningful group action. These turn out to be very restrictive conditions for the historical analysis of major institutional reforms, whose outcomes are uncertain and gains nebulous.

Even when the conditions of the Davis-North analysis are met, there is often an identification problem associated with the analysis of group action. Applying the "cost-benefit" logic to historical incidents involves the estimation of the expected gain or loss to individuals instigating the reform. The value of the outcome must be comparable to the value of the costs, and this can be most often approximated by using market prices. But what if this is not possible? Then we must assume that people have some way (unknown to us) of comparing the costs and benefits of their proposed reforms. There is a temptation in such cases to reverse the logic and assert that, in any case in which reform was actually instituted, the benefits must have exceeded the costs. By the same argument, those reforms that failed must have been instances in which the benefits were insufficient to cover the costs. Pushed to an extreme, this line of reasoning becomes tautological: Any action taken is explained as one in which the people in a group perceived a net gain; any failure to act is explained as an expectation that there would be net losses from the action. Failure to act is then seen as proof that the change was not really necessary in the

---

7 *Ibid.*, p. 10.

first place—at least from the viewpoint of participants at the time. Because it accepts the choices actually made as being the results of some assumedly rational choice process, such an argument is unable to provide insights into that choice process itself.

The shortcomings of the individualistic approach in explaining the success or failure of group actions can be traced in part to a problem inherent in any theory of group action that postulates democratic or individualistic choices. Economist Kenneth Arrow has convincingly demonstrated that reliance upon a majority voting rule within a group may produce results that are arbitrary in the sense that they cannot be derived from a given set of circumstances. According to Arrow's "impossibility theorem," even if everyone in society makes rational choices, the outcome of the voting process could depend on the order in which alternatives are presented, and therefore we can never be certain that the alternative selected is in fact superior to all the others. Arrow's proof, for which he was awarded the Nobel Prize for Economics in 1972, is a complex one. In effect, he showed that majority voting could produce results that violated the condition of "transitivity." In such a situation, the group might vote to prefer situation A over situation B, and situation B over situation C, and still vote to prefer C over A—which would not make sense in the cost-benefit analysis of Davis and North. Institutional change, in this perspective, will conform to economic rationality only by chance. One could, of course, devise voting rules that might avoid the particular paradox posed by Arrow. However, the group decisions still might not follow the cost-benefit pattern, depending on which particular rules were followed. Certainly there would be no assurance that the "best" (in a cost-benefit sense) solution would be chosen.[8]

There is, moreover, another problem with the use of voting systems to make collective choice. Voters will be induced to vote only if they expect that their vote will affect the outcome of the election. In a large group it is unlikely that a single vote will decide the outcome; hence, voters have very little incentive to vote. Requiring people to vote will not solve this problem; it will simply make the effect more subtle. Voters may vote, but they will be unwilling to make an effort to become informed on the issues of the election. As a consequence, the resulting vote will not necessarily reflect the "best" solution.[9] This problem is particularly important to the

---

[8] An excellent discussion of Kenneth Arrow's theorem and the paradox of group choice is in Norman Frohlich and Joe A. Oppenheimer, *Modern Political Economy* (Englewood Cliffs, N.J.: Prentice-Hall, 1978), Chapter 2. Arrow's initial exposition of the problem is in *Social Choice and Individual Values* (New Haven, Conn.: Yale University Press, 1951).

[9] The difficulties surrounding voter incentives and the information on which their votes are based have been examined in detail by Anthony Downs in *An Economic Theory of Democracy* (New York: Harper & Row, Pub., 1957). Also see Buchanan and Tullock, *Calculus of Consent.*

issue of institutional change, where the difficulty of making voters aware of the benefits and costs may significantly affect the way in which people vote. There have been countless reform movements which failed to get off the ground because they were unable to overcome public apathy. And, as we shall see, a major challenge to those who are successful in launching a reform is to maintain the support to press the program to a conclusion.

The Davis-North view of the capitalist industrial society is one in which individual choice remains the basis for economic and social actions. It evolved out of an approach to the problem of economic change that followed the economics of Smith, Marshall, and others. There was, however, another approach to economic change that had evolved much earlier from a rather different perspective. In the middle of the nineteenth century, the classical economists' view of society had been challenged by the man who gave capitalism its name: Karl Marx. One of Marx's great insights into the economic system and how it worked was his recognition that the consequences of industrialization in a capitalist system would fundamentally alter the entire social system through a redistribution—indeed, a redefinition—of economic power.[10]

Marx insisted that the entire framework of social action must be examined around the emergence of two new classes: *workers,* who hire out their labor and who have no control over the process of production; and *capitalists,* who control the means of production (that is, capital) in the industrial system. When Marx spoke of the capitalist "mode of production," he was referring to a *social* arrangement, rather than to some set of techniques which organize production. Marx saw this division of society into workers and capitalists as the basis for a continual struggle of opposing economic interests, and he envisioned the entire social system in terms of this struggle. Capitalists, through their control of the means of production, held enormous economic power which would permit them to control the direction of change in society to their own advantage. Workers, because they lacked the power individually to combat this tendency, were urged to band together in a common cause to resist the capitalists. The individualistic motives which dominated the Davis-North model are replaced in Marx by a "class" consciousness which becomes the basis for seeking institutional change.

---

10 It is impossible to do justice to Marx's work in a few paragraphs which touch on only a part of the entire Marxist framework. Marx's well-known (but seldom read) *magnus opus* is *Das Kapital,* which was published in three volumes between 1867 and 1895. *Capital,* (New York: International Publishers, 1967), 3 volumes. Even in a translated version it is hard reading, and not recommended for any but the most dedicated of scholars. A useful summary of Marx's thought which stresses the aspects touched in the present discussion is E.K. Hunt, *Class Conflict and Social Harmony* (New York: Wadsworth, 1978).

It is hardly surprising that Marx, writing in the middle of the nineteenth century, felt that the capitalist mode of production and the industrial system with which it was associated had come to dominate society. He was reacting to his environment in much the same sense that Adam Smith was reacting to the mercantilism of an earlier time. And one of the more obvious reasons that Marxism has survived as an economic paradigm in the United States—and exerted a much more powerful influence elsewhere—is the simple observation that a great deal of economic power remains concentrated in the hands of a rather small group of people who fit the description of "capitalists" rather neatly. The unequal division of power in society has been a consistent theme of Marxist writers, up to the present.[11]

While this point is well taken, the presence of capitalists is hardly a sufficient condition to ensure that the conclusions drawn from Marxist analysis are correct. Non-Marxist economists object to a dichotomy that divides society into only two broad classes, particularly when class distinctions are based on rather narrow economic grounds—the ownership of capital. Neither the working class proletariat nor the capitalists seem as monolithic as Marxist analysis tends to portray them. Moreover, as the modern industrial state has emerged, many would argue that the class distinctions have, if anything, become *less* distinct. The contrasting economic situations and the solidarity of purpose attributed to the two groups by Marx in the 1860s seem misplaced in the affluent American society of the 1980s.

Nevertheless, Marx's contention that the creation of a capitalist "manager" class permanently altered social relations in Britain and other western economies cannot be so easily brushed aside. Control of capital does carry with it economic power, and concentrations of wealth based on the control of capital have been a fact of life in industrial societies since the end of the nineteenth century. To pretend that these concentrations of power are disappearing, or that they have no effect on the political and economic life of the society is naive, and to formulate a notion of economic change which fails to consider the distribution of power is not likely to prove fruitful. Somewhere between the individualism stressed in the neoclassical analysis and the heavy emphasis on class distinctions of Marxist analysis lies the approach which can best reflect the American experience.

---

[11] Writings on Marxist thought have been given a boost by the "radical" movement of the past two decades. For a view of contemporary Marxist thought which illustrates the points of the text, the reader should consult Michael Harrington, *The Twilight of Capitalism* (New York: Simon & Schuster, 1976), or Howard Sherman, *Radical Political Economy* (New York: Basic Books, 1972). Marxists are not the only economists to stress the concentration of economic power in a broad social context. See, for example, John K. Galbraith, *The New Industrial State* (New York: Houghton Mifflin, 1967), for a distinctly non-Marxist analysis of economic power in an industrial society.

The two polar cases can reveal important elements of the process of change, but their overemphasis on one facet or another of human economic behavior tends to distort the analysis.

Neither Marx nor his critics were able to provide many insights into another element that has had a profound effect upon the economic development of the past two centuries: technological change. Both schools of thought note that a characteristic feature of market capitalism has been the continual and pervasive pressure for the introduction of new and better techniques of production. Producers are induced—some would say they are forced—always to seek more efficient ways to produce their products in order to gain an advantage (or to prevent some rival from gaining an advantage) in the market. The progress induced by this process is a major source of economic growth, and Marx in particular placed enormous emphasis on the impact industrial technology had on the mode of production. Yet he said very little about the sources of inventive ideas which developed the techniques responsible for the transformation of Victorian England into an industrial society. Only after an idea has developed have most economists considered the impact of that idea on the process of production.[12]

Economists have recognized, however, that the manner in which technological change altered the process of production over the past 200 years posed an unfortunate dilemma—a dilemma which represented a severe threat to competition among producers. Whenever a new process required expansion to a larger scale of production by each producer, there was a limit to the extent to which the existing market was able to absorb the additional output generated by the expansion of all firms. The price of the output was, typically, driven down by expansion of the industry, and at some point firms were unable to recoup their costs. In such a situation, it was the smaller (and less efficient) firms that were unable to sustain a competitive position in the marketplace with the new technology.

The small firm had three options:

1. The firm could expand its own production.
2. The firm could cease production and go out of business.
3. The firm could join with other firms to create a larger unit of production.

Any of the three options will result in the elimination of smaller units of production. (Economists call this situation one of *increasing returns.* As

---

[12] The problem of technological change and its role in the economic process has been receiving more attention from economists lately. See, for example, Warren J. Samuels, "Technology vis a vis Institutions in the JEI: A Suggested Interpretation," *Journal of Economic Issues,* 11 (December 1977); and Howard Sherman, "Technology vis a vis Institutions: A Marxist Commentary," *Journal of Economic Issues,* 13 (March 1979). Both articles discuss the interaction of technology and institutional change.

long as the firm's costs per unit are falling, it can increase its profits by continuing to expand output.) Such a situation has long been recognized as a threat to competitive markets, particularly in areas such as manufacturing, where the impact of technology on the structure of firms has been enormous.[13]

One of the few economists who did pay considerable attention to the role of innovation and technical change was Joseph Schumpeter. To Schumpeter, the root of progress in an industrial society was the continual influx of new ideas, which were encouraged by the capitalist system. He termed the process of innovations and economic change *creative destruction*. His choice of this term reflected on the one hand what Schumpeter saw as the positive influence which new processes of production had in creating economic opportunities, and on the other hand the dislocation and disequilibrium which the new ideas produced on the existing system.[14]

Schumpeter argued that there was a constant search for new ideas on the part of entrepreneurs who sought the rewards which the market system offered for successful innovations. In their eagerness to reap these gains, entrepreneurs would be drawn to the areas of monopoly by the lure of higher profits. Monopoly, to Schumpeter, was a dynamic phenomenon; it both rewarded those who temporarily gained an advantage and punished those who failed to change in response to threats to their market position. Described in the Davis-North approach to economic change, monopoly was one of those imperfections which entrepreneurs ("groups") were constantly seeking to turn to their own advantage. Economies of scale were one of the more obvious phenomena which encouraged entrepreneurs to expand their markets and seek changes in the economic system which would facilitate their expansion.

Schumpeter's ideas combined the technological imperative which Marx saw as a source of growth with the role of individual entrepreneurs which was emphasized by Davis and North. In doing so, he was able to deal with another feature of capitalist economic growth that has caused problems for economic theorists: the apparent tendency for the activity level of the economy to widely fluctuate. According to Schumpeter, periods of exuberant growth were a consequence of entrepreneurs rushing to cash

---

[13] For a statement of the problem as it was posed in neoclassical theory, see William Breit and Roger Ransom, *The Academic Scribblers: American Economists in Collision* (New York: Holt, Rinehart & Winston, 1971), pp. 24–30. An excellent statement of the dilemma posed by the efficiency of large scale enterprise on the one hand, and the monopoly power with which large size provides the firm on the other, is available in William N. Leonard, *Business Size, Market Power, and Public Policy* (New York: Harper & Row, Pub., 1969), Chapter 1. Also see Davis and North, *Institutional Change*, Chapter 8.

[14] Schumpeter wrote several major works on economic development, economic change, and the capitalist system. The most comprehensive summary of his thinking is in his last major work, *Capitalism, Socialism, and Democracy* (New York: Harper & Row, Pub., 1947).

in on the introduction of some new idea, thereby creating a wave of investment. When this "herdlike movement" (as Schumpeter termed it) caused the economic system to be overextended, a crisis resulted, bringing on a period of reduced economic activity. Economic growth, in the Schumpeterian model, consisted of two steps forward and one step back.

The process of creative destruction is important to our story not only as an explanation of monopoly and growth, but also as an explanation of the sources of institutional change. By its nature, the process of creative destruction was one which wrenched the economic system. New firms arose from the ashes of the old. Some people won; others lost. Schumpeter saw the problem this created; he believed that the economic instability the capitalist system produced in its creation of progress would ultimately create pressures to curb economic activity and stifle the innovative spirit which was the root of economic growth. The demise of capitalism would come not as Marx insisted, from an inexorable tendency towards collapse; it would come because the entrepreneural spirit would be stifled. Socialism would emerge as bureaucratic managers replaced the entrepreneur, not as a product of a workers' revolution.

Despite their different emphases, some common themes emerge from these theories of economic change and the process of industrialization. In all of the approaches the economic system—more specifically the market system—is viewed as the originator of many changes. The process of technological change, fostered by the incentives offered in the marketplace, is an important element in shaping economic development. And, at least to Marx and Schumpeter, the ebb and flow of economic activity—the presence of economic cycles—plays an important role in shaping change in the long run. Finally, the exercise of economic (or political) power plays a prominent role in determining the outcome of particular struggles over the exact nature of institutional change.

THE POLITICAL ECONOMY
OF ECONOMIC CHANGE

The problem of economic development in a capitalist system seems to center on the fact that the economic pressures which are produced from within the market system threaten to overwhelm every other facet of society. This is not to say that economic forces alone are responsible for institutional change. It is a recognition of the extent to which the market system, while it is geared to economic behavior, permeates all of the institutions of an industrial society, and responds to stimuli which may originate anywhere in society. On the one hand, the effects of change generated within the economic system may have ramifications far beyond the marketplace. On the other hand, changes that do not originate within the economic system are nonetheless reflected in market behavior. While in some cases the impact of change may be dampened by market responses, in others the effect will be magnified.

This pervasiveness of market influences means that decisions to effect changes in the institutional framework must be considered in the context of market forces. If proposed alterations in the structure of the economic system run counter to prevailing market pressures, then collective action based on some incentive other than the market will be required. In a society which has become geared to market behavior, such action may prove difficult to sustain. Throughout the nineteenth and twentieth centuries, those arguing for economic reforms have been confronted with the problem of coping with the argument that their suggested reforms might stand in the way of progress. Whether it involved dissolving economic and political ties with Great Britain, giving freedom to slaves, obtaining better working conditions for industrial workers, or providing greater economic security for families in an industrial society, reformers have always encountered resistance because their proposals threaten to place limits on economic efficiency. It has been an uphill battle, but not a hopeless one. The Revolutionary War was won in spite of the fact that there were strong economic forces favoring a continuation of British rule. Blacks were freed from slavery despite the vested economic interest their owners had. The plight of workers has been improved and progress made in providing economic security for Americans despite the revisions in economic power involved in such reforms.

In each of these cases, the collective action which helped to produce major reforms involved changes in the ideas of Americans. Proposals for reform must always contend with resistance from those with vested interests in the status quo. But there is another, more subtle, factor that reformers must also consider: Their ideas must be broadly consistent with the corpus of commonly held economic beliefs within society—what John Kenneth Galbraith calls the "conventional wisdom." [15] In the sphere of economic change, the conventional wisdom is often a conservative, rather than a progressive, force. It may be, as John Maynard Keynes believed, that our lives are ruled by "little else" than the "ideas of economists and political philosophers." But, as he went on to note, those ideas were likely to be from "a few years back." [16]

As we shall see, the role of ideas has not been confined to the realm of economics. Reforms of any sort which run counter to widely held ideo-

---

[15] John Kenneth Galbraith, *The Affluent Society* (Boston: Houghton Mifflin, 1958), p. 9.

[16] John Maynard Keynes, *The General Theory of Employment, Interest, and Money* (New York: Harcourt Brace Jovanovich, Inc., 1936), p. 383.

logical views are unlikely to prevail in the long run unless the mainstream views can be changed. While this is a rather obvious point, it is important to stress that the role of ideology in assisting or preventing institutional change can be very subtle. Ideology affects the ease with which groups can be organized to act as agents of reform. Proposals for significant alterations in institutional arrangements invariably involve a host of complex issues, many of which are very subtle (indeed, so subtle that they are not even noticed by the advocates of the reform). To muster sufficient pressure for change, the intricacies and subtleties must be expressed in simpler terms. Ideology offers a way to do this. Ideological beliefs create a view of the world which is accepted without questioning the logic of the explanation. Economic or political ideologies (for example any of the "isms" such as capitalism, socialism, or communism) rest on values or norms (such as freedom, individual liberty, class solidarity). On issues of major social policy, it is often easier to rank alternatives by using the value of benefits weighed in ideological preferences rather than trying to compare the estimated dollar value of benefits from each program. Ideology thus becomes an important vehicle for disseminating information.[17]

The rhetoric of reform campaigns in the United States has seldom failed to take advantage of ideological factors. Voters have been encouraged to make their decisions on the effects of some economic program based on an appeal to ideology as much as reason. As an example, we might note how President Franklin D. Roosevelt handled the issue of bank reform in 1933. He pointed out the obvious economic interest everyone had in restoring some form of order to the financial chaos. But he did so using rhetoric which was aimed at the ideology of the man on the street. Consider the following excerpt from his first inaugural address:

> Stripped of the lure of profit by which to induce our people to follow their false leadership, [the money changers] have resorted to exhortations, pleading tearfully for restored confidence. They know only the rules of a generation of self-seekers. They have no vision, and when there is no vision the people perish.
>
> The money changers have fled from their high seats in the temple of our civilization. We may now restore that temple to the ancient truths. The measure of the restoration lies in the extent to which we apply social values more noble than monetary profit.[18]

As an economic analysis of the then–recent financial collapse, that passage leaves much to be desired. But as an indictment of the banking community aimed at those who already believe that banks control our eco-

---

[17] On the use of ideology to influence information to voters, see Downs, *An Economic Theory of Democracy*, Chapter 7.

[18] Mervin Hunt, *The Public Addresses of Franklin Delano Roosevelt* (Los Angeles: De Vorss & Company, 1934).

nomic destiny through their profit-seeking manipulation of others' money, it conveys an effective message. As Roosevelt himself noted several days later, there are "comparatively few who understand the mechanics of banking." He was not the one to teach voters those mechanics. It was easier simply to assert that the government should take drastic steps to offset the selfish interests of "money changers" who controlled the system up to that point. The appeal to ideological prejudices against the banking community was an effective way to gain an audience—and eventually to gain support at the polls as well—for the bank reforms of 1933 and 1935.

Rhetoric and ideology aside, we shall discover that new ideas regarding social or economic change which challenge the conventional wisdom have seldom triumphed solely on the intellectual merits or ideological appeal of their arguments alone. They have required assistance in the form of some event that produced an atmosphere in which people were willing to experiment with new and somewhat radical ideas. In the United States there have been at least three occasions when such an atmosphere was created by crises of considerable proportions.

1. The American Revolution offered a chance to experiment with a new form of government.
2. The Civil War offered a chance not only to eliminate slavery, but to introduce other changes intended to facilitate the adjustments to industrial capitalism as well.
3. The Great Depression of the 1930s offered a chance to modify the economic and social setting in response to the collapse of the financial system and the realization of just how fragile economic security in a modern industrial society can be.

In each case, the reforms introduced—the Constitution, the Thirteenth and Fourteenth Amendments, the New Deal—would probably not have been accepted by Americans only a short time earlier. Most scholars agree that the faction supporting a break with England in the mid-1770s was barely a majority of the population, and the popular support for the Constitution may not even have been a majority. Certainly the abolitionists crusading for the elimination of slavery were a small (albeit very vocal) minority in the 1850s. And it is hard to imagine that the administrations of Presidents Hoover, Harding and Coolidge might seriously consider the legislation Roosevelt proposed in the mid-1930s. Yet, in the context of the more pressing needs of the economic crisis, the reforms were speedily enacted.

Our interest in this book concerns those instances in which the pressures for change—both economic and otherwise—became severe enough to create a crisis, as well as those instances in which more gradual pressures for change produced movements for reform which, while less dramatic (and sometimes less successful), still managed to effect some changes in the economic system. In general, our purpose will be to investigate the sort of changes in the economic system sought as a means of alleviating the problems that the existing system seemed incapable of handling. In so doing, we shall focus on those elements which were highlighted in this discussion of the process of economic change, but we shall also pursue some themes which emerge from the story itself.

Among the more prominent of these emerging themes is the constant friction between the market and nonmarket institutional arrangements. The market society of the United States provides, as we noted above, an incredible abundance of goods and services to Americans. For that reason Americans have been more than willing to accept the whims of the marketplace in the search for higher levels of output and consumption. But, as we also noted, markets expose people to risks—economic security is constantly threatened by the possibility of changes in prices, wages, and the availability of both goods and jobs. If the story of nineteenth century American growth and development seems a chronicle of the emerging dominance of market forces, then the twentieth century might be described as a gradual—but very steady—retreat from that dominance as people sought to protect themselves from the marketplace.

Finally, we should note at the outset of our journey that an investigation of what is changing will also reveal what has *not* changed. Most obvious of these constant elements is the fact that two hundred years of economic change have not caused Americans to abandon their commitment to private property. This deep commitment to individual property rights (even if the "individual" is General Motors or IBM) was a major factor in all of the reform movements we shall examine in this book. Despite the prominence of the public sector in our modern economy, the United States remains an essentially capitalist society. For better or for worse, Americans have elected to cope with capitalism rather than to restructure their economic life around some other institutional arrangements.

How they coped provides the theme for this book.

3

MAKING
AN ECONOMIC
SOCIETY

Most of the institutional arrangements that govern our economic system had their genesis many years ago. They have been modified from time to time, and the changes introduced have, one hopes, made the original institutional arrangement better suited to handle the changing economic and social situations. Rarely do we find instances in which very radical institutional changes are introduced within a short period of time. This is particularly true of the underlying foundation of laws and custom that govern our economic behavior. Colonial Americans adapted the European legal system to their needs, drawing primarily on the British example. For the most part, their heirs have not radically altered the system of property rights and protection of individual liberties which was rooted in that colonial heritage.

There were, however, two instances in which a substantial portion of the population decided that the existing system of laws was *not* suited to their needs, and felt strongly enough about the necessity for major revisions in the institutional structure that they were willing to go to war rather than compromise on the issues involved. Both the Revolutionary War and the Civil War had an important impact on American economic development because they created or modified important features of the institutional framework that was to guide subsequent development. These two episodes are important to our narrative of economic change for two reasons.

The first, and most obvious, reason for studying these periods is the extent to which the issues raised during the wars and their aftermaths touched on the most basic elements of the social and economic system:

property rights and the guarantees of individual liberty for various groups in American society. The importance of these issues is illustrated by the fact that people were willing to fight prolonged and bitter wars rather than accept compromise solutions. In each case, economic factors played a significant role in creating the frictions that ultimately prevented any peaceful resolution of the differences between groups and regions, and in shaping the changes which followed. An examination of the ways in which economic factors contributed to the process of change in these times of crisis provides insights into the evolution of the basic rules of our economic system, and the role economic interests took in shaping those rules.

The second reason for examining these two periods is to note the dynamics of change in the context of a major crisis in American history. The victories of the colonists in the Revolution and of the Northern States in the Civil War produced situations in which major revisions in the institutional framework could be introduced. Once the process of change had been set in motion by the crisis of the war, the momentum generated by these reforms produced alterations in the institutional arrangements of the United States which encompassed every facet of economic activity in every region of the country. The Constitution carefully defined a new (albeit very familiar) legal framework which was singularly well suited to the operation of a market economy, a system to which we refer today as *market capitalism*. And, although the initial efforts at reconstruction following the Civil War concentrated on the establishment of a new system of labor to replace slavery in the South, both during and after the war Congress passed laws which were clearly intended to encourage the continued development of a market system—by that time a market system dominated by the emerging industrial interests in the victorious North.

THE AMERICAN REVOLUTION

What were the major economic issues in conflict that led to a break with England in 1775? The most visible issue would seem to be the economic and commercial policies of Great Britain—particularly the infamous Navigation Acts—which were the focus of considerable debate during the decade preceding the outbreak of hostilities. The Navigation Acts were a set of laws which dated back to the seventeenth century. Their original intent was to impede the growth of Dutch commerce in the New World. By the middle of the eighteenth century, however, they had evolved into a complex set of regulations governing British and colonial trade. (If one were to look for a modern analogy, the federal regulations on personal income taxes come to mind.)[1] Upon inspection, however, one finds that both the Crown and the colonial agitators resorted to a great deal of rhetoric which seldom paid much attention to the specific claims made by the other side. Indeed, the fuss over the burden imposed by British mercantilist policies on the thirteen colonies was much ado about very little.

It is generally agreed by scholars of the period that British policy with regard to commerce and trade did *not* represent an oppressive burden to colonists. To be sure, Americans could complain of some costs and inequities stemming from British mercantilism. Merchants insisted that the myriad of laws and regulations interfered with their business by restricting the destinations of some exports and by requiring all imports be shipped to America via England. Southern planters resented the restrictions on their staple crops, which British policy dictated must be shipped to buyers in Great Britain before being re-exported (by British firms) to the continent. Farmers of various types and regions were upset over the closing of western lands in 1763 and the transfer of those lands to the province of Quebec in 1774. The discouragement—in some instances the outright prohibition—of manufacturing, which was a conscious attempt by the Crown to favor home manufacturing, hindered the small (but growing) number of colonists who sought to produce finished articles for a colonial or export market. And, of course, all colonists moaned about their taxes, a tradition which their descendants continue with great vigor to the present time.

Notwithstanding such complaints, the facts of the matter clearly reveal that taxes in the colonies were low in comparison to those in Britain itself, and recent attempts to estimate the actual burden of British policy suggest that the benefits gained by breaking away from England in the mid-1770s would have been more than offset by the costs incurred as a result of being outside the British Empire. In other words, a rational consideration of the options (according to Davis and North) would find little to favor revolution. The most ambitious effort to actually measure the value of the burden concluded that the net cost per capita was only about 26 cents—or less than 1 percent of the average income per person in the colonies at that time.[2] If they made their decision based on purely "eco-

---

[1] For a very complete description of the Acts and their development over time, see Oliver Dickenson, *The Navigation Acts and the American Revolution* (Philadelphia: University of Pennsylvania Press, 1951).

[2] Robert Thomas, "A Quantitative Approach to the Study of the Effects of British Imperial Policy upon Colonial Welfare: Some Preliminary Findings," *Journal of Economic History*, 25 (December 1965). Measuring the "burden" from the Navigation Acts has become a favorite pastime of economic historians ever since Lawrence Harper published his pioneering article, "Mercantilism and the American Revolution," *Canadian Historical Review*, 23 (March 1942). The debate has continued to the present without altering the order of magnitude of the burden reported by Thomas.

nomic" considerations, the supporters of the American Revolution were doing so in hopes of a very small gain, or on the basis of an inaccurate estimate of the immediate gains from being free from British rule. As for the king's men, it seems reasonably clear that they did not base their policy on a cost-benefit analysis. The ministers at Whitehall seem to have completely misunderstood and misgauged both the nature and the intensity of colonial displeasure with the mother country.

The differences between the king and the colonists were at least to some degree the product of the extremely slow communications of the day. Both sides were responding to news of events that had taken place a month or more earlier. But on one basic point they seemed to understand each other: The king and his ministers were adamant that the Crown retain the right to control any aspect of economic life in the colonies. The colonists were just as adamant in their opposition to this view. They insisted that such authority to control economic activity posed a pervasive threat to any long-range planning in the colonies, since it introduced a capricious element of uncertainty into the conduct of trade, manufacturing, or farming. What if some particular line of trade were suddenly cut off (as when the colonial imports of tea from China were limited to that supplied by the British East India Company)? What if the manufacture of some product was suddenly deemed injurious to "home" (British) producers and ordered ceased in the colonies (as in the case of iron manufacturing, where the only production allowed was that of pig iron)? Or what if the land needed for settlement of new farms in the west was suddenly placed under the Crown's jurisdiction rather than that of the colonial legislatures (which was the intent of the Quebec Act in 1774)?

The threat of arbitrary control of colonial economic interests from a government far removed from the scene was no imaginary fear. It was very real, and it was accentuated by the fact that, after 1763, the policy of the British ministers called for stricter enforcement of all the existing regulations. Prior to that date, regulations on colonial commerce had been enforced in a rather lax manner—a policy historians have termed *salutory neglect.* As a result of this neglect, smuggling had become quite common —even respectable—in the eighteenth century. Subsequent attempts by the Crown's officers to eliminate this illegal activity brought cries of protest from shippers accustomed to importing commodities without duties or the interference of customs officials. The stricter interpretation and enforcement of imperial regulations after 1763 magnified the actual burden on colonists who had routinely violated the customs laws. It also revealed the highly arbitrary nature of British commercial policy. The burden of British policy may not have been large, but it was unpredictable.

American economic expansion prior to 1775 had been based on a vigorous exploitation of the region's resources, involving markets both at home and abroad. To enforce a policy which seemed to place barriers in the way of that expansion was bound to excite opposition in the colonies. The economic issue posed by colonists was not whether they would be better off without English interference; it was whether lessening the interference from London could best be accomplished by demonstrating armed resistance or by negotiating with the Crown and Parliament.

"These are the times," Tom Paine wrote in his pamphlet *Common Sense,* "that try men's souls." The decision to either support the king or throw one's lot with the rebels was likely to rest on more than economic considerations. Nevertheless, economic considerations were clearly present; many who supported the war against England stood to reap economic gains—provided they won. They stood to gain little in the short run, where the interference of the war imposed considerable costs. But, over a longer period of time, when the benefits of working in an independent economy would emerge, the possible gains were large indeed. The rhetoric of the American rebels seldom emphasized the economic aspects of their cause, preferring to stress the rights of a free people. Yet many of the demands—and many of the specific complaints and petitions to the Crown —make reference to the problems posed by the arbitrary economic actions of the Crown or Parliament. Whether or not they calculated the costs and benefits of independence, most rebels fought because they placed a high value on the right to determine their own destiny—economic and otherwise.

Throughout the nineteenth century that destiny lay in the expansion to the west. The trade, commerce, and manufacturing that were generated by expansion were the mainspring of economic growth in the decades following the Revolution. This fact was already apparent in the late eighteenth century as settlers spilled over the Appalachian Mountains. Geared to the notions of mercantilist favoritism towards home producers and the control of trade to the interests of British markets, the king's advisers were simply unable to cope with the pressures emerging in a colonial economy that was expanding at such a rapid rate. Indeed, the characterization of the American economy as "colonial" in 1775 was itself a misnomer. Colonial growth had proceeded at such a pace that, on the eve of the Revolution, Britain's thirteen American colonies represented an economic system which accounted for better than one-fourth of the total foreign trade of the British Isles—more than the combined contribution of all the Northern European states.

Economically as well as politically, the American colonies had become a mature society—mature and strong enough, it turned out, to wrest their independence from Britain in a long and bitter war.

THE FRAMING OF A CONSTITUTION

Once independence was won, a new challenge appeared. What sort of institutional framework should replace the King's rule? Ironically, the same economic pressures which had pushed men to argue for freedom from England now posed serious obstacles to the unification of the thirteen independent states. The weak political confederation which had seen the colonies through the war years collapsed when the external threat was removed. Each of the new states insisted on the right to formulate an economic policy suited to its own particular needs. The new Americans appeared to have learned little from their past; each state embraced the accepted mercantilist doctrine of the time with great enthusiasm. The imposition of tariffs between neighboring states disrupted the established patterns of trade between the states. Irresponsible issue of currency by state governments resulted in monetary confusion and an inflation that greatly complicated the difficult transition to a peacetime existence outside the British Empire. The absence of any strong central authority proved as troublesome as had the autocratic rule of the king and Parliament.

What was needed was a set of rules that could preserve the freedom won in the Revolution while at the same time ensuring a greater degree of unity than existed amid the euphoria of independence. In 1787, delegates from each of the states gathered in Philadelphia in an effort (as they later wrote) "to form a more perfect union." The result was not perfect, but it was a bold attempt to create a union of individual states with a strong and representative central government. There seems little question that the draft of the Constitution proposed for ratification reflected a conservative reaction to the events and rhetoric of the previous two decades. Even a cursory glance at the composition of delegates reveals that, while the American Revolution may have broken the traditional ties with Britain, it had not yet produced a dramatic shift of economic or social power within American society. The Tories had been driven out; however, the men who emerged to lead the young nation were, for the most part, representative of the same wealthy, landed, and commercial interests in the country which had been prominent in the earlier decades of colonial life. The interruption of economic growth, first by the war and then by the political confusion of the postwar decade, had prompted these men to call for and attend the Philadelphia meeting. To many of the delegates, it seemed that political stability—and their own positions in society—demanded an institutional framework that could better cope with the economic pressures confronting the United States.

The convention's solution to this problem, however, did not explicitly deal with a rearrangement of economic institutions. The Constitution dealt primarily with the structure of political institutions of the new nation. The system of checks and balances, which represented the most novel feature of the new form of government, required few references to the economic powers of government. In fact, the Constitution touches directly on economic institutions in only two sections of the first Article. Section 9 prohibits the government from interfering with commerce between the states; Section 8 grants Congress the right to levy taxes and reserves for the federal government the sole prerogative to issue legal tender.

Nothwithstanding the lack of attention to economic matters, the Constitution *is* an economic document. It established an institutional framework intended to facilitate the operation of a market economy—a marketplace which would encourage what Adam Smith had called "a certain propensity . . . to truck, barter, and exchange one thing for another." [3] Particularly significant in this respect were the careful guarantees of private property rights which formed one of the foundations to the concept of individual freedom embodied in the Constitution. The right to hold and accumulate private wealth was guaranteed any American—as long as he was not a slave. (Women were not prohibited from owning property; however, the Constitution did not prevent states from placing restrictions on the rights of women, and most states had such restrictions in 1790).

It has been pointed out that the gentlemen at Philadelphia were protecting their own interests when they reaffirmed the right to hold property in the Constitution.[4] Such a cynical view of the matter misses a vital point with respect to ownership of property in colonial America: A system of private property rights had evolved well before the Revolution. Indeed, it was the threatened infringement on those rights by the crown that had provided one of the more compelling economic arguments for breaking ties with Britain. And not only the wealthy insisted on the right to own property. The greatest hope for advancement in late eighteenth-century America was through the acquisition of land. Legal assurances that a landowner could maintain exclusive claim on his land provided the basis for economic security in the agricultural society of the time. Land was abundant, and the reality that sustained the hope for landownership in early America was the frontier. Society was relatively fluid, and many people without land in 1775 expected someday to acquire a good deal of property for themselves. To these future farmers of America, the guarantee of title to prop-

---

[3] Adam Smith, *The Wealth of Nations,* (Chicago: Encyclopedia Britannica, 1952) p. 6.

[4] Charles Beard presented a forceful statement of this thesis in *An "Economic" Interpretation of the Constitution of the United States* (New York: Macmillan, 1913). The argument is placed in a more general context by Louis Hacker in *The Triumph of American Capitalism* (New York: Columbia University Press, 1940). The very narrow "economic" interpretation of the constitution presented by Beard is no longer generally accepted by historians. For example, see the point by point refutation of Beard by Robert Brown in *Charles Beard and the Constitution* (Princeton, N.J.: Princeton University Press, 1956).

erty was just as essential as it was to the current generation of land-owners.

The institutional arrangements established with the ratification of the Constitution provided a framework in which market forces could once again generate economic growth. By explicitly limiting the right of government to interfere in the affairs of private individuals, the Constitution served to protect the status quo, and at the same time to offer the possibility for vast change to occur as a result of individuals' pursuit of their own opportunities. The vitality of the colonial economy was retained and the threat to its continued expansion removed. The paternalism of seventeenth- and eighteenth-century mercantilism was dramatically swept aside in favor of an individualism which was to become the hallmark of nineteenth-century liberal political and economic philosophies.

The Constitution of the United States was a uniquely American document. Nevertheless, it embodied several of the latest intellectual influences from both Great Britain and the Continent with respect to political and economic philosophies. One such influence was that of the "Scottish philosophers" such as Adam Smith. The men who were instrumental in framing the Constitution (particularly Thomas Jefferson and his colleagues from Virginia) obviously believed that Smith's "invisible hand" would see to it that individual interests would be channeled towards constructive purposes. Though the checks and balances were not spelled out in the economic sphere as explicitly as they were for the political structure, it is clear that the Constitution takes for granted the beneficent result of Smith's free market system.

This confidence in market forces was evident by the manner in which the Constitution takes note of another of Smith's dicta: "[Specialization] is limited by the extent of the market." [5] The prohibition on interference by any level of government in the conduct of interstate commerce bound the various states of the union into a single marketplace—a vast area of unsettled land and unused resources. This break with the protectionist tendencies of mercantilism paid huge dividends. Left to their own interests and spurred on by the expanding markets both at home and abroad, Americans increased their production—and their material welfare—to levels never dreamed possible by Smith or the Founding Fathers.

The Constitution did contain what proved to be a tragic flaw. Americans were allowed to continue owning slaves. All the rhetoric about freedom and human rights did nothing to assist the plight of the three-quarters of a million blacks who were enslaved in 1790. They had no individual freedoms, no share in the economic gains of the new economy, no hope to realize someday the opportunities open to other Americans. The need to gain the support of the Southern states for the new union had neces-

---

[5] Smith, *The Wealth of Nations*, p. 8.

sitated a compromise. Chattel slavery would continue to be legal in the United States; however, the abominable slave trade, which brought enslaved blacks into the country from Africa and the West Indies, would be abolished twenty years after the Constitution was ratified. Unfortunately, those who had hoped for a gradual extinction of black slavery once the supply of cheap slaves was cut off greatly underestimated the vitality of the South's "peculiar institution." By the 1850s the pressure for an expansion of slavery—a pressure which derived in large measure from market forces—threatened the Union. The contradiction of slavery in a free society brought about an irrepressible conflict—a conflict which produced the bloodiest war in American history.

SLAVERY AND THE CIVIL WAR

The sectional differences which eventually erupted into the American Civil War date back to the earliest days of colonial settlement in North America. In the world of the late seventeenth and early eighteenth centuries, communities were connected by only the most rudimentary means of transportation and communications. As a result, economic development was geared to local production, with only minor attention given to external markets. Even within a fairly small geographic area, one could find highly distinctive social and economic characteristics.

The vigorous growth of international and interregional trade in the eighteenth century produced a powerful pressure to pull the regions together into a single market. The same factors, however, accentuated the economic differences between trading areas. These contrasting pressures, evident in the period immediately after the Revolution, increased as time went on. For the most part, the pressure for economic (and political) unity prevailed. The problems of economic adjustment created by external market forces were met by a continuous series of relatively mild responses, responses which usually created only minor dislocations in any year or for any locality. The gains from engaging in interregional trade were substantial enough (and obvious enough) to outweigh the costs of having continually to alter the pattern of production in response to prices fixed by conditions beyond the control of local producers. Economic growth did cause frictions which were evident in the divergent economic interests of the various regions. Representatives from the North, South, and West argued over their recommendations for national policies with regard to tariffs, transportation, land policy, banking, and immigration. But the sectional differences on these issues were not uniform, and, where sharp divisions did occur on economic matters, satisfactory compromises were worked out.

It was not economic sectionalism that ultimately posed a threat to the

Union; that threat came from an issue on which there could not be continued compromise: the moral and economic contradictions of slavery in a free society. If Northerners had been willing to tolerate slavery in their society, or Southerners willing to free their slaves, then a unified market system might have continued to function in both the North and the South. But an increasing number of Northerners viewed the continuous expansion of slavery (particularly into western lands) as a threat to their own economic and social position; and Southerners were even more adamant that the right to own slaves not be restricted. Slavery had been incorporated as one of the essential features of production in the southern states. The presence of market slavery posed an insurmountable obstacle to any attempt to reach accord on a plan that might eventually allow slave and free labor to coexist in the same market system. To understand just how powerful and pervasive the economic pressures supporting the slave system were, it is instructive to consider the economics of American slavery.

An economically rational slave system requires that slaves be considered legal property, to be used as their masters see fit. Included in this property right is the possibility that owners might sell an individual slave to someone else. Whoever owned the slave was entitled to any product or service produced by the slave. As long as the slave was able to produce some output or service whose value exceeded the cost of items necessary for the slave's living (shelter, food, clothing), the master would receive some surplus, and the slave would have a positive market value. It was the value of this surplus that determined the price of a slave. The determination of the market value of a female slave was complicated by the fact that, in addition to any output resulting from her labor, the master would also be the owner of any children she might bear. As the child grew up, the owner would realize an appreciation in its value. The promise of such gains was reflected in the price paid for female slaves of child-bearing age.

The market value—or price—of a slave thus reflected the total benefits which accrued to the owner over the slave's lifetime. As long as there was an organized market on which slaves could be traded, and as long as slaves were able to produce a surplus by performing some useful task, slavery would be profitable. Both of these conditions were met in the society of the antebellum South; economic historians have shown rather convincingly that the actual prices paid for slaves at that time reflected the economic value of slave products—including the value of children born to slaves.[6]

---

[6] For a summary of the literature on this point see Robert Fogel and Stanley Engerman, "The Economics of Slavery," in *The Reinterpretation of American Economic History*, Robert Fogel and Stanley Engerman eds. (New York: Harper & Row, Pub., 1971), An excellent collection of articles covering the historical literature surrounding the question of whether or not slavery was profitable is Hugh Aitken, *Did Slavery Pay?* (Boston: Houghton Mifflin, 1971).

It is important to stress that slavery could have been worthwhile to southern slaveowners even if the surplus produced by each slave was quite small. This seemed to be the case during the late colonial period, when the market for tobacco (which was the staple crop at that time) was depressed. The problems with depressed prices of the crop were reflected in the prices of slaves, and this was an encouraging sign to those who hoped to end slavery in the 1780s and 1790s. The closing of the slave trade within twenty years, offered as a compromise to induce the southern states to join in the federal union created by the Constitution, was supported by anti-slave forces, partly in the hope that cutting off the supply of cheap slaves from the Carribean would combine with the depressed price of tobacco to make owning slaves even less attractive. The expectation that slavery would actually die out from economic pressures proved to be unfounded, and only a few of the more zealous abolitionists of the time seem to have believed that this was a realistic possibility. On the other hand, the possibility that slavery would grow less rapidly, or that some sort of emancipation scheme—similar to those being considered in the northern states at the time—was perhaps not so far-fetched.[7]

Whatever the prospects for emancipation in the South at the time of the Constitution, the picture changed dramatically over the next few decades. In 1790 a clever Yankee inventor visiting South Carolina devised a contraption called the cotton gin. Eli Whitney's idea provided planters with an economical means of combing and cleaning the "short staple" cotton, which could be grown in the tidewater and alluvial areas of the South. Prior to the invention of the cotton gin, the amount of labor time required to remove the seeds from this short staple cotton was so great that commercial production of the crop was impractical. Long staple cotton could be cleaned economically; however, this variety of plant could only be grown along the coastal areas of South Carolina and Georgia. Short staple cotton, in contrast, could be grown anywhere in the South. Climatic conditions were not favorable to cotton production in the northern or western states—a fact which provided the South with a considerable advantage in the development of commercial agriculture.

As the demand abroad for cotton emerged and grew, Whitney's invention opened up a new vista for southern slaveholders. Cotton, they soon discovered, was a crop ideally suited for large farms and slave labor. In 1790 the total value of cotton exported from the United States was less than $500,000, almost all of it grown in the coastal areas of the South.

---

[7] See the discussion of Arthur Silversmit, *The First Emancipation: The Abolition of Slavery in the North* (Chicago: University of Chicago Press, 1967) for an account of the development of antislavery sentiment in the North, and how the opponents of slavery fought to achieve emancipation. Claudia Goldin comments on the economics of such schemes in "The Economics of Emancipation," *Journal of Economic History,* 33 (March 1973), 66-85.

Within twenty years the value of cotton exports had risen thirtyfold to $15 million; on the eve of the Civil War cotton exports totaled just over $190 million. Over the final three decades of the antebellum period, cotton accounted for at least one-half of the total value of merchandise exports from the United States. "King Cotton," as contemporary Southerners noted, stimulated economic growth not only for the South, but for the rest of the economy as well.[8] Equally important, cotton provided the impetus for southern society to continue one of the most sophisticated systems of slavery ever devised.

There can be no question but that, on the eve of the Civil War, slavery was a thriving economic system. In that year the market price of a prime field hand averaged about $1,500. In modern dollars that figure would be much higher. Considering the changes in prices and incomes, it is fair to say that the purchase of a slave in the late 1850s would be equivalent to buying an expensive automobile today—between $15,000 and $20,000. It should be noted that $1,500 is the *average* price for a young, healthy, but unskilled field hand. Slaves with special skills might sell for as much as twice that figure. As an additional indication of how important slaves were in financial terms, we can note that according to the data collected by the Census Office in 1860, the total value of slaves represented about one-half the aggregate value of all assets in the cotton regions of the South.[9] What is equally important, the high prices in 1860 were not particularly unusual; the trend in slave prices had been upward for a long time. This increase in the value of slaves seems to reflect the high returns slave labor brought to slaveowners, particularly in the fertile lands of the lower Mississippi Valley and the "Black Belt" of Alabama and Georgia. Even in those areas where the product of field labor did not provide a profit, the slaveowner need not despair. He could, after all, sell his slaves and pocket the capital gains. It is these capital gains from the increase in the slave population that many earlier writers overlooked in their analyses of the profitability of slavery. Slaves in the United States not only produced agricultural output; they produced more slaves as well.[10]

Economics even entered into the determination of how well slaves were treated. The capitalist nature of American slavery produced both benign and pernicious effects. On one hand, the slave, as a valuable economic

---

[8] On the importance of the expansion of cotton production in spurring regional specialization in all parts of the country, see Douglass C. North, *The Economic Growth of the United States, 1790-1860* (Englewood Cliffs, N.J.: Prentice-Hall, 1961). On the pervasiveness of the cotton specialization in the southern economy, see Harold Woodman, *King Cotton and his Retainers* (Lexington, Ky.: University of Kentucky Press, 1967).

[9] See the discussion of this point in Roger Ransom and Richard Sutch, *One Kind of Freedom: The Economic Consequences of Emancipation* (New York: Cambridge University Press, 1977), pp. 52-53.

[10] See the essays by Richard Sutch, Alfred Conrad and John Meyer, and Yasukichi Yasuba in Aitken, *Did Slavery Pay?*

asset, had to be well cared for. Those who defended slavery always pointed this out, noting that southern blacks were often housed and fed better than free workers in the North. But, although he took care of his valuable slaves, the capitalist master could not afford to be overly sentimental. The value of a slave, we noted, was based on net output. Thus, market conditions pressured slaveowners to drive their slaves to the limit of their endurance, and to economize on provisions of food and clothing. Poor land—which was common in the Old South, where farmers had been depleting the soil for years—meant low returns to cotton, producing a pressure to sell slaves. Few voices in the South were raised in objection to those masters who were occasionally forced to sell slaves in order to balance their books at the end of the year. Even when a master had to resort to the expediency of selling a few of his slaves for several consecutive years in order to make ends meet, this was not seen as trading in slaves. However, the aggregate effect of such individual actions looks very much like a slave trade. Those buying slaves for their labor were planters on good land—and the best land was in the West. Consequently, the old slave trade with the Carribean was replaced by a new slave trade between the various southern states. How large this new trade was is hard to say. Estimates of the movement of slaves for the last decade before the Civil War imply that as many as 250,000 slaves were sent from the exporting states of the South Atlantic to the importing states to the west. If these estimates are accurate, the impact of the slave trade must have been far-reaching. The odds that a slave would have some contact with the slave trade— whether by sale or by movement of a master—were very high indeed.[11]

Cold statistics, while they point out the magnitude of the problem, cannot reveal the harshness of the slave world in the antebellum United States. By most accounts it was a grim existence indeed. Simon Legree, the overseer in Harriet Beecher Stowe's novel *Uncle Tom's Cabin,* may not have been as typical as many abolitionists insisted, but if we are to judge from the "rules" put forward by the more enlightened slaveowners, he was not all that atypical, either. The economic situation of the slave and master had much to do with the treatment they received. If the plantation was well off, the master could afford to be generous and provide for his slaves. If not, the slave was likely to suffer deprivation. The slave plantation's bottom line, after all, was income. Southern slavery was a very efficient system of production. But its efficiency was the result of considerable sacrifice on the part of those at the bottom of the system—the slaves. The economic pressures of the market system produced a morality among

---

[11] The best statistics on slave migration are those developed by Richard Sutch, "The Breeding of Slaves for Sale and the Western Expansion of Slavery, 1850-1860," in *Race and Slavery in the Western Hemisphere: Quantitative Studies,* eds. Stanley Engerman and Eugene Genovese, (Princeton, N.J.: Princeton University Press, 1975): 173–210.

planters which those who objected to slavery could point to as an unmitigated evil, whatever the economic benefits from slavery might be.[12]

The economic robustness of the slave system in southern agriculture was an extremely important factor in shaping the alternatives which could be considered by those seeking to find a compromise between slavery and abolition, or at least some containment of the slave system. To the abolitionist, of course, the only acceptable solution was the adoption of some scheme of peaceful emancipation. However, there was the nagging problem of whether or not the slaveowner should be compensated for his emancipated property, as the capitalist ethic would suggest. Because the value of a slave was already high (and expected to rise still more), the monetary costs of such a scheme would pose problems. The most noteworthy example of such a plan pursued to conclusion—emancipation in the British West Indies—was a case in which the slave population was relatively small and the costs of buying the slaves could be spread over a large number of people. Such was not the case in the United States, where the number of slaves was great, and the capital investment in slaves represented a sizeable sum even when shared by the entire population. The value of slave capital in the United States on the eve of the Civil War exceeded $3 billion. Finding a way to finance a sum that large would have been a major task, since the gross output of the United States in 1859 was only slightly more than $4 billion.[13] The costs of emancipating the slaves were large, and the benefits diffused among many people, only a small minority of whom (the abolitionists) really seemed to place a very high value on assisting the enslaved blacks in their quest for freedom.

The total abolition of slavery was never a very likely political outcome during the antebellum years. A more limited objective, which was the focus of political debate, was containment of slavery within some distinct territorial bounds. The two great Compromises, in 1820 and 1850, reflected efforts to define "slave" and "free" territories. Ultimately that attempt failed amid the bloodshed of Kansas and Nebraska. This clash of slave and free forces sheds additional light on the economic issues behind the Civil War. The push for western lands by both western and southern farmers brought the proslavery and antislavery factions into direct con-

---

[12] This point is not conceded by all scholars. Thus, for example, Fogel and Engerman argue that the economic considerations of capitalist slavery worked to mitigate the harshness of slave life in their study, *Time on the Cross* (Boston: Little, Brown, 1974). Their analysis, however, has a number of serious flaws. See Roger Ransom, "Was It Really All That Great To Be A Slave?," *Agricultural History*, 48 (October 1974). A series of more detailed critiques can be found in Paul David and others, *Reckoning with Slavery* (New York: Oxford University Press, 1975). For still another look at "the world the slaves made," see Eugene Genovese, *Roll, Jordan, Roll* (New York: Pantheon, 1974).

[13] These problems are discussed by Goldin in "The Economics of Emancipation," and by Gerald Gunderson in "The Origin of the American Civil War," *Journal of Economic History*, 34 (December 1974).

flict on an issue central to farmers in both regions. The "yeoman farmers" of the South, confronted with the rising price of slaves, saw cheap land to the west as the necessary means for acquiring a stake in the prosperous cotton culture. With land, a family might hope eventually to acquire slaves —and slaves were the key to wealth in the antebellum South. To the northern or western farmer, cheap land was equally essential, and the prospect of having as neighbors slave planters, with their large holdings of both slaves and land, was not appealing. The "Free Soilers" were especially adamant in their demands for free land and were extremely hostile to the prospect of living in an area inhabited by Negro slaves. Viewed in this light, the economic interests of both the large slaveholders and yeoman farmers of the North and the South, are seen to be much more subtle than a simple defense of past investment.[14]

The argument that economic factors blocked any hope of reconciliation between the North and the South should not be pushed too far. It seems unlikely that the South seceded from the Union solely to reap the economic gains of continuing slavery. Southerners went to war to preserve a way of life based on the enslavement of almost 4 million black Americans, a system of racial slavery which happened also to be remunerative to slaveholding capitalists. Both northern and southern observers knew that southern society could not exist as it was in 1860 if any kind of emancipation took place. I find it difficult to accept an argument that explains the Civil War as a product of some sort of economic reasoning on the part of Northerners and Southerners.[15] Even in the narrowest economic sense, the costs of the Civil War could not be justified in terms of any reasonable calculation of benefits (to those who fought the war) from abolition. Viewed from another perspective, the war was "irrational" because there was an alternative which might accomplish the same ends at a much lower cost. Substantial though it may have been, the price of compensated emancipation did not approach the fiscal or human costs incurred by either side during the war. In economic terms alone, the Civil War does not make sense.

Historians—and economic historians as well—may never settle the debate of whether slavery caused the Civil War. Clearly it was an important factor, and the argument of this chapter claims that the economics of slavery increased rather than mitigated the frictions caused by pres-

---

[14] For a recent attempt at "making economic sense of cotton, slavery and the Civil War," see Gavin Wright, The Political Economy of the Cotton South (New York: W.W. Norton & Co., Inc., 1978), Chapter 5.

[15] Gunderson, in his article "The Origin of the American Civil War," does develop such an argument. He claims that the "expected costs" did indeed about balance the "expected gains," and that the two sides were "economically" rational. The argument, in my judgment, is not convincing; Gunderson's hypothetical world seems far removed from the realities of 1860.

sures to abolish slavery. What is not a matter of debate is that the war did eliminate any legal foundation for chattel labor in the United States. The Thirteenth Amendment abolished involuntary servitude; the Fourteenth Amendment provided legal assurances that the civil rights of all citizens would be equally upheld. After nearly 250 years, black Americans were finally set free.

They were free, but not yet truly equal, for the assurances provided by legal emancipation proved too weak to ensure equality. Freedom, in the sense that it had been enjoyed by white Americans, remained an elusive dream for black Americans.

RECONSTRUCTION IN THE SOUTH

If the freeing of four million blacks was the great accomplishment of the Civil War, then the years of the Reconstruction which followed represent an equally great failure to capitalize on the opportunity created by emancipation. The dream of a "New South," a South without slavery and patterned after the northern free market, never materialized. The South after 1865 lapsed into economic stagnation that saw it become the economic backwater of a vibrant and expanding American system.[16]

What accounts for this failure? Why did the opportunity to rebuild the South slip by? Ironically, Reconstruction failed partly because there was so much that could be done. The emancipation of slavery was a sudden and traumatic shock to the South. Within the space of a few short months an entire social and economic system was almost totally destroyed. The financial institutions were bankrupt, the plantation system gone, and whites were now expected to consider the "freedmen" as members of a free labor force. In short, a new economic system had to be devised to replace the old regime.

There was, unfortunately, no real plan for the most sweeping set of institutional reforms attempted in United States history. The slaveowners had been "whupped," the blacks set free; the rest was expected to follow naturally enough from the elimination of slavery. No one believed it would

---

[16] There is a vast literature on the Reconstruction, and recently the interest in the economic facets of the period has picked up considerably. The discussion that follows in this chapter draws heavily on Ransom and Sutch, *One Kind of Freedom: The Economic Consequences of Emancipation* (New York: Cambridge University Press, 1977), and Ransom and Sutch, "Growth and Welfare in the American South of the Nineteenth Century," *Explorations in Economic History,* 16 (April 1979). Robert Higgs presents a rather different analysis in *Competition and Coercion: Blacks in the American Economy, 1865-1914* (New York: Cambridge University Press, 1977). For a historian's view of the economic side of Reconstruction in the South, see Woodman, *King Cotton;* and Jonathan Wiener, *Social Origins of the New South: Alabama 1865-1885* (Baton Rouge: Louisiana State University Press, 1978).

be easy, of course. Civil rights legislation was passed by Congress, and in the early years of Reconstruction Congress even toyed with the idea that a redistribution of land—property which had been seized by the Federal Army during the war—might aid in the reorganization of southern society. But most Northerners were not prepared to accept an idea as radical as giving expropriated property to ex-slaves, and the question of land reform never even came to a vote. President Andrew Johnson's general pardon in 1865 extended amnesty to all but a few ex-confederates, and most farms were restored to their antebellum owners.

Land, which represented the basis for economic power in the agricultural South, remained in the hands of a few large planters—by and large the same class of men who had controlled the economic and political fortunes of the antebellum South. By the early 1870s, interest in reconstructing the South was already disappearing in the North. Once the ex-slaves were employed in the production of crops, the "invisible hand" of the market—guided by the law of supply and demand—should have been sufficient to provide the necessary direction for institutional reorganization in a "New South."

In the context of the turmoil surrounding the collapse of slave society in the South, this faith in the restorative powers of the market proved sadly misplaced. The legacy of slavery to both blacks and whites effectively undermined the establishment of a free market for labor and credit after the war. Slavery had left blacks totally unprepared for freedom. Virtually all ex-slaves were illiterate, and fewer than one out of six black men (and a still smaller fraction of black women) had managed to learn some rudimentary trade or skill to practice as freedmen. The ex-slaves were cast adrift in the marketplace without assets, skills, or experience in coping with the challenges and responsibilities of freedom. To whites, slavery left a more subtle, yet in the long run equally crippling, legacy of racist attitudes and fears. Two-and-a-half centuries of black slavery had produced a deep seated conviction on the part of whites that the black race was inferior—incapable of functioning in a free society. Manifestations of this racism—most strikingly revealed in the violent activities of the Ku Klux Klan—can be seen in the resistance to providing blacks with land and education. The racism not only affected white behavior toward the social position of blacks; it also shaped their evaluation of black abilities in the labor market—a labor market controlled by white landlords.

Whites' solution to the problem of how to combine land and labor now that the blacks were free was to reinstate the plantation system with gangs of wage workers replacing the slaves. Blacks, not surprisingly, were not at all enthusiastic about such conditions. These differing points of view were resolved by the introduction of a new form of tenure arrangement: *sharecropping*. Sharecropping was an agreement that stipulated that the tenant and landlord split the farm output according to some agreed-upon ratio (typically in halves). The "cropper" supplied the labor; the landlord provided the land and most of the farm capital.

Sharecropping was one of the most significant institutional changes to emerge from the Reconstruction era. It was not planned; working for a share of the crop was very uncommon in the South before the war, and neither the planters nor the northern advisers in the Freedmen's Bureau favored it when it began to appear in 1866 and 1867. An arrangement which seemed to elevate the Negro to a position of copartner in the farm management had little appeal for the whites. Despite this displeasure, white landlords found (often to their surprise) that the ex-slave worked well under the cropping agreements. For their part, blacks saw sharecropping as a chance to improve their lot much more readily than would be possible under the gang system. Though it has subsequently come under considerable criticism as an inefficient and exploitive form of tenure, share-cropping began as a compromise which suited both labor and landlord. The eagerness with which blacks initially embraced sharecropping reflected the promise which that system offered.[17] Certainly, it was preferable to the terms of wage labor offered by planters in the first seasons after the war, and it must have seemed infinitely superior to the conditions of slavery.

If the only change in the post-emancipation period had been the introduction of a new tenure arrangement, then it is possible that share-cropping could have provided a basis for economic advancement for blacks —and for white farmers as well. But land tenure was not the only change. A sharecropping contract provided the tenant with only one factor of production—land. The farm family could supply the second factor—labor. But where was a tenant to find the third factor of production—capital? Who would provide credit? As in the case of land tenure, a new institutional arrangement had to be developed. Gradually, it become clear that the task of extending credit to farmers could be handled most effectively by the rural merchants scattered throughout the South. These storekeepers could concentrate on a relatively small geographic area, and, because they were near their customers, they were willing to accept the risks associated with loans secured by nothing more than a lien against the coming crop.

The new credit structure and tenure arrangements succeeded in providing a means of financing the crop each year. But the manner in which they did so involved a monopolistic arrangement. Farmers without assets

---

[17] The argument of the text can be found in Ransom and Sutch, *One Kind of Freedom*, Chapters 4 and 5. Several writers have insisted that sharecropping remained an effective means of Negro advancement. See in particular Higgs, *Competition and Coercion*, and Stephen DeCanio, *Agriculture in the Postbellum South* (Cambridge, Mass.: MIT Press, 1974).

or land became dependent upon the credit offered by a single merchant. The price of agricultural credit reflected the extent of this monopoly; the average rate of interest charged by rural merchants in Georgia during the 1880s was 60 percent. To make matters worse, the merchant insisted that the farmer grow cotton to ensure that there would be sufficient cash at the end of the year—and, coincidently, to increase the farmer's dependence upon supplies purchased at the merchant's store. Southern agriculture became entangled in a monopolistic credit system which limited opportunities to the farmers. In the words of one observer, the South was trapped in a system of "debt peonage." [18]

Why was such an economic system—which was both exploitive and inefficient—allowed to persist in the midst of an economy which elsewhere was undergoing rapid economic growth and enormous changes? The answer to this question reveals an important aspect of economic change in a market society. As we noted in the last chapter, market forces can resist, as well as promote, changes. This seems particularly true when the market has found an equilibrium. In the case of the American South, one of the mitigating factors against economic change was the low income equilibrium that the agricultural markets had created for the majority of southern farmers. Operators of small farms—tenants and owners alike—remained poor year after year precisely because they were unable to take advantage of the escapes offered by the market for their products. They were continually pressured into borrowing against a future which remained permanently mortgaged. In the logic of the Davis-North model, one could argue that their poverty closed off effective collective action by denying them the means with which to organize. Farmers accepted the situation of debt peonage because it was the only alternative they could afford. The costs of breaking free from the control of a merchant were too high.

The economics of the agricultural system, moreover, served a very important social objective: blacks were effectively kept in their place as a landless, rural class. The stagnation of the cotton economy produced a very efficient form of race control. To be sure, the price was high; economic progress for many whites was also held in check. But it was blacks, not whites, who were at the bottom of the economic scale. In this case, the definition of "class" according to race coincided with that of an economic class. Southern whites as a racial and economic class had a strong common interest in preserving an economic system which effectively kept blacks in agriculture as laborers with no claim to land. The imperfect eco-

---

[18] George K. Holmes, "Peons of the South," *Annals of the American Academy of Political and Social Science,* 4 (September 1893). The issue of debt peonage is currently a matter of considerable controversy. See the articles by Ransom and Sutch, Joseph Reid, Peter Temin, Goldin and Wright in *Explorations in Economic History,* 16 (January 1979); the issue is devoted to the discussion of arguments on the postbellum system of credit and tenure.

nomic institutions which had emerged from the wartime adjustments were allowed to become permanent because they were consistent with—indeed, they reinforced—social objectives which sought to keep blacks segregated from whites in the postbellum South.

ECONOMIC CHANGE AFTER THE CIVIL WAR

The economic changes of the post-Civil War were not confined to the Reconstruction of the defeated Confederate states and the freeing of black slaves. Indeed, for Northerners, the plight of the ex-slaves and their former masters held only a momentary interest. Outside the South, the impact of the Civil War was very different. Historians Charles Beard and Louis Hacker have termed the Civil War a "Second American Revolution" which culminated in the "triumph" of industrial capitalists as the dominant economic and political class of the United States.[19] The Hacker-Beard thesis stresses two main points:

1. The Civil War accelerated industrialization of the United States by providing a direct stimulus to industry.

2. The major reforms enacted during the war and immediately afterwards fundamentally altered the institutional structure of the American economy in a fashion that favored industrial development.

Though this thesis has been challenged by many writers who point out that the rate of growth during the Civil War decade hardly supports a claim that the war directly boosted industrial growth, the argument that there was a fundamental change in the direction of American economic development following 1865 has persisted. There were, after all, a number of important changes inaugurated after the War, and these changes appear to have been made possible through the political power of the northern Republican Party—a party whose voice reflected the interests of the industrial capitalist class.

That the Civil War produced a new alignment of political groups in the United States is obvious. The issue we wish to address is whether this new political coalition introduced changes which clearly changed the direction of economic policy and institutions in the United States.[20] The

---

[19] Charles Beard and Mary Beard, *The Rise of American Civilization* (New York: Macmillan, 1927); Hacker, *The Triumph of American Capitalism*, Chapters 23-26. An updated statement of these views was provided by Hacker in his book, *The Course of American Growth and Development* (New York: John Wiley, 1971).

[20] For an excellent summary of the debate over the effects of the Civil War, see the articles in Ralph Andreano, ed., *The Economic Impact of the Civil War*, 2nd ed., (Cambridge, Mass.: Schenkman, 1964).

Hacker-Beard thesis focuses on the manner in which the new ruling class of capitalists managed to shape changes in the structure of the American economic system to suit their own interests. As Professor Hacker observed, the men who put the Reconstruction Acts through Congress

> . . . were neither Abolitionists nor egalitarians: The unequal status of the Negroes and poor southern whites was of no interest to them. But, as spokesmen for industrial capitalism, the war furnished them the opportunity to round out the economic program of the class they represented.[21]

Hacker proceeded to identify several areas that illustrate his point. The National Bank Act of 1864 established a system of federally chartered banks with restrictions that favored larger, urban banks and the industrial-commercial interests they served. The promotion of railroads through the granting of federal lands and subsidies allowed capitalists to exploit the settlement of vast areas of the West. The Homestead Act sought to open up the West to anyone by offering 160 acres free to anyone who would settle on the land. The Morrill Act laid the foundation for an extensive system of publicly funded higher education by giving land grants for the establishment of colleges. The imposition of more restrictive tariffs protected domestic manufacturers at the expense of consumers, while at the same time immigration was encouraged to keep the costs (that is, the wages) of labor low. Finally, the government pursued a policy of restrictive credit and debt retirement which created a decline in prices—thus favoring the creditor class over the debtors. Even the Fourteenth Amendment was, in Hacker's view, meant as a protection of corporate rights, not the rights of ex-slaves, in the South.

Two lines of criticism have been leveled against this sweeping indictment of the Republican programs of reform after the Civil War. First, critics point out that the benefits from many of the changes enacted by the Reconstruction Congresses were not restricted to capitalists. Subsidies to railroads, for example, benefitted western agriculture through greatly reduced transportation costs—whatever the profits reaped by capitalists. Benefits from acts such as the Homestead Act and the Morrill Act were directed as much towards the western farmers as they were towards capitalists in the east. Such changes could easily be viewed as the result of a consensus reached between various groups—all of whom stood to gain from the distribution of gains—rather than the product of a single group's narrow interest. To argue that the reforms were the product of a conspiracy by a single group overlooks the possibility that these acts stimulated economic growth and settlement to the west which benefited many people, not just a privileged few.

A second criticism of the Hacker-Beard approach to economic

---

[21] Hacker, *The Triumph of American Capitalism*, p. 340; italics in the original.

change in the postbellum period points out that many of the actions taken did *not* represent breaks with past arrangements. That is, the legislative reforms of the Reconstruction Congresses represented little more than the extrapolation of past trends. Viewed in this light, the legislation was not a pathbreaking switch in institutional arrangements, but rather the more usual situation in which incremental responses were made to the continual pressures for economic change.

The National Banking Act is an example. There is indeed evidence that the act made it easier for eastern banks to obtain federal charters. It also seems to have been the case that restrictions on minimum capital investment and loan policies made the formation and operation of National Banks more difficult in the West and the South. But the act did not alter the fundamental tenet of American banking in the nineteenth century: freedom of entry. While National Banks were restricted, banks chartered by the states were not. As a result, the impact of the National Bank Act's restrictive provisions was lessened through the chartering of state banks. Despite its narrow intent, the National Bank Act proved to be just one more episode in the tug of war between "hard" and "easy" money forces in the nineteenth century. If the banking reforms of 1864 were a victory for the capitalists, then the reemergence of state banks shortly thereafter was a victory for the "other side." And the dominant feature of banking in rural areas—small banks scattered in many markets—remained unchanged by the reforms pressed by urban interests.[22]

Nor were the Homestead Act or the railroad subsidies new policies. The Pre-emption Act of 1843 had clearly established the principle of "squatter's rights"; the Homestead Act merely extended this notion by promising every settler 160 acres. Railroad subsidies were consistent with a pattern of government aid to transportation dating back to the early nineteenth century; the only change was an increased role for the federal government.[23] In other words, a strong case can be made for the view that the Reconstruction reforms were not a break with the past, and that the

---

[22] On the problems of rural banks under the act, see Richard Sylla, "Federal Policy, Banking Market Structure, and Capital Mobilization in the United States, 1863–1913," *Journal of Economic History*, 29 (December 1969). Congress placed a 10 percent tax on state bank notes, which curtailed activities of state banks for several years in the 1870s. However, by the 1880s the rise of deposit banking had largely offset this obstacle everywhere except in the South, where the problems discussed in regard to credit continued to pose an obstacle to banking of any sort. For an argument that the National Banking Act had relatively little impact on the monetary situation in the country as a whole, see Milton Friedman and Anna Schwartz, *A Monetary History of the United States, 1867-1960* (Princeton, N.J.: Princeton University Press, 1963).

[23] For a collection of articles which deal with the emergence of federal land policy, see Vernon L. Carstensen, ed., *The Public Lands* (Madison, Wis.: University of Wisconsin Press, 1963). On the role of government in transportation during the nineteenth century, see Carter Goodrich, *Government Promotion of American Canals and Railroads* (New York: Columbia University Press, 1960).

emerging power of the manufacturing and commercial interests would have been heard from in any case. The Hacker-Beard interpretation of Reconstruction as a product of class interest oversimplifies the many different interests within the fledgling capitalist class and the equally diverse interests of their opponents. By stressing the essential continuity of policies before and after the Civil War, their critics have pointed to the diversity of interests which formed coalitions to effect economic policy. Not all of the coalitions were successful, and the results of their efforts were at times different from what they intended. As Davis and North might point out, the bargains reached were based on the perceived interests of the groups—and those perceptions were not always correct.[24]

Notwithstanding their critics' arguments, Hacker and Beard seem to have a valid point when they argue that the capitalist interests of the Republican Party emerged stronger from the Civil War than had been evident in the antebellum period. Industry in the United States had come of age. As Hacker argued, more than ever after 1865 it would be the voice of *capital* that shaped the economic policies of government, both in Washington and in state houses across the nation. Whether or not this was a new trend, it was a reality which foreshadowed a new set of challenges to the American system.

---

[24] The criticisms of the Hacker-Beard thesis are summarized by Stanley Engerman in his essay reprinted in Andreano, *The Economic Impact of the Civil War.*

4

THE TRIUMPH
of AMERICAN
CAPITALISM

In the half century which elapsed between the meeting of Grant and Lee at Appomattox and Woodrow Wilson's trip to Versailles in 1919, the United States was transformed from an economy whose industry had only begun to flex its muscle into an industrial giant. Though the process of change which brought about this transformation was far more subtle than the fighting of the Revolutionary or Civil wars, the impact of the changes proved to be just as great. By the end of the nineteenth century, Americans found themselves confronted with a set of new and perplexing problems.

The problems were new because the technology and organization of an industrial society were new. They were perplexing because, unlike the situations which precipitated the wars, industrialization did not produce crises that served to concentrate activity at a few points; the pressures of the industrial economy were scattered everywhere. Farmers, workers, merchants, and small-businessmen all were affected, but not always in the same way. Consequently, the pressures for reform during this period were more diffuse, and the objectives of reformers were correspondingly less focused. The farm revolt, the struggle for better working conditions, and the efforts of "progressives" to achieve economic reforms all represented responses to the cumulative impact of a half-century of industrialization. And, to varying degrees, they succeeded; the reformers had some victories in their fights with the railroads, the trusts, and the concentration of economic power.

They did not, however, succeed in fundamentally altering the distribution of economic power in America. The Progressive Era witnessed major efforts to alter the economic system, and those efforts prompted counterproposals by those who felt threatened by the original reforms. In the course of jockeying back and forth, the economic system *was* changed. However, both the concentration of economic power and the economic ideology that supported that power remained intact. Large corporations remained a part of our economic life, and the principle of *laissez faire,* which had dominated economic policy throughout the last quarter of the nineteenth century, survived (though proponents were forced to concede that areas did exist in which the market could not be allowed to operate without some limitations). Industrialists had their victories, too.

The process of economic change around the turn of the century is fascinating, partly because there was no pressing crisis nor any clear resolution of the conflicting pressures which were prompting reform and reaction to reform. Our study of the period focuses on two crucial issues which dominated the discussion of the day and reflected the emerging industrial revolution:

1. The reaction of farmers to the increasing dominance of the marketplace, and the growing importance of the industrial sector in shaping forces within that marketplace.
2. The control of economic power that emerged with the growth of vast corporate empires. Through their control of capital, these groups—most notably the trusts—could manipulate markets to their own advantage, and in the process affected the economic welfare of millions of Americans.

ECONOMIC GROWTH IN THE GILDED AGE

The expansion of production achieved by the American economy during this interval is one of the most remarkable examples of sustained growth ever recorded, and the benefits can be duly noted in the statistics on income and production. After adjusting for changes in prices, gross national product—the total value of goods and services produced in a year—was six times larger in 1919 than it had been in the decade following the Civil War. This means that the annual rate of growth over those fifty years was just over 3¾ percent, and per capita output more than tripled in two generations.[1]

---

[1] Prior to 1890, the estimates of GNP are presented as an average for each decade. For the decade 1869-1879, total GNP (in 1958 dollars) was $23.1 billion; in 1919 GNP totaled $146.4 billion. Per capita GNP during that time averaged $531; in 1919 it was $1,401. See U.S. Bureau of the Census, *Historical Statistics of the United States from Colonial Times to 1970,* Bicentennial Edition, 2 Parts (Washington: G.P.O., 1976), Chapter F. Unless otherwise noted, descriptive statistics in this chapter are from *Historical Statistics.*

Less obvious but equally important were the many adjustments required of the nation to adapt to the pressures created by the emergence of an industrial system. These adjustments were seldom easy, and in many instances they were forced upon people who were not anxious to change their way of life simply to accommodate a changing economic system. Their anxiety was exacerbated by the manner in which the process of economic change took place; those who were reluctant to yield to the needs of industrialization were for the most part rudely pushed aside by the momentum of progress during the "Gilded Age."

Evidence of the impact of industrialization could be seen in every facet of American life as the second decade of the twentieth century came to a close. Whereas farmers in the Civil War era were still experimenting with the newfangled equipment that might eventually ease their labor, the operation of intricate—and every expensive—farm machinery had become commonplace on commercial farms by 1920. The gasoline-powered tractor had by that time served notice that it would replace the horse (and mule), which had served as the primary source of power on American farms for three centuries. Farming, like everything else in America, had become a business—a business managed by capitalist farmers.

Increasingly, Americans were abandoning the farm for more lucrative jobs in the expanding industrial markets of the cities. The mines and factories which produced the raw materials and the finished products consumed by twentieth-century Americans had grown by astonishing proportions. What had been a large industrial enterprise of the Civil War era would be dwarfed by the huge plants, employing hundreds of workers and involving hundreds of thousands of dollars in investment, that had become typical of heavy industry by 1920. Technology, which had only begun to transform industry in the middle of the nineteenth century, had by the end of the century drastically altered the nature of production. Thus, for example, in 1860 the Bessemer process for producing steel was still a novelty which promised to greatly enlarge the size of steel plants. By 1920 that process had been replaced by a new technique (the open hearth furnace) which was still larger and more efficient. America's first oil well was drilled in 1859; sixty years later there were forests of oil rigs covering portions of California, Oklahoma, and Texas—areas which, at the outbreak of the Civil War, were hardly even settled. The oil wells pumped their crude oil into a network of refineries and marketing facilities extending coast to coast. The process of freeing man from his dependence on animal power had only begun in 1860; by 1920 the steam engine had been joined by new forms of power—electricity and the internal combustion engine.

These changes involved much more than simply the introduction of new and bigger machines. To cope with the expanding technology the entire organization of production had been drastically altered. The concept of an assembly line had carried Adam Smith's notion of division of labor to the point where production had been systematically broken down into a seemingly endless repetition of simple tasks. Though this greatly increased productive efficiency, it also significantly altered the nature of work. Scientific management, continually seeking ways of further improving the efficiency of production in every aspect of the production process, was seldom inclined to make work challenging or individualized. Indeed, just the opposite was sought; the ideal worker was an automated robot, perfectly trained in his or her specific task.

Large-scale production required the movement of a huge volume of materials over long distances. The arteries which carried the lifeblood of American commerce constituted an immense transportation network. Here also, the impact of the technological revolution was evident. At the end of the Civil War decade the dream of a railroad which spanned the continent had only just been realized with the completion of a single set of tracks across the vast western plains and over the Rockies to the Pacific. By the end of the century there were five major trunk lines and numerous other railroads that could offer less direct connections from coast to coast. The total mileage of track operated in the United States during 1920 could have circled the globe ten times.

People as well as goods moved along this vast system. Even the common folk could speed between cities on express trains whose picturesque names—the Hiawatha, the Twentieth Century Limited, the Crescent Limited—proclaimed that they were the pride of a nation that moved on rails. Yet already the nation was moving off the rails for a new and exciting experiment in transportation—the automobile. As Henry Ford turned out his Model T's and others copied him, Americans took to the roads in ever increasing numbers to enjoy the advantages offered by this new form of transportation. As Will Rogers wryly noted a decade and a half later, the United States was a country that could go to the poorhouse in an automobile.

The mechanization and commercialization of farming, the development of huge industrial complexes, and the construction of a massive network of railroads and asphalt roads were all manifestations of the industrial revolution which were clearly evident to any observer of the American scene of that period. The forces produced by industrialiation were evident in another part of the new social system which had emerged: the cities. At the time of the Civil War, only two cities in the United States (New York and Philadelphia) had more than half a million inhabitants, and only one of five Americans lived in a town or city with a population of at least 2,500. By contrast, the 1920 census reported twelve cities with 500,000 or more people and a total of thirty cities with at least 250,000 people. Some, like New York, Philadelphia, Boston, and Baltimore, had always been among the largest cities, and had simply grown larger. (The combined population of these four cities totaled just over 2 million in 1860; in 1920 their population totaled just under 9 million.) Others, such as Chicago, Detroit, and Cleveland, were smaller cities which had expanded into major metropolitan areas in the sixty years following the Civil War. (The population in these three cities increased from a total of around 200,000 in 1860 to 4.5 million in 1920.) Several of the thirty largest cities in 1920 (Seattle and Denver, for example) had reported no urban population at all in 1860! The 1920 census statistics are the first to show that more Americans lived in urban areas than lived in rural areas.

These obvious changes were accompanied by less visible, but equally profound, changes in the structure of the economic and social system. Of particular interest to our study is the extent to which the industrial and urban explosion had dramatically altered the sources and distribution of economic power in the United States. For while the impact of industrialization had been spread ubiquitously over city, town and countryside, the control of this giant octopus remained concentrated in the hands of a relatively small group of people who controlled the corporations that dominated the industrial and financial resources of the United States. By the last decade of the nineteenth century, these "trusts," as they styled themselves for a time, not only provided their owners with direct control over productive facilities; they provided additional power through the intricate maze of interlocking directorates, financial arrangements, and market ties which inexorably linked one giant to another and the rest of the economy to the heart of industrial production. The "Captains of Industry" (or, as their critics preferred to call them, the "Robber Barons") who managed these corporate empires had within their own lifetimes become household names. Several generations later they are still familiar to most people: Rockefeller, Ford, Stanford, Carnegie. Each of them built and operated a large economic empire, and their decisions regarding production and prices affected millions of other Americans who had come to depend on the products or services these firms offered in the markets. Many people were also dependent in another way: These enterprises created the jobs which were the sole source of family incomes.

This power, which at times seemed even to exceed the power of the government itself, was rooted in the corporate organization of the economic system. The use of incorporation as a device to attract investment capital was hardly new to the United States in the nineteenth century. As a form of business organization, the joint stock company dates back to medieval Italy, and such companies had become a part of English law prior to the settlement of the New World. (Indeed, several of the thirteen American colonies were established using joint stock companies to finance the initial costs of settlement.) However, apart from banking, transportation, and certain commercial ventures which required large sums of capital, the use of the corporate structure as a form of business organization had not been required for the limited scale of operations pursued by antebellum manufacturers. But for the greatly enlarged scale of operation that became typical of postbellum industry, incorporation seemed to be a very advantageous form of organization. Incorporation limited the liability of the investor to the amount of the stock purchased—an attraction to those wishing to risk some, but not all, of their assets in a venture. From the perspective of management, incorporation allowed the operation of the firm to be turned over to specialists who could go about their jobs with a minimum of contact with (and therefore potential interference from) stockholders who were content to collect the rewards of their investment *in absentia.*

Though incorporation was a well-known method of business organization by the time of the Civil War, becoming incorporated was still a complicated process in most states, and there was some ambiguity regarding the extent of control retained by states issuing corporate charters. The first problem was eased by the enactment in most states of legislation that removed the need for special chartering of each group applying for incorporation. However, it was not until the Supreme Court finally provided an interpretation of an amendment to the Constitution that the second difficulty was cleared up. The Fourteenth Amendment to the Constitution was passed in 1867, ostensibly to guarantee due process of law for every U.S. citizen, particularly the newly freed black citizens of the South. However, this change proved to be a convenient vehicle for establishing and protecting the rights of corporate individuals as well. In a series of legal opinions in the 1870s and 1880s, courts ruled that the due process clause ensured that, once chartered, a corporation had rights before the law equivalent to those of an individual citizen.

There can be no doubt that the court's ruling facilitated the expansion of corporate power in the late nineteenth century. Historians who stress class interests as a force in directing economic change have argued that the Fourteenth Amendment was instituted primarily as a device to protect the interests of capitalists after the Civil War. The court's ruling on the due process clause represented a significant change in the institutional environment—a change which was consciously engineered by those who stood to gain from the use of incorporation as a means of organization.[2] The advantages of the corporation as a legal entity in organizing

---

[2] See the discussion by Louis Hacker in *The Triumph of American Capitalism* (New York: Columbia University Press, 1940), pp. 387-92. While Hacker's analysis is no longer generally accepted by mainstream historians, it still appeals to some modern radical economists and historians. For example, see the comments in E. K. Hunt, *Property and Prophets* (New York: Harper & Row, Pub., 1971).

industrial production and commercial ventures were such that some definition of the legal status of corporations, which stressed their freedom of
action, was likely to emerge in the years after the Civil War. The inclination of the courts to uphold the rights of individuals—an inclination which,
we might recall, was a bulwark of the slave property right before the war
—could have been supported by the existing legal framework even if the
due process clause had not been added to the Constitution. In fact, the
prohibition against interference of interstate commerce proved to be almost as significant in the judicial reviews of government regulation as did
the due process clause. To the extent that the courts were already of a
mind to discourage government intervention, any company doing business
across state lines could plead that regulation was an interference of interstate commerce. Granting corporations rights as individuals did not extend
to them immunity from public control; like any citizen, they could still be
held accountable for their actions.

The removal of legal ambiguities cleared the way for the widespread
use of the corporation as a means of organizing firms. However, it was the
success of large firms such as the railroad companies which provided the
economic stimulus for the acceleration of incorporation during the postbellum period. Spurred on by the ease with which railroads sold their
shares of stocks to the public, entrepreneurs engaged in all sorts of ventures
that required the acquisition of large amounts of capital. One way to obtain such capital was by "going public." The corporate age was in full
swing before the end of the century, and the consequences of this new
form of business organization proved to be profound.

THE FARMERS' REVOLT

As the dislocations and changes brought on by the industrial expansion became evident, groups sought to respond by changing the institutional framework of the American economy. Some of these revisions, as
we noted in the last chapter, were intended to facilitate the economic
growth of the industrial sector. More liberal incorporation laws, a national
banking system, subsidies to transportation, and the encouragement of
immigration all aided the expansion of the industrial system. At the same
time, reforms were proposed by groups seeking to alleviate some of the
pressures created by the new economic order. These attempts at reform are
of particular interest to us because they focus on economic aspects of life
during the latter part of the nineteenth century. Farmers and city dwellers
alike found themselves drawn into the market process to an increasing
degree. It seemed to many of them that their lives were becoming more and
more controlled by those who ran the industrial system. Not surprisingly,

they searched for ways to limit that degree of control, and the large corporations became a focus for their efforts at reform. The balance of economic power was shifting from farm to city, from agriculture to industry. Many of the reforms of the Progressive Era concurred with that change in power in the United States.

Concentration of power—economic or political—is not an unusual phenomenon in societies, now or in the past. Despite the influence of corporate power, the United States at the turn of the century probably had a political and economic framework that diffused power more fully than most at that time. Indeed, the distribution of wealth, income, and power in the United States of 1900 or 1920 was not noticeably more concentrated than it had been in earlier times. Statistics on wealth and income are notoriously unreliable, but such data as we have suggest that a large fraction of wealth and income has always been controlled by a very few people.

The earliest comprehensive and reliable data on wealth and income date from the middle of the nineteenth century. Estimates of the concentration of land—the primary form of wealth in the agricultural sector—suggest that while the ownership of land may have been widespread, the wealthiest 5 percent of landowners owned between 40 percent and 50 percent of all farmland.[3] These figures are probably higher for the South than elsewhere; however, data on landholdings from 1910 show that even in the midwestern areas, large landholdings were common. A study of landholdings in several northern states just before the Civil War found that the top 5 percent of owners held about 50 percent of the wealth.[4] Nor does the evidence suggest that there was a marked trend towards greater equality of income over time. A study that examined the distribution of income for the years 1867–72, 1894, and 1913 concluded that the degree of inequality was slightly greater in the earlier interval than in either of the later years.[5] Studies of income changes in more recent time indicate that while there was some diminution in the concentration of wealth during the 1930s and 1940s, the distribution has remained fairly stable since.[6] Although

---

[3] See Gavin Wright, " 'Economic Democracy' and the Concentration of Agricultural Wealth in the Cotton South, 1850-1860," *Agricultural History,* 44 (January 1970); Jonathan Wiener, "Planter Persistence and Social Change: Alabama, 1850-1870," *Journal of Interdisciplinary History,* 3 (Autumn 1976); and Roger Ransom and Richard Sutch, *One Kind of Freedom: The Economic Consequences of Emancipation* (New York: Cambridge University Press, 1977).

[4] Lee Soltow and Dean May, "The Distribution of Mormon Wealth and Income in 1857," *Explorations in Economic History,* 16 (April 1979), Table 3, p. 158.

[5] Lee Soltow, "Evidence on Income Inequality in the United States, 1866-1965," *Journal of Economic History,* 29 (June 1969), pp. 279-86; also see Soltow, *Men and Wealth in the United States, 1850-1870,* (New Haven: Yale University Press, 1975).

[6] See Robert Lampman, "Changes in the Share of Wealth Held by Top Wealthholders, 1922-1956," *Review of Economic Statistics,* (1956); and James Smith and Stephen Franklin, "The Concentration of Personal Wealth," *American Economic Review,* 64 (May 1974).

the data used in these studies are imperfect, they suggest that economic power has always been fairly concentrated in the United States.

What did change was the *basis* of wealth and economic power. Prior to the industrial revolution, *land* had been the foundation of economic power. In a society dominated by agricultural production, the control of land provided its owner with rent (land's share of agricultural output), and was the only certain means of security. As we noted in our discussion of the Revolutionary period, colonial leaders tended to be men of property. Put more bluntly, they were landlords. The ownership of land in early America was probably fairly concentrated; in most rural areas the economics of farming were dominated by the few large landholders who not only managed large tracts of land, but also exerted a major influence on the provision of credit and marketing facilities as well.

As time passed, the influence of the large owners almost surely increased. While it is quite true that small holdings of land were still common in the late nineteenth century, the contribution of small farms to the total production of agricultural commodities was dwarfed by the volume of output produced on the large, commercially-oriented farms. Whether he was a tenant landlord of the Midwest or Plains, a planter of the cotton South, or a cattle baron of the West, the wealthy farmer-landowner was a dominating influence in all matters of rural life.

Even in those farm communities where the ownership of land was considerably more diffuse than was typical, monopoly was usually present. The small size of the rural market invited the establishment of businesses that catered to the local farmers, and the isolation of that rural market precluded the possibility of most farmers having a wide range of alternatives from which to choose in making purchases. In areas such as the cotton-producing regions of the South, this fact of life created, as we have seen, a monopolistic control so powerful that contemporaries described it as a form of peonage. Elsewhere the situation was less severe, but the country store owner and the small-town banker were typically in positions where they could exert substantial control over customers unable to find ready competitors.

The power wielded by those rural monopolies was just as exploitative as that exercised by the corporate monopolies that controlled national markets. But there is a difference between monopolists whose power is based in the communities in which they live, and monopoly power that has its roots far away from the locality and is exercised by people who are remote and seemingly beyond the reach of customers. The country store-keeper or banker exacted profits from their trades—but they generally recognized a social responsibility that went with that monopoly. Thus, Thomas Clark insisted that the country stores were much more than places to purchase supplies; they were:

. . . the heartbeat and pulse of a good portion of American business. In their own communities they were centers of every sort of neighborhood activity. Everything of importance that ever happened either occurred at the store or was reported there immediately.[7]

Though they were not necessarily the most popular members of the community, the storekeeper, banker, and landowner were invariably counted among a town's "leading citizens." They comprised an oligarchy based in part on economic position and power. Yet it was also supported by a strong social involvement with the community on the parts of these prominent families. They possessed considerable economic power, but the use and impact of that power was tempered by their presence in the community.

The personal involvement of the storekeeper or banker did not always work to the advantage of the customer. As we noted in the discussion about the southern store, there was a great deal of control exercised by the monopolist, who was able to dictate the terms on which credit could be obtained. In "company towns," where townsfolk depended upon a single source of employment, the closeness of control also was not an unmitigated advantage. In these cases, the local monopolist could use his proximity and familiarity with workers or customers to keep troublesome people in line. While such situations undoubtedly made it more difficult for those seeking to break away from the system of exploitation, they were not likely to promote substantial pressures for change since they were invariably cast in terms of local issues. Only in the most extreme situations—such as in the mining areas of the West or the mill towns of the South—did confrontations develop over this sort of "local" monopoly power.

Monopoly power which arose from industrial expansion was of a far different sort. The railroad agent represented corporate interests that spanned many communities; the local manager or representative of a national equipment or supply company, or the local broker of a commission house or wholesale firm, acted on directives emanating from markets far from the scene of his own decisions. Local politics and economic conditions were of only secondary importance to such concerns—and the employees who ran the local branch had no choice but to reflect that lack of concern. Prices and policies were set in markets centered in Chicago, Kansas City, St. Louis, Cincinnati, or the urban metropolises of the East, not in the hundreds of small towns of rural America. Like the farmer, the mercant was himself caught in the grip of supply and demand from distant markets, a fact he frequently pointed out to customers unhappy over

---

[7] Thomas Clark, *Pills, Petticoats, and Plows* (Norman, Okla.: University of Oklahoma Press, 1944), p. 15.

some price or delivery schedule. At least there was a personal tie to the boss of the local establishment, someone to whom to complain when things went wrong. Even if that only resulted in commiseration over the general state of things, it was business on a personal basis.

It was not just that the industrial system created large, impersonal firms whose influence dominated local markets. The problem was compounded by the manner in which industrialization forced people to deal with these corporate giants. If the farmer could just have ignored the changes taking place in the cities and continued his old ways, all this would have been of little consequence to him. But he could not. As long as he wished to sell his products in an organized market, the farmer found himself inexorably drawn into the commercial arrangements which had come to dominate so many facets of economic activity in the United States. He needed the services of the railroad because the prices received on the farm for crops reflected the greater efficiency of the "iron horse" compared to the other horses available for transporting crops to the buyers. He needed the machines offered by the equipment manufacturers because farmgate prices also reflected the much higher output per man possible with their machines. Even if he chose to ignore the new methods, others would not. And they would then have an advantage on the market for crops. But the purchase of transportation and machines required cash. As the farmer sought to respond to the pressures created by the markets for his "cash crops," he became increasingly dependent upon the industrial system for his flow of funds.

The anger expressed by farmers during this period was in large measure due to his frustration over this increased role of the market. As one historian has commented:

> "Farmers were objecting to the *increasing importance of prices;* . . . they were protesting a system in which they had to *pay* for transport and money rather than the specific *prices* of transport and money." [8]

If he owned his farm and could finance his capital needs, the farmer became—willingly or unwillingly—a capitalist who managed land, hired labor, and invested capital in an effort to produce output to sell in the commercial markets for agricultural products. If he could not afford the increased scale of farm operations, the farmer either capitulated to the industrial system and joined those entering the urban labor force, or he hired himself (and, in all probability, other members of his family as well) as tenant farmers or farm labor to work some other capitalist-farmer's enterprise. Some tried to resist the pessures of commercial farm-

---

[8] Anne Mayhew, "A Reappraisal of the Causes of Farm Protest in the United States, 1870-1900," *Journal of Economic History*, 32 (June 1972), p. 469. Italics in the original.

ing and remain self-sufficient, producing simply for their own needs. But this option was viable only in the more remote regions, such as the hill country of the East and South, the fringes of settlement on the western Plains, or the isolated areas of the Far West. Wherever farm land was fertile and accessible to markets, those who sought to use land for commercial use could invariably bid it away from those seeking to escape from market pressures. Escape was possible only by moving to the periphery of the system, where the cost of leaving land in the hands of "walk-away" farmers was low enough that no one cared to interfere with their isolated existence.

To the farmer, no single group or organization epitomized this threat of economic domination better than the railroads. In the 1870s and 1880s, the railroad had come to be viewed as an American institution, one synonymous with progress. Towns fought for the privilege of having a railroad station. Civic-minded groups bought stocks and bonds; city fathers offered choice land along the routes, built facilities, and not infrequently offered outright bribes which were only thinly concealed. All this was done in an effort to ensure that the town had access to transportation facilities. The stakes in this game were high. More than a few towns became doomed because they lost such bidding; more than a few owed their survival and subsequent growth to success in obtaining rail facilities. Everyone—farmer, merchant, tradesman, banker—had come to depend upon the railroad's low-priced transportation. President Dillon of the Union Pacific Railroad summed up the situation accurately when he asked: "What would it cost for a man to carry a ton of wheat one mile? What would it cost for a horse to do the same? The railroad does it at a cost of less than a cent." [9] People knew the answer to Dillon's query. They knew how great their dependence upon the railroad was.

People were also aware of another economic reality Dillon chose not to stress. In rural areas, economic logic seldom dictated that two railroads serve a single small town. Once a railroad was built, a second line was likely only to bid traffic away from the first, and, as a consequence, *both* might prove unprofitable. Railroads, after all, were very expensive to build, and investors—even those who were local townspeople—wanted a return on their investments. In most communities, therefore, the railroad that got there first remained the only game in town, a single producer which controlled a service vital to the well-being of virtually every person in town.

Economic and geographic circumstances gave railroads serving rural areas a powerful monopoly, and their behavior towards customers accentuated this fact. The prevailing practice among railroaders was to charge

---

[9] Cited in John D. Hicks, *The Populist Revolt* (Norman, Okla.: The University of Oklahoma Press, 1961), p. 62.

what the traffic would bear, and the "bearers" had little difficulty in seeing that this was the case. Since rate schedules were published, shippers could easily figure out that charges varied according to the degree of competition on a particular line. And if they were located some distance from a trunk line, producers could see that it was their traffic which bore the heaviest burden. Dillon's point—that this burden was much lighter than would be the case with no railroad at all—was readily conceded. What irritated shippers in rural areas was that it seemed to them that the burden could be lower still.

This is a point worth emphasizing, because those who cite the fact that railroad rates were relatively low and falling throughout the 1870s and the early 1880s as evidence that the farmers' complaints were unfounded miss one of the basic points of the protest. To be sure, farmers hoped that by protesting the rate schedules, a lower level of rates to rural shippers could be established. But they expected this to occur primarily through removing the discriminatory practices and enforcing equal treatment for all railroad customers. The favoritism shown to large shippers through rebates and various other forms of preferred service was resented by all those customers whose business was too small to net them similar favors—and who recognized that the higher rates they were paying financed the subsidies offered to powerful organizations such as Rockefeller's Standard Oil group. This situation provided the common link among the many groups that joined farmers in protesting the railroads' abuse of power in the 1870s and 1880s.[10]

Confronted by the economic power of the railroads, the farmers realized that as individual customers they were helpless. On the other hand, if several million of them banded together, they might represent an effective economic and political force which could be brought to bear against the railroad interests. Even before the Civil War, farmers had begun to organize; after 1865 the pace quickened. The Granger Movement, which began as a secret society called the "Patrons of Husbandry" in 1867, took up the antimonopoly cause and expanded their membership to more than three-quarters of a million by the mid-1870s. In the subsequent decade the Granges gave way to the farmers' Alliances, whose more militant outlook gave added political leverage to the complaints of those farmers who were struggling against the pressures of commercialization of agriculture and the vicissitudes of the marketplace. Finally, in the 1890s, the Peoples'

---

[10] There is a considerable literature on the movement toward railroad regulation at this time. Among the most useful works are: Lee Bensen, *Merchants, Farmers, and Railroads* (Cambridge, Mass.: Harvard University Press, 1955); Gabriel Kolko, *Railroads and Regulation, 1877-1916* (Princeton, N.J.: Princeton University Press, 1965); Paul MacAvoy, *The Economic Effects of Regulation* (Cambridge, Mass.: MIT Press, 1965); and George Miller, *Railroads and the Granger Laws* (Madison, Wisc.: University of Wisconsin Press, 1971).

Party—more commonly known as the *Populists*—emerged as a significant political force. In 1892 the party managed to run successful campaigns at the state and local levels in several western and southern states. James B. Weaver, the Populist candidate for president of the United States in that year, received one million votes, about 9 percent of the total votes cast for president.

The farmers' revolt involved more than economic issues. Nonetheless, the antimonopoly issue served as a rallying point in the early years of the Grange, and, together with the desire for "cheap money," continued to spur on the Alliance Movement in later years. The activities of these farm groups provide a useful example of how the economic interest of diverse groups of individuals can be molded into a common goal. The farmers formed groups based on the premise that cooperative action was an effective device for countering the railroads' power. On a local level, this involved the organization of farm cooperatives which could act on the behalf of a number of farmers together in the purchase of equipment and supplies, provide members with some of the services normally controlled by middlemen (particularly storage space and marketing arrangements), and disseminate information on prices, the latest farming techniques, and other matters of interest to farmers. The cooperative movement met with varied success. Some have survived to the present; many failed because of poor management or because they were unable to maintain an effective coalition in the face of market pressures. The successes were frequent enough to provide examples of what cooperative ventures could accomplish, and set a pattern for subsequent years.

Beyond the local level, the Grangers supported enactment of laws in Illinois, Iowa, Minnesota, and Wisconsin that gave legislatures or commissions varying degrees of control over the setting of railroad rates. These "Granger Laws," as they became known in later years, represented the first efforts to establish the principle that a state government had the power to regulate private interests engaged in business. The railroads, not surprisingly, insisted that states did not have a right to interfere with the private affairs of legally chartered corporations. In a series of decisions handed down in March of 1887, the United States Supreme Court agreed with the farmers by upholding the Granger Laws. A state government's right to curtail monopoly power was affirmed; the corporate right to act without regard to the public interest was denied.[11]

Encouraged by this success, the antimonopoly groups pressed on for a national law which would regulate rates. In 1887 Congress passed the Interstate Commerce Act, which established the first major regulatory

---

[11] For an excellent discussion of the early efforts by farmers to curb railroad monopoly, see Miller, *The Railroads and the Granger Laws*.

agency of the federal government—the Interstate Commerce Commission. The creation of the ICC, with its mandate to see that only "just and reasonable" rates were charged, and that such rates did not discriminate against particular groups, was seen as a triumph of the "little guys" over the corporate Goliaths of the transportation industry. Farmers were not the only railroad customers eager to see such legislation; the Interstate Commerce Act was supported by many other groups as well—including, as we shall see, some of the railroads who would be regulated by the new commission.

The cooperative effort by farmers to produce measures which might curb monopoly power seems a case of successful collective action by individuals who clearly identified their economic interests and tried to reap the gains that would stem from the removal of monopoly power. The costs of such collective action in this case were small enough that the gains, though broadly distributed, warranted the effort. Viewed in this light, the farm movement of the 1870s and 1880s was a response based on "economic logic," the type of institutional change economic analysis can readily explain.[12] While the attention farm groups devoted to the monopoly issue suggests that this approach has some merit, preoccupation with economic interests as they pertain to the power of railroads may tend to obscure some broader influences underlying the protest. For while it fits the individualistic economic model of social action quite well, the antimonopoly campaign by farmers also reveals distinct class divisions within the rural community.

Rural life in the United States has always been characterized by class distinctions, and those distinctions were traditionally based on the control of land—a control which, we noted above, has been restricted to a relatively small group of individuals or families. The commercialization of agriculture served to accentuate the distinctions between those who farmed land owned by others and those who farmed their own land or rented out land to be farmed by others. The market also gave added emphasis to the presence of a third very distinct group: the middlemen. By the postwar period, control of capital was becoming as important in the determination of one's status in the rural community as the ownership of land. The rise of a capitalist class—capitalist merchants and bankers as well as capitalist farmers—created new frictions in rural America. Each spring, the farmer —whether a planter, a small "yeoman" farmer, or a tenant—had to obtain credit for the coming season. And each fall, he had to arrange to sell his crop and repay the advances from the past season. The middlemen provided these necessary services. Their interests, divided between the farmer

---

[12] Lance Davis and Douglass North present such an analysis in their treatment of farm discontent and railroad regulation. See *Institutional Change and American Economic Growth* (New York: Cambridge University Press, 1971), pp. 93-96; 157-62.

and his crops on the one hand and the buyers of agricultural products on the other, set them apart from both.

Commercialization also exacerbated the landlord-tenant relationship. To what extent should the landlord assist in obtaining (or providing) credit for his tenants? He had an obvious interest in seeing that those working his land were provided with working capital, but as a landlord he might have very little interest in becoming involved with the intricacies of credit and merchandising. There was no "correct" answer. The landlord could be damned if he did help (he might be exploiting his tenants or taking risks he did not want), and damned if he did not help (he might be regarded as an absentee landlord with no interest in his tenants). The dilemma not only strained his relationship with his tenants, but was also a potential source of conflict with the merchant if the landlord decided not to supply credit or supplies to his tenants.

The antagonisms which might arise from these roles could be set aside in the presence of a dominating external threat, such as that posed by railroad monopoly. Middlemen, landlords, and farmers of all sorts enthusiastically joined together to curb the power of the railroads. But the success of the antimonopoly crusade in controlling the railroads carried with it the seeds of dissent. The Farm Alliances, which superseded the Granger Movement as the dominant farm coalition of the 1880s, sought to exclude the wealthier farmers (the landlords), and attacked middlemen (including local merchants and bankers) with the same virulence they directed towards the railroads. By the 1890s, when the Populists became the political voice of many farmers, class distinctions had shattered the solidarity of the farm bloc. The cooperative spirit of the 1870s, which had succeeded in mobilizing a broad base of support among diverse segments of the rural community, had turned into a crusade against special interests which pitted tenant against landlord, farmer against merchant or banker, and, in the South, black against white. Economic interests had been blended with broader considerations of class interest, and these class interests produced neither the unanimity nor the cooperation that the antimonopoly campaign had elicited. The objectives of the Populists were defined only in very broad terms, and the calculation of benefits and costs that might have been attached to their program of reform was no longer a simple matter of estimating the savings from a lowering of monopoly prices. More than economic calculus was required to assess this broader program. Many—indeed most—of the specific reforms sought by the Populists in the 1890s eventually came to pass. But this occurred later, when the activism of farmers was reinforced by that of other classes which could identify gains from such actions.

The political agitation that culminated in the Populist Party of the 1890s points up another problem beginning to trouble Americans both on the farm and in the city. The political as well as economic institutions of the United States were predicated on the premise that individual choice was inviolate. But as that concept was expanded to included such "individuals" as the giant trusts, people began to question whether there might not be a conflict between the interests of such entities and the interests of the thousands of farmers working the soil. The Populists, and later the Progressives, called for limits to be placed on the power of individuals with as much economic power as the large corporations. And those limits could only be enforced by the government. The "liberalism" that had sprung from Adam Smith was encountering the first faint stirrings of discontent—discontent that would gradually evolve into a full-scale attack on the notion of "laissez-faire."

Our emphasis on the monopoly issue has caused us to ignore the other issues—both economic and social—that bothered farmers during the last quarter of the nineteenth century. One such economic issue which generated a great deal of debate (though very little substantive reform) was the question of "hard money" and the alleged hardships the deflationary policies following the Civil War imposed upon certain groups—particularly farmers. Not surprisingly, farmers supported proposals that would expand the basis on which credit could be extended. They clamored for "easy money" (i.e., an expansion of the money supply) in the hope that such policies would ease the pressures from falling prices in the 1870s and again in the 1890s.

When government policy went in exactly the opposite direction, farmers were vociferous in their opposition. During the Civil War, the Union government had issued large quantities of paper money—called "greenbacks"—that could not be redeemed for gold. Once things had settled down, the administration of President Grant decided to return to the prewar situation in which all currency issued by the government could be redeemed for gold. The greenbacks were therefore gradually retired from circulation—thus reducing the currency in circulation. The decision to return to a gold backing for the currency—later termed the "Crime of '73" by its critics—was a major source of irritation to farmers in the years of declining prices between 1873 and 1896. Farm lobbies consistently supported legislation to expand the monetary base by including silver as well as gold in the monetary reserves of the economy. These efforts did meet with limited success. The Bland-Allison Act of 1873 required the Treasury to purchase and coin silver, and the Sherman Silver Purchase Act expanded this commitment. Nevertheless, it was gold, not silver, which formed the principal basis for issuance of currency by the government. The relatively slow growth in the stock of gold during the last quarter of the nineteenth century was seen by the farmers as an inhibiting factor which curtailed the expansion of money and credit.

The call for abandonment of this commitment to gold was most eloquently expressed by William Jennings Bryan, who received a thunderous ovation (and his party's nomination for President of the United States) when he told the Democratic convention of 1896:

> You shall not press down upon the brow of labor this crown of thorns; you shall not crucify mankind upon a cross of gold.[13]

Farmers may or may not have understood the complex mechanisms that produced the drastic decline in prices following the Civil War. But they knew firsthand the problems that declining prices brought to the farmer selling his produce in the marketplace each year. The pressure for abandonment of the tight relation between gold and the currency in circulation was one more manifestation of the farmer's struggle with market forces. Bryan's rhetoric struck a responsive chord among his rural constituents.

It is easy to see why this agitation was so intense. Prices fell by over 60 percent from the peak in 1865 to the trough in 1896. As the value of their products fell, farmers found it necessary to increase their output in order to meet payments for fixed commitments on land mortgages and capital needs.

Although the problem of declining prices was aggravating, the fuss over gold and the money supply was really a question of changing a policy rather than mounting a movement for reform. When, in the late 1890s, a marked increase in the supply of gold caused the price decline to be reversed, the money issue died down. It is interesting to point out that the pressure for reform of the banking system—culminating in the Federal Reserve Act of 1914—came at a time of monetary expansion and general prosperity, not as a consequence of the deflation that characterized the latter third of the nineteenth century.[14]

THE RAILROADS FIGHT BACK

The movement to control the railroads reveals an important facet of the process of institutional change: the extent to which changes proposed by one group will elicit reaction by other groups. One would expect that the monopolies which were the focus of the farmers' attacks would resist

---

[13] Bryan's speech is cited in George F. Whicher, ed., *William Jennings Bryan and the Campaign of 1896* (Boston: D.C. Heath & Co., 1953), p. 36.

[14] For an excellent review of nineteenth-century banking developments, see Richard Sylla, "American Banking and Growth in the Nineteenth Century: A Partial View of the Terrain," *Explorations in Economic History*, 9 (Winter 1972). Anne Mayhew presents a very concise analysis of the broad sources of populist unrest in "The Causes of Farm Protest in the U.S., 1870-1900," *Journal of Economic History* 32 (June 1972). Also see Hicks, *The Populist Revolt*, and Norman Pollack, *The Populist Mind* (New York: Bobbs-Merrill, 1967).

any curtailment of their power. And so they did. The railroads fought the Granger Laws tooth and nail, carrying the battle to the Supreme Court. Confident of judicial vindication, they largely ignored the statutes under review. Yet they did not let their confidence blind them to the growing popular support for control of railroad rates, and the possibility that some limits might eventually be placed on their freedom to set rates. When they lost the Granger cases—when the right of government to regulate monopoly was upheld by the nation's highest court—the railroads immediately sought to turn the farmers' victory to their own advantage.

The ink had hardly dried on the landmark decision (*Munn vs. Illinois*) before the railroad men had determined their strategy. If, as now seemed likely, railroad commissions were to be given power to control rates in each state, then the railroads must see to it that this regulation offered a protection of fair return on their investment, rather than posing a threat to their economic position. In fact, upon reflection, the prospect of regulation—particularly regulation on a national scale—seemed to offer some distinct advantages over prices set by the marketplace. Historian Gabriel Kolko sums up the situation immediately after the decisions of the Granger cases by arguing that:

> In 1877, the main danger posed to the railroad was not from state and federal governments that had provided cash in time of need and troops in time of labor conflicts, but from cut-throat competition, rate wars, and the manipulators of stocks.[15]

In the words of Walt Kelly's cartoon character Pogo: "We have met the enemy and they are us."

Kolko insists that, far from resisting the pressure for creation of a national regulating body, railroad leaders supported the passage of the Interstate Commerce Act. They had discovered that their own informal agreements (which were not enforceable in court) could not be policed, so they hoped to use the authority of a national regulatory body as a means of bringing recalcitrant "rate cutters" into line. The rate-fixing and pooling arrangements which were not binding before the creation of the ICC would be legitimatized under the supervision of a government agency.

The railroad tycoons largely succeeded in their efforts to eliminate competition from the railroad sector. By the time the authority of the ICC to establish rates had finally been upheld through judicial review and legislative amendment (a process which, ironically, was prolonged by the judiciary's concern for defending the railroads' right to remain free from regulation), the question of who actually controlled the setting of rail tariffs was no longer in doubt. Assured by the courts that the owners of private enterprises were entitled to a "reasonable" return to their invest-

---

15 Kolko, *Railroads and Regulation*, p. 17.

ment, the railroad capitalists set out to earn at least that—without having to cope with the bothersome worries of competitive pressures from rivals. Writing in 1904, John Moody argued that the ICC had "gradually evolved into a mere bureau of railroad statistics." [16] Moody was wrong, of course. The bureau that collected the statistics put them to use in enforcing proper behavior on the part of railroads. Whether or not they took sufficient notice of the need to protect customers, the ICC commissioners saw to it that the interests of the railroads were well served.

This argument should not be pushed too far. The security gained through the elimination of price competition was not obtained without some strings being attached. As the regulation of prices came to be accepted, so did the regulation of other facets of railroad transportation. Here again, class as well as individual interests lie behind the process of economic change. Given a choice of all possible alternatives, it seems likely that many railroads—and almost certainly all of the very large railroads—would have elected to have no controls from outside the industry. Individually, each would have preferred to keep the freedom of action offered by laissez faire economic policy. But collectively, the presence of regulations might prove a boon if it could be manipulated into restricting competition among rivals.

The reaction of the railroads to the institutional change effected by the farmers was to use their power to manipulate the very commission established to curtail their power. In this sense, the reform movement had failed; the railroad magnates had managed to escape with their wings only slightly clipped. The reason for this failure to regulate monopoly power is evident enough. The Interstate Commerce Act did nothing to remove or reduce the *source* of monopoly: the economic power that accompanied the ownership and control of huge capital investments. That power enabled the larger lines to quickly capture the ICC. The concerted efforts of a few powerful capitalists could offset the idealistic hopes of several million farmers. Idealism proved no match for economic power in the marketplace.

THE TRUTH ABOUT THE TRUSTS

The railroads were only the tip—albeit a very visible tip—of the monopoly iceberg. By the end of the nineteenth century, monopoly had become characteristic of most American industries. To some extent this development was a result of the increased scale of operations that accom-

---

[16] John Moody, *The Truth about the Trusts* (New York: Moody Publishing Company, 1904), p. 497.

panied the industrial growth of that period. The larger plants required by new methods of production made it impractical for many efficient firms to compete within a limited market for their product. Concentration of industrial production went hand in hand with industrial progress. However, the need for size to ensure that firms were technically efficient was only part of the pressure that fueled the waves of industrial mergers during the 1870s and again at the beginning of the twentieth century. The establishment of *trusts,* corporate entities which resulted from an integration of all the major producers in a given industry, involved a baser motive as well.

Like the railroad men, industrialists who were operating in large national markets found that they all had an unfortunate tendency to disregard the "gentlemen's agreement" so carefully worked out to stabilize competition whenever it seemed to their individual advantage to do so. The result was "cut-throat competition" which took a heavy toll in foregone profits (and realized benefits to consumers), not to mention an occasional business failure. The formation of a trust eliminated this tendency by creating a single unit to control all production. Those who created these trusts made no secret of their intentions: They sought to form monopolies to protect themselves from the uncertainties of competition. Their success in achieving this rather ignoble objective eventually caused a definition of "trust" to be entered in American dictionaries that stands in rather marked contrast with the other meanings of the word:

> A combination of firms or corporations for the purpose of reducing competition and controlling prices throughout a business or industry.[17]

How pervasive was this trust movement in American industry? To its critics—nicknamed *muckrakers* by those they attacked—the organizers of trusts had succeeded in monopolizing the entire American economy. What the trusts did not control outright, they allegedly controlled through intimidation or by the indirect influence of their dominant market position. Lincoln Steffens, Ida Tarbell, David Graham Phillips and their colleagues presented persuasive rhetoric, supported with seemingly irrefutable facts, that illustrated just how powerful the industrial capitalists were at the turn of the century.

However, measuring monopoly power is, at best, an imprecise art. As some economists (then as well as now) are quick to remind us, the pressure from even a single rival (or, for that matter, a potential rival) will exert a mitigating effect on the exercise of monopoly power by a dominant firm. Apart from those firms which were called "franchised trusts" (that is, trusts which were licensed by the government to be a monopoly), instances of pure monopoly were extremely rare even in 1900.

---

[17] William Morris, ed., *The American Heritage Dictionary of the English Language* (New York: Houghton Mifflin, 1969).

Like a constitutional monarch whose powers were limited by the presence of some higher authority, the industrial monopolist had to keep a wary eye on that portion of the market which he did not control, lest some aspiring entrepreneur seek to take over his position. As Joseph Schumpeter argued, the process of "creative destruction," whereby firms with new ideas effectively undermine the market position of existing firms, gets its dynamic impetus from the quest for monopoly profits. Schumpeter believed that it was the scramble for monopoly rewards which gave the capitalist system its enormous energy. In his model, the static inefficiency created by monopoly pricing was offset by the dynamic effects of progress through the process of creative destruction.[18] This being the case, a mere counting of firms or comparison of market shares controlled by each firm will not suffice for establishing the extent of monopoly present in a given industry. (Indeed, the very definition of "industry" becomes difficult, since the possible competition between industries could also affect the measure of monopoly power within each industry.)

Such warnings, well meaning though they are, should not deter us from pressing on. There is, after all, a rather strong prima facie argument that the degree of competition is likely to be positively associated with the number of firms in the industry. We can obtain some appreciation of the degree of monopoly power by looking at the statistics of industrial concentration around the turn of the century.

The most important statistical compilation on trusts at this time is the exhaustive compilation of data undertaken by John Moody in 1904.[19] Moody identified more than 300 "important industrial trusts," and estimated their total capitalized value of stocks and bonds to be $7¼ billion. While this seems like a modest enough sum to a reader living in an age when the federal government spends that much in a week, we must remember that in 1900 the total estimated value of all stocks and bonds was only $19 billion. There were in 1900 about 1.2 million business enterprises, of which perhaps one-fifth, or 240,000, were incorporated. By this reckoning, Moody's 300 trusts, representing about 1¼ percent of the corporations, controlled better than one-third (37 percent) of the total value of corporate stocks and bonds in the United States.[20] For the most important of these trusts, Moody provided more detailed information, in-

---

[18] See Joseph A. Schumpeter, *Capitalism, Socialism and Democracy* (New York: Harper & Row, Pub., 1947); and the discussion in Chapter 2 of this text.

[19] Moody, *The Truth about the Trusts*.

[20] Moody's figures are from *The Truth about the Trusts*, p. 469. The estimate of the value of corporate stocks and bonds is from *Historical Statistics*, Series F401-403, U.S. Census Bureau, p. 253. There are no figures on the total number of incorporations in 1900. The total number of business enterprises is from *Historical Statistics*, Series V20, p. 912. The fraction of these enterprises which were corporations was calculated from the figures for 1916, which estimated a total of 341,000 corporations out of a total number of business enterprises in 1916 of 1,708,000. (*Historical Statistics*, Series V41, p. 914).

cluding a rough estimate of what businessmen commonly call "market share." In fifty-five of the 72 markets Moody examined, the trust controlled 60 percent or more of the market; in twenty-five of those markets the market share of the trust exceeded 80 percent.

Moody's data have been buttressed by subsequent research. A more recent study of monopoly in the United States since 1900 concluded that one-third of all industrial output in 1900 was accounted for by the activities of only eight-tenths of one percent (0.841 percent) of all firms. Put another way, this set of data showed that the ten "most monopolized" industries in 1900 produced just over one-half of the total "value added" of firms in the manufacturing sector.[21] Of course, figures can be made to represent the particular purpose of the author, and one must always be skeptical of this sort of data. In that regard, it is illustrative to note that the statistics just cited were accepted by authors seeking to support an argument that insisted that the effects of monopoly power were rather *small*.

What are we to make of these "facts"? At the very least, it would seem as though a great deal of power was held by a tiny fraction of the corporations. Nor did most people need a statistical abstract to see this point; the trusts, like the railroads, were highly visible. The popular conception was that most economic activity was controlled by a few corporate groups. In fact, our friend Moody, who was in an excellent position to view the corporate structure of the United States in the early years of the century, concluded that just two groups—one controlled by Rockefeller's Standard Oil and the other by financier J. Pierpont Morgan's banking group—dominated American business. As he rather colorfully described it:

> These two mammoth groups jointly . . . constitute the heart of the business life of the nation, the other [trusts] all being the arteries which permeate in a thousand ways our whole national life, making their influence felt in every home and hamlet, yet all connected with and dependent upon this central source, the influence and policy of which dominates them all.[22]

ECONOMIC REFORM
IN THE PROGRESSIVE ERA

The antimonopoly campaign that the farmers directed against the railroads was soon expanded to include the industrial trusts as well. And

---

[21] G. Warren Nutter and Henry A. Einhorn, *Enterprise Monopoly in the United States: 1899-1958* (New York: Columbia University Press, 1969). The term *value added* refers to the increase in value a firm contributes to the value of its final output (that is, the total value of output minus the cost of materials).

[22] Moody, *The Truth about the Trusts*, p. 493. The apparently hostile tone of the quotation should not obscure the point that Moody, as we shall see, was a defender of the trusts.

the rural crusade found strong support among the urban workers and small-businessmen throughout the country. By the end of the 1880s an effective coalition had emerged which succeeded in having an antimonopoly law approved in Congress by an overwhelming majority. The Sherman Antitrust Act did not mince words: "Every contract, combination in the form of trust or otherwise, or conspiracy, in restraint of trade or commerce among the several states" was declared to be illegal. Lest the intent of this clause was lost on any would-be monopolists, the act went on to note that, henceforth, it would be a misdemeanor to "monopolize or attempt to monopolize" any market.

As any reformer knows, words alone are not enough to effect real reform. Having passed the legislation outlawing the trusts and monopolies, it proved much more difficult to press the attack further and actually reduce the market power of corporate trusts. In the first decade following enactment of the Sherman Act, not one of the major industrial trusts identified by Moody had been successfully challenged by the government. Not until 1911, twenty years after the antitrust act was passed by Congress, was Rockefeller's Standard Oil Trust finally broken into more modest-sized giants. Over two decades, Standard's monopoly power had been eroded far more by market forces than by the government's effort to break up the country's most infamous trust. Largely because of the increase in production in the western states (where Standard's market position was less dominant), the share of the market controlled by Standard of New Jersey fell from about 90 percent in 1890 to only 66 percent by 1909.[23] The intent of the Sherman Antitrust Act seems clear, and the huge majorities with which it passed both the House and Senate were probably a reasonably accurate barometer of public opinion on the question of monopoly. Yet after twenty years, many court battles, and the passage of additional legislation, market forces proved to be as effective in eroding the economic power of trusts as had the Justice Department of the U.S. Government. Why?

In part, the answer lies in shortcomings within the Act itself and the approach to monopoly power implicit in the legislation. However emphatic the language of the law might be, the Sherman Act could not enforce itself. Enforcement depended upon both the vigor with which the government (or private parties) pressed lawsuits against the trusts, and upon the degree to which the process of judicial review supported the challenges to monopoly power. Neither provided much encouragement to those seeking to break up the trusts. Theodore Roosevelt was the first president to profess much of an interest in enforcing antitrust legislation,

---

[23] See the discussion of the company in Harry N. Schieber, Harold G. Vatter, and Harold U. Faulkner, *American Economic History*, 9th ed., (New York: Harper & Row, Pub., 1976), pp. 235-36; 313.

and his reputation as a "trust buster" rested chiefly on a single victory —the dissolution of J. Pierpont Morgan's Northern Securities Company in 1904. Understaffed, underfunded, and frequently undermined by their own superiors, lawyers in the antitrust division of the Justice Department counted few victories even at the peak of the Progressive Era.

This lack of success does not reflect a complete lack of effort, however. Roosevelt's administration helped launch over thirty cases against companies; his successor, William Howard Taft, introduced another eighty during his tenure in office; and Woodrow Wilson continued the pressure in the early years of his administration. Still, the number of suits was small compared to the magnitude of the problem (recall that Moody was able to identify 300 "major" trusts in 1904), and many of the cases failed to produce any significant changes in the market structure they attacked. In 1914 Wilson and Congress sought to bolster the basis for antitrust action through the passage of a second major bill. The Clayton Act defined several practices that were declared illegal and established the Federal Trade Commission to help oversee the regulation of monopolistic practices in industry.

The Clayton Act also sought to provide some additional protection for labor unions. Several of the early court tests of the Sherman Act had been directed against union attempts to organize the labor force, and the courts had shown themselves to be far more receptive to discouraging such labor conspiracies than to restraining the monopoly power of large firms. The continued harassment of unions through antitrust actions in the early years of the twentieth century is another illustration of the success with which capitalists turned some provisions of the antitrust acts to their own advantage.

The early rulings by courts on antitrust cases were not encouraging to those seeking to dissolve the trusts. The courts tended to interpret each clause of the act in its narrowest sense—a procedure that made it extremely difficult to find firms in violation of the law. In an 1899 case against the Sugar Trust, the U.S. Supreme Court ruled that manufacturing was only indirectly related to "trade and commerce," thus questioning whether the trust could be in restraint of trade and commerce! While such a narrow view gradually gave way to a more encompassing definition of trade and commerce, the Sugar Trust decision also posed another problem with the Sherman Act: Was large size prima facie evidence of monopoly power? In that particular case the court insisted that size was not "proof" of monopoly—even though no one contested the fact that the Sugar Trust controlled over 90 percent of the U.S. market!

The question of size posed a dilemma inherent in an approach to monopoly which sought to restore competitive behavior by eliminating large concentrations of market power. To the extent that economies of

scale are significant enough to preclude the presence of many firms competing in a single market, attempts to bring about competition by insisting on
many firms will reduce efficiency. Yet leaving them efficient (and large) does
nothing to reduce the monopoly power. Either option involves costs in the
form of impaired economic performance. The compromise that eventually
emerged to handle this problem was the "rule of reason." Holding to its doctrine in the sugar case, the court eventually decided that size alone was *not*
grounds for antitrust action. Nevertheless, the government could successfully
pursue an argument which demonstrated that size had produced monopoly
power that was used in an unreasonable manner to restrain trade. This
argument suggested that the true issue was not the existence of monopoly
power, but rather its use. It left the judgment of "reasonableness" to the
specific case. In the 1911 Standard Oil case, and in the Tobacco Trust
case of the same year, the court ruled that the exercise of monopoly power
had been unreasonable and ordered dissolution. Several years later, the
court decided not to break up the United States Steel Company, despite the
fact that the firm was a dominant force in the market and the acknowledged
price leader for the entire industry. The U.S. Steel case is generally regarded as the landmark case which established the principle that domination of a market simply because of size would not constitute prima facie
cause for antitrust action.

By 1920, then, the institutional changes implemented in 1890 with
the Sherman Act had been worked out. On the one hand, the government's
right, and indeed its responsibility, to act against monopoly abuses had
been clearly established. On the other hand, the definition of just how
much monopoly power warranted prosecution under the acts remained up
to the courts, and the courts chose to leave a degree of ambiguity as to
how much power was too much. As it turned out, the courts, to a far
greater extent than those who pressed for regulation of monopoly power,
were willing to let market pressures mitigate the ills of monopoly power.
Except for transportation and municipal public utilities, the control of
monopoly power in the United States remained a very indirect process.

Such an outcome kept with the individualism of nineteenth-century
America. The role of individualism points up another problem for those
who hoped that the Sherman Act would curb monopoly. Popular support
for antimonopoly legislation was intense, and support for laws such as the
Sherman Act could be mustered. But the people who pressed for this
legislation were an amorphous group. Once the law(s) had been passed,
who was going to press suit against the offenders? In a sense, the Sherman Act leaves the initiative for such action with those who have been
damaged by monopoly. But few victims of a monopoly will have been
damaged to the point where they will step forward and become involved in
a court action with a large industrial firm. Each person's loss from monop-

oly (and therefore the gain from removing monopoly) will be quite small—too small to go to court in person to complain; too small to spend a great deal of time organizing a group to go to court; and perhaps too small to provide an incentive to support the taxes necessary to fund the efforts of the Justice Department to take the case on one's behalf. To the man on the street, the Sherman Act made the monopoly of large trusts illegal. That should have been the end of it.

Ironically, it was in part the sweeping language of the law—language meant to provide a basis for indicting even the most trivial monopolist—that in fact protected many of those accused of antitrust violations. As we noted above, proving that a firm was actually acting in restraint of trade was not a simple task, and the law provided no guidelines with which to determine the presence or impact of monopoly power. Since size alone—even when that size meant controlling 90 percent of the available market—was not accepted as proof of misbehavior by a monopolist, the problem of providing evidence to prove that a firm had misused monopoly power was almost impossible.

The vagueness of the act also meant that the remedial action to be taken under the act was left unspecified. The law ruled out very few specific practices that might be declared illegal because they were monopolistic; the usual remedy was to seek dissolution of the large trust or holding company. But this was a drastic step which sometimes flew in the face of the economic realities of the marketplace. As a result, even many of the cases that were won turned out to have little impact on the eventual distribution of market power. Like the attempt to regulate the railroads, the antitrust efforts did little more than stem the tide of industrial mergers. And since that effort was aimed primarily at the giants, the typical businessman probably noticed little, if any, effect from the efforts by the government to create a more competitive environment.

It would be tempting to conclude at this point that the efforts at economic reform around the turn of the century were a failure, insofar as the curbing of monopoly power was concerned. The attempt to control the railroad monopoly had resulted in a government commission whose main accomplishment was the enforcement of collusive pricing on a scale that could never have been maintained in a market situation. The struggle to break up the trusts had seemingly been thwarted by the obstinacy of the courts together with the pressures of economic efficiency and monopoly profits associated with the control of large markets.[24]

There is no question that the reforms did not live up to the expecta-

---

[24] Gabriel Kolko has presented the most forceful argument that the reforms of the progressive era fell far short of their goals. In addition to *Railroads and Regulation*, see *The Triumph of Conservatism: A Reinterpretation of American History, 1900-1916*, (New York: Free Press, 1963).

tions of those who fought so hard to see them enacted. Nevertheless, an assessment of the long range impact of the antimonopoly reforms reveals a number of respects in which perceptible progress had been made. Those who lament the shortcomings of the movement are often comparing the actual historical record with what might have been in the absence of the legislation (or any other set of antitrust laws). The nature of the "counterfactual" world devised for such a comparison determines how one will view the impact of the change resulting from the passage of the antimonopoly acts. If the economic historian imagines a world that is far better than the one which actually emerged, then there is a danger that he may overlook the gains which were actually recorded because such an analysis stresses the opportunities which were lost, not the accomplishments actually achieved. It is not my purpose here to debate the merits of using such a methodology, but only to point out that in this particular case—in which we wish to assess the importance of some rather specific changes—our judgment must rest on some idea of what the economy would have been like had the laws not been passed. Although the "counterfactual" in this case would be any number of possibilities, I shall concentrate on the possibility that no action at all might have been taken to curb monopoly power.

If we consider what was actually accomplished, one cannot ignore the fact that the Sherman Act, for all its shortcomings, remains the cornerstone of antitrust policy in the United States today. While it has not always struck fear in the hearts of businessmen, the ghost of Sen. Sherman is still an *ex officio* member of every corporate board of directors. Critics of the act maintain that the senator's ghost has not felt out of place in that role, easily joining hands with those who defend monopoly power. Yet the fact remains that there is legislation that allows the government to set limits on monopoly practices. Though they tried to evade it; though they often fought it with prolonged court battles; though they tried to bend it to serve their own ends, businessmen could never completely ignore the antitrust laws and the government action those laws permit. The triumph of conservative forces emphasized by writers such as Kolko was by no means complete. The decision to empower the government with broad powers to stem the tide of monopolistic mergers was, in itself, a major accomplishment. The fact—cited by critics of the Sherman and Clayton acts—that concentration has not diminished appreciably in the last seventy-five years must be judged in light of the enormous increase in concentration and mergers that took place in the period prior to the enactment of the antitrust laws. The Sherman Act did not restore a competitive environment to the U.S. economy, but it may have helped to preserve those elements of competition which still existed in 1900.

The Interstate Commerce Act introduced a similar element into the industrial structure by allowing government to influence (and eventually to control) the price of transportation. While it may be true that the railroadroad companies were able to control the ICC—and in so doing reduce its effectiveness as an impartial regulatory agency—it is also true that the railroads no longer had the freedom of action they enjoyed before 1887. Rates were not always stabilized at levels the railroads (particularly the more efficient railroads) would have selected on their own. Gone were the opportunities to take full advantage of extreme monopoly over isolated areas. Gone were the opportunities to change (or deny) service in areas that no longer proved lucrative. The "common carrier" principle meant that routes could only be started or dropped with permission. If they had ever enthusiastically endorsed regulation by the ICC, the restrictions on action that came with regulation were already causing railroad owners second thoughts by 1920. The competitive warfare of the 1870s had its problems, but the government regulation of railroads, which reached its peak during World War I (when the government virtually took over the country's rail transportation), must have convinced most rail executives that their power was in fact severely limited. Indeed, the first two decades of this century must have caused them to wonder whether private interests still dominated the railroad industry. Certainly the good old days of the years immediately following the Civil War seemed gone forever.

Nor is it clear that the regulation of railroads was a failure from an economic standpoint. Several writers have insisted that the ICC actually made things harder on rail customers by causing rates to rise after the 1880s.[25] However, such a conclusion is again based on what might have been, and one should be skeptical of claims that the trends of railroad rates in the 1870s and 1880s would have persisted into the twentieth century had there been no regulation. The one thing that most people—railroad men, shippers, farmers, and financiers—agree on is that the rail tariffs in 1890 were the product of imperfect (monopolistic) markets, and that the existing rates could not have remained unaltered. The ICC was created to deal with this problem, and it did have an effect. Rates were stabilized (perhaps to the benefit of the railroads) and routes were regulated to provide more even service (perhaps to the benefit of the consumers). The public interest was represented, albeit faintly, in the provision of transportation to the economy.

It is important also to remember that the accomplishments of the reformers should be judged in light of the events and pressures that existed at the time of the reforms. The antimonopoly movement was a response to a new and puzzling problem in America: the accumulation and concen-

---

[25] MacAvoy, *The Economic Effects of Regulation*, provides the most detailed indictment of the ICC pricing policy. Also see Robert Higgs, *The Transformation of the American Economy, 1865-1914* (New York: John Wiley, 1971).

tration of monopoly power in a democratic society. The source of the power was clear enough, but the manner in which to deal with it was not. By 1900 industrial capitalism had made the United States into the wealthiest, most powerful nation in the world. However irritated they might get over monopoly, Americans were hesitant to embrace schemes which threatened (or even seemed to threaten) the source of their economic progress. Throughout this period of rapid industrialization, a striking ambivalence was apparent in the reactions of people to the problem of monopoly power. On the one hand, they clearly wanted the abuses of the monopolies—and particularly of the trusts—curbed. On the other, they did not wish to infringe upon individual property rights as a means of doing so. Even when laws were enacted to regulate the railroads, the courts took care to assure investors that such regulation could not preclude earning a "normal" rate of return on their capital. The Sherman Act, for all its flowery language prohibiting monopoly, dictated only mild penalties for the persons convicted of monopoly behavior, and, in the few cases where large conglomerates were broken up, the assets were distributed in an orderly fashion which protected the market value of the monopoly assets. Breaking up monopolies under the Sherman Act thus did not involve any huge penalties, but only a diffusion of wealth over a large number of concerns. The public did not seek retribution for past sins, only a promise of better behavior in the future. (It should be noted that this lax attitude did not extend to union leaders prosecuted under the acts. To them, the fines were not trivial, and the impact of an adverse judgment was a serious blow to the union.)

This reluctance to strike at the root of the monopoly power accounts in large measure for the inability of antitrust legislation, as well as regulatory agencies, to deal with the problem of monopoly effectively. As long as the market forces created a pressure for large units of production, and as long as those units of production remained private, economic power was left concentrated in the hands of a few people. The power—political as well as economic—that their market position afforded them enabled them to evade, change, or subvert the laws to their own interests.

The ambivalence Americans felt towards the trusts involved more than a simple materialistic calculation of the gains and/or losses from monopoly. The social philosophy of the Gilded Age strongly reinforced the arguments of business leaders that the corporate economy should be left to its own devices. Adam Smith's "invisible hand" had always fit well with the American emphasis on individual freedom. Smith's rationalization of a laissez faire economic policy was bolstered by a new scientific doctrine based on Charles Darwin's *Origin of the Species,* first published in 1859. Darwin argued that animal species evolved slowly through a process of "natural selection" in which only the stronger members survived to carry on the line. This evolutionary theory fit very nicely into the prevailing thoughts regarding the workings and evolution of the economic system at the time of the Sherman Act.[26]

Social Darwinists applied Darwin's notion of evolution to the economic model of competition and growth. They viewed change as a process by which the institutional features of society were gradually molded through evolution into the most appropriate framework. This evolutionary explanation of change appealed to Americans for two reasons. First, it provided a comfortable rationale for defending the status quo. The existing institutional framework was seen as the result of selective evolution in which only those features that served a useful social function had survived. To a nation just coming into its own as a world power, Social Darwinism offered a convenient bridge with the manifest destiny which had supported the vigorous expansion of a younger society earlier in the century. America had evolved into an industrial giant. The second appealing feature of Social Darwinism was that, while it defended the status quo, it also offered the hope of change to correct faults which might emerge. The corrections would not come through hasty or ill-advised meddling of social legislation, but rather through the orderly evolutionary process that had brought us this far. Social Darwinism thus offered a dynamic explanation of economic change.

The changes that would come, however, would not be swift. To the ills so evident in the industrial world of 1900, Social Darwinists offered little encouragement. Henry George, a prominent American economist of the time who was not at all impressed with the extent to which market forces had alleviated poverty, asked his friend Edward Youmans what could be done about the problem of poverty. Youmans, an outspoken advocate of Social Darwinism, replied:

> Nothing! You and I can do nothing at all. It's all a matter of evolution. We can only wait for evolution. Perhaps in four or five thousand years evolution may have carried men beyond this state of things. But we can do nothing.[27]

Not everyone had the patience of Youmans. But Social Darwinism was a popular and pervasive intellectual force at this time. Whether found in the intellectual exchanges of academics or the thoughts of the ordinary work-

---

[26] These "prevailing thoughts" on economics were best summarized in the newly published textbook by Alfred Marshall, *Principles of Political Economy* (London: 1890). Marshall became the most widely used text for economics and had gone through eight editions by 1920. A current edition is New York: Macmillan, 1961. It remains the standard reference for interpreters of neoclassical economics today.

[27] Quoted in Sidney Fine, *Laissez Faire and the General Welfare State* (Ann Arbor, Mich.: University of Michigan Press, 1956), p. 44. Youmans was a close friend of Herbert Spencer, the leading proponent of Social Darwinism. Fine's study is an excellent account of the influences of this line of thought on contemporary policy and its acceptance by a broad spectrum of the population.

ers, the idea that there was a systematic pattern to the way in which America was emerging rested easily with a broad spectrum of Americans at the turn of the century.

The evolutionary explanation of social change also fit easily into the economic functioning of markets. Only those firms which were strong enough to survive the rigors of competition would succeed. In the dog-eat-dog struggle of the industrial jungle, survival was proof of superior economic performance. This being so, interfering with the operation of firms would, in all likelihood, produce inefficiencies and undermine the evolutionary process. The effect of this sort of reasoning can be seen in the conclusions of John Moody regarding the power of the trusts. As we have seen, Moody was quite cognizant of the extent of that power, and as a practical businessman he understood the threat that power posed to competition in the marketplace. Yet he opposed both the Interstate Commerce Act and the Sherman Act. His description of the trust as a business enterprise explains why:

> The modern trust is the natural outcome or evolution of societary conditions and ethical standards which are recognized and established among men today as being necessary elements in the development of civilization.[28]

The attack on monopoly in the United States was constrained from the beginning by this strong belief in the correctness of institutions that had been forged from years of economic competition. While concessions might be made to allow for dealing with the more obvious abuses of monopoly power, the underlying structure of production and distribution was to remain unchanged. America was not yet ready to be convinced that the concentration of power brought on by industrialization posed a fundamental threat to its way of life. The system seemed to be working well enough, and the importance of the inequalities that had emerged were rationalized by combining an economic doctrine that insisted people earned what they were worth with a social doctrine that argued that the institutional framework was the product of a carefully worked out response to the real needs of society. In the face of these views, the antimonopoly reforms faltered. The effort to curb economic power had not been entirely in vain, but it proved premature in its expectation that the distribution of economic power in America might be significantly altered through controls in the marketplace.

Soon the problems of inequality and power would pale in comparison with another more pressing difficulty: the threat to economic security. Americans could be complacent about both their future and their past as they headed into the Roaring Twenties. But ahead lay a series of events

---

[28] Moody, *The Truth about the Trusts,* p. 494.

that would shatter their faith in American capitalism. The Great Depression, symbolized by the stock market crash of 1929 and the unemployment lines of the early 1930s, provided the impetus for both significant institutional realignments and an intellectual revolution. Social Darwinism—and indeed for a time the entire framework of laissez faire economics—was buried under an avalanche of events too pressing to be put off for "four or five thousand years."

5

THE GREAT DEPRESSION

The quarter-century following the Civil War witnessed a remarkable expansion of economic activity in the United States—a period of economic growth which, we argued in the last chapter, produced profound changes in the structure of the economy of the United States. However, in the final decade of the century, the economy floundered; the 1890s witnessed the first "Great Depression" in the history of modern capitalism. The economic optimism which had been a characteristic of Americans up to that point momentarily wavered amid the financial crisis of 1893 and the protracted unemployment of the mid-'90s.

Had the impetus for growth in the American economy disappeared? Some feared that it had. The west, so long a source of economic expansion, had been settled. In 1890 the superintendent of the census wrote:

> Up to and including 1880 the country had a frontier of settlement, but at present the unsettled area has been so broken into by isolated bodies of settlement that there can hardly be said to be a frontier line.[1]

The closing of the western frontier was taken by some as signalling a major change in the pattern of American development. Writers such as Frederick Jackson Turner insisted that the presence of a frontier had produced many of the distinctive features of American growth, and that the

---

[1] The quotation was cited by Frederick Jackson Turner in his essay "The Significance of the Frontier in American History," which he read to the American Historical Association in 1893. See George Rogers Taylor, ed., *The Turner Thesis,* (Boston: D.C. Heath & Co., 1956), p. 1.

existence of a vast area of unsettled land was an essential part of the American growth experience. Though many elements of Turner's thesis have been criticized by subsequent researchers, some of the factors he pointed out as mechanisms that fostered growth in the nineteenth century were later identified as important variables in explaining the stagnation of the 1930s. The railroad network, which had provided so much of the impetus for new investment in the post-Civil War economy, had been finished. The steady stream of migrants from farm to city continued, but they found to their despair that, for the time being at least, the jobs were no longer available in the depressed urban economies.

But the obituaries were premature. The first three decades of the twentieth century suggested that good times had returned. After struggling through the troubles of the 1890s, the American economy bounced back into another period of sustained economic growth, which culminated in the "Roaring Twenties." The pattern of economic expansion was very uneven, with minor recessions in 1907, 1921, 1923, and 1927. Nevertheless, substantial gains in real product were made during the first three decades of the century. In 1899 per capital income in the United States was approximately $500; gross national product totaled just under $38 billion (measured in 1929 dollars). Thirty years later, per capita income had risen to almost $850, and GNP had for the first time topped $100 billion.[2] Small wonder that President Calvin Coolidge was able to "regard the present with satisfaction and the future with optimism" in his 1928 State of the Union message.

The recent past gave particular emphasis to Coolidge's optimistic assessment. After a sharp economic downturn immediately after the war, the decade of the twenties saw a substantial rise in production and real incomes. Unemployment was low (it averaged only 3.3 percent of the labor force between 1923 and 1929), and per capita income soared from about $600 to $850 in the space of only eight years. In terms of the production of goods and services, then, the 1920s appear to have been a decade of substantial prosperity. Coolidge's optimism may seem unwarranted in light of the events that followed, but it was based on a historical record of economic growth which hardly seemed to point towards a total collapse of the economic system.

Not, that is, until October of 1929.

---

[2] The estimates of GNP cited in the text have been adjusted to reflect the changes in the price level between various years, using the "implicit price index" presented with the series in *Historical Statistics*. Prices in 1899 were substantially below the level of 1929, though they were stable in the interval 1921-1929. See U.S. Bureau of the Census, *Historical Statistics of the United States, Colonial Times to 1970*, Bicentennial Edition, (Washington: GPO, 1976), Chapter F.

THE GREAT CRASH

On Friday, October 25, 1929, the front page of *The New York Times* carried the banner:

WORST STOCK CRASH STEMMED BY BANKS: 12,894,650-SHARE DAY SWAMPS MARKET LEADERS CONFER, FIND CONDITIONS SOUND

"The most disastrous decline in the biggest and broadest stock market of history rocked the financial district yesterday . . ." began the lead story of the day, which went on to describe what was to be known as "Black Friday."

The stock market crash that Friday ushered in a decade of economic stagnation and depression which has left an indelible mark on American economic history. The 1930s represented, in a very literal sense of the word, a *collapse* of the American economic system. And while it would be oversimplifying the situation to say that the Depression was "caused" by the stock market crash, it can certainly be argued that the overall collapse was triggered by the events on Wall Street.

There are a myriad of statistics which can be presented to describe the extent of the collapse in the 1930s. The same data on per capita income and GNP which showed the economic expansion of the twenties graphically demonstrate the turnaround of the following decade. The 1929 level of $100 billion for GNP was not reached again until 1941, and real income per capita did not get back to the 1929 level until 1940. The economic decline which began in late 1929 continued uninterrupted until mid-1933, by which time real income had fallen to only two-thirds the level it had been three years previously. The fall in incomes seemed even greater at the time, since the price level was also falling. In terms of current dollars (that is, if we ignore the fact that things are cheaper when prices fall), the fall in per capita income was 48 percent (from $847 to $442) between 1929 and 1933! Over the same period GNP fell from $103.1 billion to $55.6 billion—or by 46 percent.[3] To make matters considerably worse, between one-fifth and one-fourth of the labor force was out of work each year between 1932 and 1935. If we consider that most of this unemployment was in the urban nonagricultural labor force, the workers who

---

[3] The figures are from *Historical Statistics*, Chapter F.

were unemployed probably represented more than 30 percent of the urban labor force during those three years! The nonagricultural unemployment rate did not fall below 20 percent until 1941—the year the United States entered World War II.[4]

While these grim statistics portray the economic hardship of the Depression years, no single statistic captures the change in the economic spirit of the country so completely as the movement of prices on the New York Stock Exchange. Just as the soaring stock prices of the late 1920s represented the epitome of that decade's economic outlook, so the plunging stock prices of the early 1930s chronicle the confusion and despair of the Depression. By examining the pattern of the decline and the reactions to the stock index, we can get a glimpse at the way in which Americans reacted to the economic events that were overwhelming them.

Figure 5–1 presents the movement of stock prices as measured by *The New York Times'* composite index of stock prices.[5] A glance at this index reveals two things about the collapse of 1929–1933:

1. The enormity of the collapse is evident from the chart. From the level of 100 fixed for October 1929, our index of stock prices fell to a low of 12.3 in 1932. This means that the value of stocks had declined by 87.7 percent. To the extent that the index measures a general drop in stock prices, persons holding stocks saw nine-tenths of their savings disappear in the space of a few months.

2. It is also apparent from the examination of stock prices that the steady erosion of confidence of investors in the market continued well past the initial panic of late October 1929. Stock prices at the end of the first week were about 100 points, or approximately 30 percent, below the index of stock prices just before the crash. The weeks which followed were to set a pattern which persisted throughout the period 1929–1932. Panic selling would be followed by a rally that recouped some of the recent losses; however, each rally was invariably followed by a plunge that wiped out the gains and carried the index to a new low. If we were to smooth the ups and downs to determine a trend,

---

4 For many years the standard work on the Great Depression was Broadus Mitchell, *Depression Decade* (New York: Holt, Rinehart & Winston, 1947). John Kenneth Galbraith's *The Great Crash* (New York: Houghton Mifflin, 1955) is an excellent account of the collapse of the financial sector of the economy. Lester Chandler, *America's Greatest Depression, 1929-1941* (New York: Harper & Row, Pub., 1970), provides an exceptionally thorough treatment. The initial chapters of that book present an excellent statistical overview of the Depression years. More technical analyses of the onset of the Depression and its causes can be found in Milton Friedman and Anna Schwartz, *A Monetary History of the United States, 1867-1960* (Princeton, N.J.: Princeton University Press, 1963), Chapters 7-9; and Peter Temin, *Did Monetary Forces Cause the Great Depression?* (New York: W.W. Norton, & Co., Inc., 1976), Chapter 1.

5 The monthly data for Figure 5-1 are given as Table A at the end of this chapter. The data represent a simple average of the high and low prices reported in *The New York Times* at the conclusion of each week. The *Times'* index has been converted into an index where October 1929 equals 100 to facilitate the discussion.

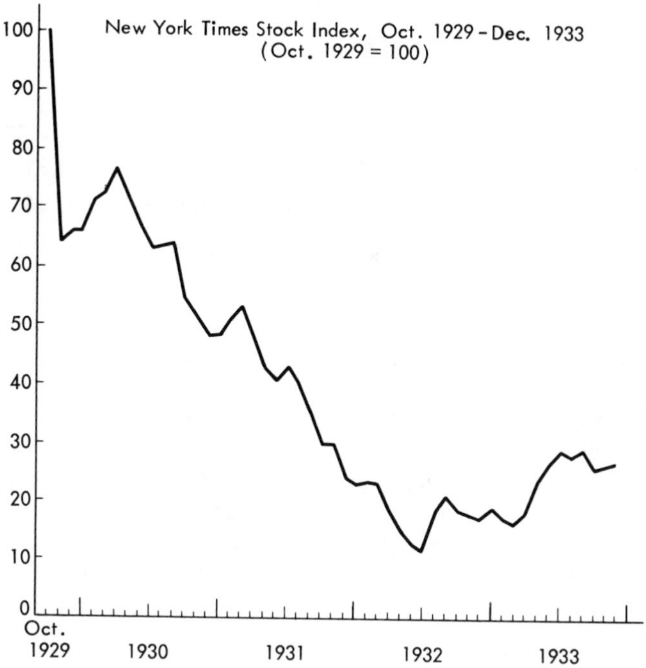
New York Times Stock Index, Oct. 1929 - Dec. 1933
(Oct. 1929 = 100)
100
90
80
70
60
50
40
30
20
10
0
Oct.
1929
1930
1931
1932
1933

Figure 5–1

we would find that between October 1929 and July 1932 the index of stock prices declined by an average of 6 percent per month.

People at the time certainly seemed to feel that the stock market was a barometer of the economic situation. The previous day's business on Wall Street was the lead story in the Times virtually every day for the next few months, and the diminishing level of optimism was reflected in both the stock prices and in the headlines of stories carrying the latest financial news. Initially, the stories sought to bolster the sagging confidence of investors. On October 26, the Saturday after the crash, President Hoover echoed his predecessor's optimism by insisting that "[t]he fundamental business of the country—that is, production and distribution of commodities—is on a sound and prosperous basis." [6] Bankers seemingly agreed; on page 2 of the same issue was a headline which claimed that:

ONLY YAWNS RECALL BIG DAY IN WALL STREET

[6] *The New York Times,* October 26, 1929, p. 1.

The complacency did not have time to settle in. The following Wednesday (October 30) the Times' lead story reported that once again:

STOCKS COLLAPSE IN 16,410,030-SHARE DAY, BUT RALLY AT CLOSE CHEERS BANKERS

Bankers Believe Liquidation
Now has Run Its Course
and Advise Purchases

But as the weeks went by and the stock market failed to rebound from the losses, the confidence began once again to falter. Mounting concern developed over the issue of unemployment. On November 24 the president asked for cooperation from all forty-eight governors in "speeding up" public works to stimulate employment. The results, he hoped, would provide jobs and bolster economic morale. As Mr. Hoover noted on December 6:

> . . . [C]onfidence has replaced fear in the business world and the country may now look forward to the future with hope. . . . The most important single thing that can be done now is for each one of us to continue normal, reasonable buying.[7]

However these were not "normal, reasonable" times. As the new year came in, business and government leaders continued to grope for answers to the continuing economic decline. But the answers were not there. Banks lowered their interest rates according to the accepted argument that such a reduction in the cost of funds would stimulate investment and generate a recovery of stock prices. But the decline continued. Assurances that the crisis was past and that the country was on its way to recovery gave way to puzzlement over the failure of the system to respond to any of the stimuli that should have generated a recovery. On Sunday, May 4, 1930, the inside pages of the Times carried a story dealing with:

PARADOX OF LAST WEEKS' EVENTS— FALLING BANK RATES ALONG WITH FALLING STOCKS

The traditional cures were not having an effect. By April of 1931 the prime rate in New York had fallen to only 1½ percent, the lowest ever recorded.

---

7 *Ibid.*, December 6, 1929, p. 2.

Unemployment, which had reached 3 million by March 1930, continued to rise. (It eventually would reach more than 12 million.)

The prevailing spirit was hardly optimistic. The Hoover administration frankly admitted that it was unable to stem the tide; the only cure officials offered was to let the liquidation "run its course." As Andrew Mellon, the influential banker who had been secretary of the treasury through three administrations of the 1920s, noted in May of 1932:

> Today, like other nations, America is bewildered in the face of forces which have overwhelmed the world. We have found that the machine civilization which has evolved in recent years cannot be made to function with ever-increasing speed, and that new inventions and overproduction have necessitated a period of slowing down until the world adjusts to the conditions that have arisen since the war.[8]

Not everyone was quite so fatalistic about the country's economic prospects. In April of 1932 Franklin Roosevelt, then governor of New York and bidding for the Democratic nomination for president that year, insisted:

> The country needs and, unless I mistake its temper, the country demands, bold, persistent experimentation. It is common sense to take a method and try it: If it fails, admit it and try another. But above all, try something. The millions who are in want will not stand by silently forever while the things to satisfy their needs are within easy reach.[9]

Roosevelt had not mistaken the temper of the country. Seven months later he was elected president of the United States by a commanding majority: 22.8 million votes to 15.8 million votes for Herbert Hoover.

THE THREAT TO ECONOMIC SECURITY

The economic collapse of 1929–1933 revealed serious flaws in the institutional structure of the American economy—and indeed, in American society as a whole. No other period of our history brings together in a single episode so many of the major factors in the process of economic change we discussed in the opening chapter of this book. The cries for institutional change came from all directions. While Roosevelt's call for

---

[8] Cited in Burton Hersh, *The Mellon Family: A Fortune in History* (New York: Morrow, 1978), p. 307. We shall return to the inability of economic thinking in the early 1930s to develop an economic policy to prevent the collapse—or at least to slow it down appreciably.

[9] Cited in Wallace E. Davies and William Goetsmann, eds., *The New Deal and Business Recovery* (New York: Holt, Rinehart & Winston, 1963), p. 4.

experimentation did not identify specific programs, it was clear at the time that whatever reforms were proposed to correct the problems which had surfaced in the early 1930s would have to consider the possibility of changing economic institutions. Moreover, the response to the economic catastrophe had to look beyond the immediate problem of economic recovery towards the more fundamental issues of economic stability posed by the emergence of an industrial society. The New Deal was, in a sense, an attempt to confront some problems which had been building up for many years. At the heart of these problems was the increasing insecurity of individuals in the United States—insecurity which was a consequence of threats such as unemployment and job insecurity, financial instability, and support for the elderly. These were not new concerns, but they involved aspects of economic life in America which had changed drastically over the years—changed to the point at which the collapse of the economic system released enormous pressures for economic change.

The New Deal is important to our narrative not only because of the major reforms it introduced, but also because it demonstrated that major changes could be made in the economic system through a process of consensus rather than through conflict. The reforms of the 1930s permeated every part of the economic system. They were introduced, debated, and implemented in a way that involved a wide spectrum of people and interests—some of whom were included in such a process for the first time. The New Deal set a pattern for implementing economic change on a continuing basis which has become a part of our present day economic policy.

In order to assess the importance of the New Deal reforms we must deal with the overriding economic concern of that time: the problem of economic security in a market society which was in the grips of a depression far worse than anyone had imagined possible.

The United States in 1929 was a market society, a society which had come to depend almost exclusively on the smooth operation of markets for the solution to the economic problem. The collapse of 1929–1933 caused an interruption in economic activity that ultimately affected every facet of life in the United States. Things which for years had been taken for granted were suddenly no longer certain. If anything, things in 1933 seemed to be getting still worse after three years of disastrous economic decline. The institutional structure of the economic system had failed to provide safeguards against the possibility of economic instability. The market's invisible hand seemed to be pushing the United States towards chaos, not equilibrium.

Most obvious, of course, was the chaos created by the problems in the financial sector. Like any market economy, the United States depended upon the use of money both as a medium of exchange in market transactions and as a store of value over time. The stock market crash and the disruption of other financial institutions—particularly commercial banks—threatened to undermine both of these functions and completely paralyze economic activity by spring of 1933. People used to holding money in the form of demand deposits (checking accounts) in banks found banks closed and their money unavailable for use in paying bills. For a week in 1933 they had virtually no medium of exchange at all! People who had invested their savings in stocks and bonds saw the value of their savings wiped out by the sudden plunge in asset prices, with little assurance that they would subsequently recover their earlier values. The continuing slide in the prices of stocks, bonds, and commodities influenced decisions on production and planning throughout the economy, and even those who had neither bank accounts nor investments in the stock market felt the effects of the uncertainty and loss of confidence produced by the problems in the financial world.

At the center of this problem were the group of public and private institutions which we call the "banking system." Banks provide the money and credit which fuel transactions in a market economy. We tend to think of money as "legal tender"—currency issued and backed by the government. In fact, this is not so; a major portion of the money supply consists of deposits in banks, which are *private,* not *public* debt. As a practical matter, "money" is whatever people are willing to use as money. For this reason, the definition of what constitutes money is a matter of considerable debate among economists. The most commonly accepted definition considers the money supply to be currency issued by the government (including obligations of the Federal Reserve System) plus demand deposits held in commercial banks. Such a definition is useful, but it is important to remember that there are many "near-monies" (highly liquid assets such as savings deposits, short-term treasury bills, and the like) which, although not treated by people as money in normal times, become money substitutes in periods of financial panic, when they are pressed into service. In such situations banks—and the monetary authorities as well—must scramble to find some way to satisfy the public's demand for money.

The banks, of course, do hold reserves of legal tender to meet those occasions when someone insists on currency rather than a bank draft. So long as people will accept bank drafts in lieu of currency, banks do not need to keep sufficient reserves on hand to cover the eventuality that *all* deposits will be withdrawn at one time. In normal times, people have confidence in the soundness of their bank, and this practice of keeping only a small fraction of deposits as cash poses no problems. Even if an individual bank becomes pressed for cash to meet unexpected obligations, it can borrow from other banks—or from the Federal Reserve Bank. If, however, the increased demand for cash becomes so widespread that *all* banks become pressed for reserves, they may no longer be in a position to help their distressed comrades. The banking system as a whole will then experience what is termed a "liquidity crisis"—a situation in which the liabilities outstanding in the form of demand deposits exceed the reserves (currency) available to be placed in circulation by banks. Some banks will be forced to suspend payment of cash to people wishing to withdraw funds deposited in the banks. The problem can quickly spread, because even if only a few banks initially are faced with this trouble, the possibility that other banks might experience difficulties produces a fear throughout the community that encourages depositors to withdraw their money at once. Even perfectly sound banks will then be caught in the rush to get cash and be unable to meet their obligations.

Problems with the liquidity of the American banking system date back to the early nineteenth century. Major panics occurred in 1837, 1857, 1873, 1893 and 1907, and the elimination of such episodes was a major objective of the Federal Reserve Act of 1914, which established the Federal Reserve System. The act provided for such crises by stipulating that the "Fed" would be a "lender of last resort" for banks. That is, member banks were entitled to borrow funds from the central bank in order to raise short-term capital, using their illiquid assets as collateral. In theory, at least, the discount privilege should have forestalled banking crises such as those which had plagued the American banking system in the nineteenth century.

But that theory did not work in 1929–1933. The Federal Reserve Banks did not accept some of the securities offered by banks for rediscount, nor did they offer assistance to those banks who were not members of the Federal Reserve System. The reluctance of the Fed to assist many of the banks experiencing difficulties at this time reflected a strong feeling on the part of the governing board that the problems of many banks—and particularly the small country banks—stemmed not only from the present liquidity squeeze, but from more deep-seated problems as well. The board, which mirrored the interests of the large city banks, felt that many of the smaller banks should not be rescued because they were not viable banking units. The system would be stronger, and better able to withstand the pressures from the panic, if the smaller banks were simply allowed to go under. The problems of the banking system were seen as a process of weeding out "weak sisters." The Fed was therefore not eager to answer the cries for help.

As a result, many banks were unable to meet the sudden demand for cash which developed in early 1930. The central bank's unwillingness to provide cash produced a rash of bank failures, and that in turn produced still greater pressure on the remaining banks. In the three years from 1930 to 1933, at least 5,000 banks failed because of problems of liquidity; between 1929 and 1933 the number of commercial banks operating in the

United States declined from about 25,000 to 14,000.[10] Even allowing for the fact that the smaller banks were most vulnerable to the panic, the loss of assets involved in these bank failures was enormous. Despite the fact that the reserves available to banks *rose* over this period, the total money supply *fell* by almost 30 percent.[11] In addition to the financial losses this involved, the uncertainty in regard to bank deposits meant that the usefulness of such deposits as money was seriously impaired. A society which had become geared to the use of this medium of exchange found its use rudely interrupted on March 6, 1933, when President Roosevelt declared a "banking holiday." A week later, 4,200 banks were no longer in operation, having been unable to reopen for business as usual. While some of these did eventually resume business, their failure to reopen immediately added to the difficulties experiencd by depositors who had left their money in banks, and further weakened the public's confidence in the monetary system.

The magnitude of the financial collapse was in part a reflection of the very high level to which security prices had been driven prior to the fall of 1929. The crash put a sudden end to a prolonged period of rapidly rising prices of stocks and bonds—a rise which had been fueled by strong speculative pressures. The speculative proclivities of investors of the 1920s are well known. As Professor Galbraith rather succinctly notes in his description of how investors behaved during that decade:

> One thing in the twenties should have been visible even to [President] Coolidge. It concerned the American people of whose character he had spoken so well. Along with the sterling qualities which he praised, they were also displaying an inordinate desire to get rich quickly with a minimum of physical effort. The first striking manifestation of this personality trait was . . . the great Florida real estate boom.[12]

The Florida land boom saw prices of real estate along the eastern coast of Florida soar in the mid-1920s. By the fall of 1925, lots within forty miles of Miami commanded prices of $8,000 to $20,000, while choice seafront lots were priced as high as $75,000—four to five times their value only a few years before. The rise was checked in late 1926 when the combination of rising interest rates and the effects of two devastating hurricanes discouraged a continued increase in demand. What is

---

[10] See Chandler, *America's Greatest Depression*, pp. 83-84. Chandler estimates that the failure rate (as a percentage of all banks in operation at the beginning of 1930) was 21.5 percent. The failure rate was highest in the midwestern and southern states. For a vivid account of the approaching bank crisis as viewed from the perspective of a single community—Akron, Ohio—in early 1933, see Ruth McKenney, "Bank Crisis," in *The New Deal: A Documentary History*, ed. William E. Leuchtenburg (New York: Harper & Row, Pub., 1968).

[11] The money supply in 1929 was $26.4 million; in 1933 it was $19.4 million. Temin, *Did Monetary Forces Cause the Great Depression?*, p. 5.

[12] Galbraith, *The Great Crash*, p. 9.

remarkable about the boom in Florida land, Galbraith notes, is that "[e]ven as the Florida boom collapsed, the faith of Americans in quick, effortless, enrichment in the stock market was becoming every day more evident." [13]

Though it may have surfaced with particular enthusiasm in the 1920s, the speculative trait which Galbraith emphasized was hardly new in the United States. Throughout the nineteenth century land had provided a source of capital gains for those who were patient—and who had access to capital for investment. In the twentieth century the possibility of playing a similar game with the ownership of capital intrigued investors. For the first two and a half decades of the century, the gains from such speculation were anything but automatic. Between 1900 and 1919 the index of stock prices on the New York stock exchange showed only a modest tendency to rise, and the fluctuations from year to year were sufficient to make short-run speculation in stocks a risky enterprise, unless you possessed the skill (or luck) to accurately predict the particular issues whose prices might advance. But by 1925 a strong upward trend in all stock prices had become evident, and the rise seemed to be accelerating. Between 1925 and 1929 Standard and Poor's Index rose by an average of 23½ percent per year. This means that the speculative gains were being compounded at an average of 1¾ percent per month! [14] It did not take any financial wizardry to earn a handsome return in such a situation—anyone who bought stocks expected to receive substantial capital gains simply as a matter of course. The ability to pick particular stocks on the basis of their performance was not necessary; even an average stock brought profits to the investor.

Speculative pressures such as those in land and stocks during the 1920s are fed by more than a promise of quick riches. In order to speculate one must have the means of acquiring title to the asset whose price is expected to change. In other words, someone must be willing to pay for the opportunity to take a chance on the speculative venture. The problem which invariably confronted the individual speculator was obtaining cash with which to purchase the stock. The "margin" or "call" loan solved this problem for the investor-speculator of the 1920s. Borrowing "on the margin" also solved a problem for banks and brokers who sought safe, liquid assets as an investment for funds which otherwise would have to be held as idle cash reserves. With a margin loan, an individual could buy a stock while paying only a small fraction (as little as 10 percent) of the total cost in cash. The remainder of the cost would be loaned to the cus-

---

13 *Ibid.*, p 12. Galbraith provides an excellent synopsis of the Florida boom.

14 The trends in stock prices cited here are based on Standard and Poor's index of common stocks presented in *Historical Statistics*, Chapter X.

tomer by the stockbroker. The speculator gained enormous leverage through this arrangement. With a margin of 10 percent, a $100 investment bought $1,000 worth of stocks. If the price of the stock went up by only 10 percent the speculator would double his original capital!

There were risks, of course, but in the market of 1925–1929 they seemed easily outweighed by the potential gains. Even in those rare cases where the value of the stock did not appreciate, the investor would lose his venture capital, but no more. The broker had a hedge against any loss because he had the power to sell the securities if, in his judgment, the margin loan was threatened by changes in the prices of stocks held as collateral. It was this guarantee of safety which appealed to bankers and brokers who scrambled to lend money on such terms at 5 percent. In a period when banks needed liquid assets, margin loans on stocks were particularly attractive commercial paper. The risks, after all, were entirely on the shoulders of the borrower; the broker got his 5 percent whatever happened to the price of the stock. Nothing could be more secure.

Or so it seemed in 1927. As the speculation continued to grow, a few people began to have concerns that the "bull market" might end. The danger which had been created by the financing of speculation was becoming increasingly evident to anyone who did not have blind faith in the continued rise of stock prices. The Achilles' heel in this seemingly secure financial world was that investors depended upon the continued rise of prices to provide them with a return to the capital which they had borrowed. Dividends from stocks purchased at highly inflated prices would not cover even the interest costs, much less provide profits from the investment. As early as mid-1928 there were warnings that the continued rise of stock prices could be interrupted—and perhaps permanently reversed—by the instability which had been built into the financial system.

Ironically, it was the very feature which made margin loans and call money so sound to the bankers that ultimately brought down the entire network of speculative debt. It was rather like the diplomats in 1914 who tried to ensure peace and security through a network of treaties which guaranteed that each country would go to some other country's aid in time of crisis. The problem with their system was that even the most trivial incident among major powers could touch off a chain reaction guaranteed to bring on a major war. So it was with the financiers in 1929. They had created a potentially explosive situation in which, by late 1928, any significant downward movement (or even a noticeable slowing of the upward movement) in stock prices could easily escalate into a major disaster if everyone tried to sell at the same time. The margin loans which were designed to be "self-liquidating" provided protection only if the stock could be sold at a price to cover the loan. Normally, these loans protected the lender against minor shifts of the market or isolated stock issues which suffered price declines. But in the event of a decline in *all* stock prices, the widespread use of margin arrangements made things much worse by creating an enormous pressure to liquidate assets quickly. In the scramble to sell stocks before the price dropped below the value of the loan, prices were driven down very quickly. In fact, there were several scares in mid-1928, when the volume of stocks traded reached record levels, and the prices of many issues did fall sharply. However, these episodes were followed by periods of recovery; those who depended on a continued rise in prices of stocks to produce capital gains on their speculation were reassured.

Then came October of 1929. As we have already seen, the bubble burst at that point. Each new wave of selling was followed by a rally which served only as encouragement for additional selling. The optimism which had fed the speculative rise turned into a pessimism which fed the decline. And the same institutional features which had encouraged the boom now reinforced the downward movement of stock prices. The need to liquidate loans created a persistent pressure to sell stocks whenever the opportunity arose. "Profit-taking" (if only to cut one's losses) developed at the least sign of a rally, making it extremely difficult to sustain any rise in prices over a period of time.

There were those who insisted that the decline in prices on the market was nothing more than a correction of the speculative bubble of the late 1920s. As late as May of 1930, the annual report of the New York Stock Exchange referred to the slump in prices as "security indigestion," suggesting that once the liquidation had run its course, the stock prices would regain their upward momentum. And, in fact, it was true that despite the crash, stock prices had only fallen back to the level which had generally prevailed during the first twenty years of the century. But the debt which had been created in the process of bidding up stock prices remained. The impact of the default of this debt on the financial institutions—particularly the banks—was not confined to those who had speculated in stocks. If the institutional arrangements of the 1920s had been able to somehow insulate the banks from defaults on speculative loans, the Great Crash might have been one of those curious financial phenomena that seems terribly important to the bankers and financiers, but whose effects never reach the typical person. Financial panics, after all, were hardly unique in American history.

But this panic was unique. Because the banks were intimately linked to the provision of credit in the markets for securities, the collapse of the securities market spread to the banks. And because so many other areas of the economy were tied to both the banks and the securities market, the collapse of financial markets spread to most other markets as well. The panic of 1929, therefore, became more than just a financial phenomenon; it grew to the point at which, by 1933, the entire economic system in the

United States had almost ground to a halt. No other financial collapse had created this degree of confusion. The "Great Crash" did not become just a passing memory; it became the "Great Depression."

The failure of the institutional arrangements of the financial sector to provide safeguards against economic collapse was compounded by the absence of effective institutional arrangements to cushion the impact of that collapse on most Americans. In 1930 four out of five workers were employed in nonagricultural occupations, and by 1933 one out of three of these people were out of work. Laborers depended on a wage for their income, and even self-employed persons relied upon the marketplace to provide some demand for their product or service. When the demand for labor declined precipitously after 1930, these people lost their only visible means of support. Not only did many people lose their jobs; many more were left with only part-time jobs, and still others simply gave up and left the labor force.

The problem of insecurity did not appear for the first time in the 1930s; the Depression merely brought into focus the degree to which laborers had become exposed to the vicissitudes of the market. Of course, the return to all factors of production had always fluctuated in response to the changing pattern of demand in a market society. As we stressed in the last chapter, one of the persistent sources of complaint during the nineteenth century was the continual pressures of the market to respond to a changing situation. Farmers and urban workers alike were faced with the need to adjust. The person who operated a farm at least had some minimal support to protect against the impact of a severe shift in demand for farm output. Even a very small farm in America—20 acres in crops—provided a subsistence income. The farm income declined considerably at times, but it did not fall to zero. As one midwestern housewife recalled a half-century later:

> We gardened and gardened and canned and canned. . . . Many was the time we didn't have a dollar in the house, . . . but we always had food on the table. My late husband used to complain that we always ate the same meals. I'd tell him "What do you mean? I fixed corn and beans for dinner and beans and corn for supper." [15]

As the comment suggests, farmers were severely affected by the Depression. In fact, the money income of farmers almost certainly fell more than wages did in the industrial sector. It is only in comparison with the *unemployed* urban worker that the farmer's security looked so appealing. And even that security could be threatened by natural forces, as the experience of the Dustbowl dramatically showed. Moreover, the loss of

---

[15] Quoted in *The Wall Street Journal*, September 6, 1979, p. 16.

money income was not inconsequential to the farmer; many lost their land through inability to meet the payments on their mortgages.

Nevertheless, farmers who clung to their land at least had a basis for subsistence. The produce from their land provided a form of economic security on the farm which was absent in the urban industrial setting. In the city or town one had either to keep a job or to accumulate capital to provide an income. In good times both were possible. Workers saved a portion of their wages and accumulated security for the future, much as the young farmer saved in order to buy some land. But wage earners faced some significant obstacles in their quest for economic security. To begin with, consider the problem of insuring a minimum level of income. Farmers who had land received a return to their savings in the form of physical output the farm family could consume. The value of that output fluctuated with the swings in agricultural prices, but the farm family had tangible rewards for its labor nonetheless.

People seeking security through the accumulation of savings invested in capital faced a different situation. Both the value of their savings and the monetary return which they received from investment depended on the market conditions. Thus, someone who thought they had prudently invested their savings in the stock market saw the return to those savings decline—and possibly disappear altogether—in the early 1930s. Nor could this problem be avoided by the accumulation of capital through investment in "real" capital, such as a small business. The return to that business still depended on the market for its output, and the value of the assets of the business reflected the market conditions. Small businesses did not fare well in times of depression. The 1930s saw the demise of thousands of entrepreneurs who had risked their savings in some market enterprise. Like the wage earners, such persons found themselves without means of support.

There was also the difficulty surrounding the magnitude of an investment required to establish economic security in the industrial sector. Small parcels of land provided farmers who worked them with income to see them through bad times. By contrast, it took a sizable stock of capital to provide a subsistence money wage. Suppose we set the figure of $1,500 as a reasonable poverty level during the Depression.[16] To provide that minimal level of money income indefinitely would require a capital stock of $30,000 if the interest rate were 5 percent; $25,000 would be required if the rate were 6 percent. To guarantee $1,500 for only twenty years would still necessitate the accumulation of between $17,200 and $18,700 at those rates of interest. And that would leave nothing at the end of the twenty

---

16 In 1935-36, about 15 percent of the families received incomes of $1,000 or less; about 30 percent received $2,000 or less. The $1,500 figure would cover about 20 percent of the population. See *Historical Statistics*, Chapter G.

years! [17] Trying to accumulate such a sum from an income at or near the minimum level was obviously not easy. The insecurity of the wage-earning poor was brought to light by the shattering experience of having so many people thrown out of work at once. A small group of unemployed workers could be handled by the charitable groups which assisted the less fortunate people of the community. But a third of the labor force could not be supported by such means; the institutional arrangements to cushion the effects of cyclical unemployment were inadequate to meet the challenge of 1931–1935.

The threat of unemployment was only one of the sources of insecurity among the wage laborers. The large sums of capital required to ensure even the most minimal income without employment posed a threat to the economic security of the elderly worker in the labor force even in good times. How can old people support themselves—or be supported by a family whose income fluctuates with the level of economic prosperity? Here again, the presence of land in an agrarian society provided security. On the farm the elderly could perform tasks of some sort to provide support. Their contribution might be small, but the family structure saw to it that all family members were cared for from the product of the land. In theory the same system could work in the urban setting. And for some it did. But two factors worked against the accumulation of savings sufficient for retirement as a viable option for the average worker.

The first problem concerns the threat from economic instability. If the worker was called upon to cover periods of unemployment (or underemployment) when income was decreased, then savings of the lower income groups would be exhausted (or at least greatly diminished) long before retirement. A second obstacle to accumulating an adequate retirement fund was what the economists call the "rate of time preference" of an individual. The "rate of time preference" is an individual's "personal" (or internal) interest rate. The higher a person's rate of time preference, the lower the value he or she places on income which is postponed until some future date. In a world which is very uncertain, individuals tend to place a very high premium on present events and income payments, and will tend to heavily discount the prospects of income that will not be received until sometime in the distant future. To illustrate the effects of a high rate of time preference, consider the fact that at an annual rate of eighteen percent (the rate commonly charged by commercial credit companies until recently), an investor should be willing to pay only $200 for

---

[17] The capital requirements are computed as the present value of an annuity for twenty years at 5 percent and 6 percent interest respectively. The actual rate of return available to small investors in the 1930s was almost certainly less than 5 percent or 6 percent, so the capital required to assure an annuity of $1,500 would have been greater than the examples in the text.

a note promising to pay $1,000 ten years hence. If the note were payable at the end of twenty years, it would be valued at less than $50 today! In oher words, with high rates of discount, the individual has little incentive to put away his current earnings for some future consumption. (One way to see this effect is to ask yourself how much $1,000 today would be worth ten years from now if inflation proceeds at a rate of 12 percent or so each year.) In good times, the failure to save for one's retirement was disguised by the ability of older workers to maintain their employment. But the Depression, both by its severity and by its longevity, revealed the problem of old-age insecurity in an industrial society. The existing institutional arrangements failed to provide an effective buffer to protect a large segment of the population from the insecurity of the market society.[18]

THE NEW DEAL

I pledge you—I pledge myself—to a new deal for the American people. Let us all here assembled constitute ourselves prophets of a new order of competence and courage. This is more than a political campaign; it is a call to arms. Give me your help, not to win votes alone, but to win in this crusade to restore America to its own people.[19]

With that stirring call to action Franklin Delano Roosevelt accepted the Democratic nomination for president in 1932, and launched the *New Deal.*

Despite the great deal of attention devoted to the period, the New Deal and the Great Depression remain something of an enigma to historians and economists alike. Historians have not yet agreed on the extent to which the policies of Roosevelt changed the direction of the American economy in the 1930s. Carl Degler has termed it the "Third American Revolution," while Paul Conklin insists that "[t]he New Deal solved a few problems, amelieorated a few more, obscured many, and created new ones." [20] Economists also offer mixed appraisals. In the conclusion to his study of the period, Lester Chandler poses the question of whether or not the debacle of the 1930s could happen again:

---

[18] For an excellent discussion of this problem and the struggle to correct the situation in the United States, see Roy Lubove, The Struggle for Social Security, 1900-1935 (Cambridge, Mass.: Harvard University Press, 1968), Chapter 1, "The Constraints of Voluntarism."

[19] "Address of Franklin Delano Roosevelt Accepting the Presidential Nomination, July 2, 1932," in The Public Addresses of Franklin Delano Roosevelt, Mervin Hunt (Los Angeles: De Vorss & Co., 1934).

[20] Carl Degler, Out of Our Past (New York: Harper & Row, Pub., 1959), pp. 379-416; Paul Conklin, FDR and the Origins of the Welfare State (New York: Harper & Row, Pub., 1967), p. 106.

The answer must surely be "No" . . . Since the Great Depression, and partly because of that experience, almost revolutionary economic changes have occurred—changes in our state of economic understanding, in our attitudes towards the role and responsibility of government, in economic aspirations, and in institutional arrangements. These make it almost inconceivable that depressions will again be allowed to become so deep and so prolonged.[21]

That is not to say, however, that we know what caused the Depression or what the chances of recovery from a similar shock might be. Chandler goes on to hedge his bet by noting:

Another stock market crash of the magnitude of that in October and early November 1929 is by no means inconceivable. Neither regulation of the use of credit for purchasing or carrying securities nor regulation of trading practices by the Securities and Exchange Commission can prevent surges of optimism and pessimism that become reflected in fluctuations of stock prices.[22]

Theodore Rosenhof put it more succinctly when he observed that: "The depression of the 1930s came to an end, but it was never really solved." [23]

While they may differ on the importance of the New Deal as a program which was effective in bringing about economic recovery, virtually everyone agrees that the period 1933–1936 witnessed a social experiment on a grand scale—a scale comparable, in many ways, to that attempted after the Civil War. In fact, one can see a number of interesting parallels between the two reform periods—parallels which underscore the pitfalls of undertaking a program of planned institutional change in a society. Both the New Deal and the Reconstruction programs were launched in the wake of a major crisis in American society; indeed, it was that crisis which offered the opportunity for major institutional realignment. Partly as a consequence of the recent crisis, the "reform" or "radical" groups initially had substantial support in the national legislature. The Civil War had removed slavery and presented the challenge of establishing a free labor system in the South. With the defeated South no longer in the government, the northern Republicans had large majorities in both the Senate and the House of Representatives in 1868. The economic collapse of 1929–1933 had decimated the financial sector and exposed the difficulties associated with the fluctuations in aggregate demand. In 1932 the voters sent an overwhelming majority of reform-minded Democrats to Congress, and four years later gave a still larger margin of victory to the "New

---

[21] Chandler, *America's Greatest Depression,* p. 241.

[22] *Ibid.,* p. 241.

[23] Theodore Rosenhof, *Dogma, Depression, and the New Deal: The Debate of Political Leaders over Economic Recovery* (Port Washington, N.Y.: Kennikat Press, 1975), p. 3.

Deal" party. In both cases, the opposition party had been largely discredited. The reforms were shaped by people who "had the votes." Their only problem was what to do with them.

Although the need for change was recognized, and the votes to pass the reform legislation were there, neither the Reconstruction radicals nor the New Deal reformers had a well-defined game plan. Each began with a program for reform that identified some broad objectives they hoped to attain. However, the various groups which comprised the reform coalitions had not reached any firm consensus regarding the specific goals that should be pursued to reach the larger vision of a new society. This lack of a specific plan meant that many of the reform measures were enacted in response to particular problems rather than as a part of some larger scheme.

Finally, in both the Reconstruction and post-1933 periods, the proponents of reform were careful to accept major tenets of the existing ideology and intellectual paradigms. They sought, for the most part, to work to change an existing system, not to create a new order. Thus, for example, the unwillingness of many Republicans to endorse the confiscation of rebel lands in 1866—an action which effectively ended any hopes of a comprehensive land redistribution in favor of the newly freed blacks—reflected the strong commitment of most Republicans to property rights. In the same vein, Roosevelt and his advisers were careful to stress the need for a "partnership" of all economic groups—including the capitalists —in his call for reform in 1932. The New Deal was not intended to be the end of capitalism in America; it was intended to save capitalism.

Both reform movements were characterized by an ambivalence that stemmed from the need for major reforms on the one hand and the importance of maintaining the broader features of American society on the other. In part this ambivalence was simply a manifestation of the short-term demands for change to restore some semblance of economic and political order, and the long-run need for a stable institutional framework. In neither case was there any clear-cut path to follow, since the enormity of the crises had created situations contemporary economic and social theories were ill-equipped to analyze. And in both cases the ambivalence produced a situation where the reforms stopped well short of those steps which might dramatically alter the distribution of power in our society. If improving the lot of the blacks in 1865 or the poor in 1930 infringed too much on the positions of others, then the enthusiasm for change was quickly diminished. As Norman Thomas said of Roosevelt: "[He] is willing to experiment, but he always oscillates on the same plane." [24]

The similarities between the two periods should not be pressed too far, however. Particularly with regard to the formulation of major policies of reform, the New Dealers had several distinct advantages over their

---

[24] Quoted in Rosenhof, *Dogma, Depression, and the New Deal*, p. 11.

counterparts three generations earlier. To begin with, the Great Crash, unlike the Civil War, produced a strong unifying force throughout the country. Roosevelt had a *national* mandate, confirmed by his margin of victory in 1932 and dramatically reaffirmed four years later. Together with the presence of a charismatic leader, this meant that the New Deal reforms were pressed with a vigor and solidarity not possible in the situation of a bitterly divided nation recovering from four years of civil war and the assassination of a strong president in 1865. Moreover, whereas the issues debated during Reconstruction centered initially on broad issues of *social* policy, the focus in 1933 was on the *economic* crisis and what could be done about it. Regional differences, which were dominant in the 1860s, were submerged beneath the need for a systemwide reconstruction of the economic system in 1933.

The initial proposals of the New Deal stressed the need to inject a new spirit of confidence and cooperation into Americans who had become dispirited by three years of economic collapse. "The only thing we have to fear" declared Roosevelt in his inaugural address, "is fear itself. Our distress," insisted the new president, "comes from no failure of substance. We are stricken by no plague of locusts." On the contrary, he pointed out, "Plenty is at our doorstep." Roosevelt's call for cooperation was a theme which was to be repeated time and again during the ensuing months, months which saw the formulation of legislation designed to reshape the institutional framework of the American economy.

The emphasis on cooperation was more than an appeal to rally together in times of crisis (though it served that purpose well). The changes Roosevelt introduced to restore economic equilibrium to the system brought the government into virtually every sector of the economy. In the early period of the New Deal, Roosevelt hoped that he could effect his changes without seeming to abrogate the prerogatives of private interests in the economy. By asking for cooperation rather than taking more direct action to control private interests, Roosevelt hoped to stem the opposition which might (and, indeed, eventually did) arise from a more obvious lessening of economic power in the hands of private producers. In the confusion of 1933, when the entire economy seemed on the verge of collapse, he was able to avoid coming to grips with the problem of economic power. For the moment, everyone was in the same boat—and unless they cooperated with the captain, the boat might sink. Roosevelt's reluctance to seriously tackle the issue of economic power did not disappear, however, even after the crisis passed. As we shall see, the New Deal continued to seek solutions which would accomplish its ends without making major alterations in the distribution of economic power.

In the four month period of March through June of 1933, Congress passed, and the president signed, bills which were to have major implications for the financial sector, the farm sector, the situation of labor in the industrial sector, and the economic security of the elderly. Many of the bills represented only beginnings, and most were modified within a year or so of their origin. But the principles they set forth remained, so much so that we largely take them for granted today. What is remarkable about the reforms introduced in the early days of the New Deal is that, although they were formulated in a context of impending crisis and urgency which made long-range considerations of only secondary importance, they laid a lasting foundation for substantive reform over a long period of time.

The New Deal legislation was directed at both economic reform and economic recovery. Our concern in this study is with those measures that eventually produced significant changes in the institutional setting. These measures fall into three broad areas: banking and finance; agriculture; and the problem of economic security for labor. To appreciate the magnitude of the changes, we shall briefly summarize the major laws enacted between 1933 and the end of 1935—the period generally termed the first New Deal.[25]

Banking and Finance

Immediately upon taking office, Roosevelt addressed the crisis in banking. He declared a "bank holiday" and convened a special session of Congress to consider emergency measures to shore up the failing banks. The banks remained closed for over a week—a week in which a society which had come to take the use of deposit banking for granted was forced to make do without their principal form of money. The medicine was drastic, but it worked. The banks which were reopened after little more than a week had managed to get their houses in order. It would be some time before the public's confidence in banks was completely restored, even though the fear of bank failures was lessened by the emergency legislation. The fraction of the total money supply which was held in the form of currency rather than bank deposits remained more than twice what it was before the Crash, a clear indication that people were more reluctant to place their funds in banks after 1933. By the same token, bankers were hesitant to return to the pre-1929 habits with regard to the amount of cash kept on hand; they showed a marked tendency to hold excess reserves just in case the public decided they wanted more cash. This skepticism persisted throughout the remainder of the decade; not until the post-World War II period would banking truly return to normal.

---

[25] Almost any introductory text in economic history includes a summary of the legislation discussed in this section. A very good, concise, source is Chandler, *America's Greatest Depression*, Chapters 9, 11, 12, and 13. The division of the New Deal into "first" and "second" parts reflects the changing emphasis Roosevelt placed on the importance of cooperation with industrial and financial interests, and his increasing reliance upon direct intervention to alleviate unemployment.

Nevertheless, the actions taken in 1933 provided the basis for restoring some semblance of financial stability for the first time in almost three years. In June Congress passed the Banking Act of 1933. After more than a century of experiencing banking panics generated by a fear of losses on the part of depositors, a solution was finally adopted. The Federal Deposit Insurance Corporation (FDIC) was established with an initial capital subscribed by the U.S. Treasury, the Federal Reserve System, and member banks themselves. Under the terms of the law, the FDIC guaranteed any depositor's money, even if the bank failed. Initially the maximum insurance for a single account was $2,500; two years later it was raised to $5,000. (The limit was doubled again in both the 1950s and 1960s; it currently stands at $20,000 per account.)

The creation of the FDIC seems a rather modest reform. Yet it accomplished what two previous revisions in the banking system (the National Banking Act of 1864 and the Federal Reserve Act of 1914) had failed to do. Since 1933 no depositor has lost money in an account insured by FDIC. Consequently, the fears which fed the banking panics of 1930–1933 have not reappeared. Despite a major recession in 1937–1938, the wave of bank failures was not repeated.

The 1933 Banking Act also forced commercial banks to divorce themselves from any affiliates involved with the financing of securities. Restrictions were placed on interlocking directorates among banks, on the acquisition of corporate stocks by banks, and on the involvement of banks as agents for individuals purchasing securities on credit. Two years later, the Banking Act of 1935 reorganized the leadership of the Federal Reserve System by replacing the Federal Reserve Board with a seven-person Board of Governors appointed for 12-year terms. At the same time, the powers of the system to control the money supply were substantially increased. Though not as significant as the earlier banking reforms, these changes underscored Roosevelt's determination to create a sound banking system able to withstand the pressures that had created panics in the past. Monetary authorities were politically more independent and free to pursue policies which might head off any future economic cycles.[26]

The stock market—widely regarded as the villian who had started all these troubles—came under particular scrutiny by those seeking new arrangements. The reforms enacted were intended to make more accurate information available to the investor. The Securities Exchange Act of 1934 required more complete information regarding stocks traded on the market

---

[26] The 1935 changes consolidated power within the system by eliminating the secretary of the treasury and the comptroller of the currency from the governing board, and authorized expanded authority for controls on member bank reserves. The act also increased the role of the Federal Open Market Committee as the primary vehicle of implementing monetary policy through purchases of securities in the open market.

to be made public. The Securities Exchange Commission was established to monitor the registration of new issues and to see that information provided on all issues was accurate. This, it was hoped, would eliminate some of the more flagrant abuses of "inside information" and fraud which many people thought had contributed to the speculation of the 1930s. Another reform aimed at curbing the excesses of speculation was the authority given to the Board of Governors of the Federal Reserve System to set limits on the margin requirements on loans—reducing the enormous leverage which had helped fuel the speculation just prior to the Crash.

As testimony to the success of the New Deal legislation on banking and finance, it can be noted that after 1935 few additional changes have been instituted. The concept of deposit insurance backed by the government has been extended to savings and loan societies as well as commercial banks. While not everyone gives the Board of Governors of the Federal Reserve System high marks for their management of monetary policy since 1935, their mistakes do not seem to stem from any glaring deficiencies in institutional arrangements of the banking system. As we noted above, the failures and panics that had been endemic to the system prior to 1933 have not reappeared. For nearly a half century of turbulent economic activity, the Federal Reserve System has kept its member banks solvent, a significant accomplishment when viewed in the context of the history of banking in this country up to 1933. Finally, although the changes were less dramatic, the Banking Acts of 1933 and 1935 created a buffer between the financial operations of the investment markets and the operations of commercial banks. If, as many argue, the very close links between those markets contributed to the overall collapse of the economy in 1930–1933, then the reforms have lessened the probability that any subsequent fluctuations in asset prices will be mirrored in the commercial banking sector.

Agriculture

The reforms of the banking system were supported by virtually every group in society. The obvious need for a stable banking system—and the costs of financial instability—were apparent to all. But other New Deal measures did not have such a sweeping appeal. The efforts to provide assistance to farmers and to labor necessitated the formation of a political coalition which would enact measures that rather explicitly conferred benefits on a specific group—sometimes at the expense of others.

One such group was the farmers, who constituted an important part of the political alliance Roosevelt forged for his victories in 1932 and again in 1936. We stressed in the previous chapter the discontent of farmers over the vicissitudes of the marketplace. The major concern of farmers in 1933—as it had been for several years—was the depressed prices for farm products. Prices received by farmers fell 51 percent from 1929 to 1933, compared to a fall in nonfarm prices of only 31 percent. The effect of this price movement can be seen in the fact that whereas in 1929 the net income of farm operators totaled just under $6 billion, by 1932 this had fallen to only $2 billion. Since the number of farms did not change significantly over this period, this means that the income per farm fell to only one-third its 1929 level.[27] Hoover's administration had tried to provide some relief by implementing the provisions of the Agricultural Marketing Act of 1929 to stabilize commodity prices. The results were not impressive; despite the expenditure of almost $500 million between 1929 and 1933, farm prices had plummeted. More drastic action was clearly needed.

The New Deal response to the agricultural problem was in many respects the most comprehensive and carefully planned reform attempted by the Roosevelt administration. It involved three major thrusts:

1. The support of agricultural prices to ensure a "parity ratio" comparable to the period just before World War I.
2. An emphasis on soil conservation and better land management.
3. Relief for farmers burdened with debts facing foreclosure on their land and equipment.

While all of these objectives played a part in alleviating the distress of farmers in the mid-1930s, the commitment to maintaining parity prices had the most significant repercussions for future farm policy. This commitment was spelled out in considerable detail in the Agricultural Adjustment Act which Roosevelt signed into law on May 12, 1933. The act stated as one of its objectives the restoration of farm prices "at a level that will give agricultural commodities a purchasing power with respect to articles that farmers buy, equal to the purchasing power of commodities in the base period." In other words, farm prices in 1933 were to be raised to a point at which they would be as high relative to other prices as they had been in the years 1909–1914. To accomplish this, the Act enumerated seven agricultural products whose prices were to be supported at a parity with the earlier years.[28]

The AAA's commitment to higher prices for farm products did not repeal the law of supply and demand which had ruled agricultural markets all those years. To sustain a higher price, the government was authorized to impose production controls or quotas, grant subsidies to farmers producing supported crops, and enter the market as a purchaser of farm prod-

---

[27] The statistics on farm income are from *Historical Statistics*, Part 1, Chapter K.

[28] The seven commodities were wheat, cotton, corn, rice, tobacco, milk products, and hogs. Over the next few years, eight more commodity groups were added to the list: rye, flax, barley, sorghums, sugar beets, sugar cane, potatoes, and cattle.

ucts to sustain demand. The Agricultural Marketing Board was also empowered by the AAA to enter into agreements which, in effect, meant paying farmers *not* to grow crops where supplies had pushed prices to extremely low levels. This was to prove to be one of the most powerful controls the government exercised to maintain the prices of supported crops.

All of these actions authorized by the AAA were subsequently undertaken by the Roosevelt administration. The result was an intervention by the government in agricultural markets on an unprecedented scale, and some of the actions brought strong protests from people who questioned the wisdom of imposing restrictions on output in the midst of a severe depression. Two rather famous examples of decisions that stirred considerable controversy were the attempt to raise pork prices by slaughtering (but not marketing) 6 million pigs in the spring of 1933; and the decision in May of the same year to pay farmers $11 per acre to plow under about 10 million acres of cotton—which was selling for 4½ cents per pound at that point.

The AAA proved to be one of the more successful New Deal programs in meeting its stated objectives. By 1937 net farm income was almost back to the 1929 level—a record far better than that recorded by production in other sectors of the economy. The success in restoring prices to their pre-Depression levels did not eliminate the problems farmers had with prices of their output, however. A considerable variation in both total farm income and income per farm persisted throughout the 1930s because of the year to year fluctuation in farm prices. Thus, while the income per farm was 96 percent of the 1929 level in 1937 (having climbed steadily since 1933), it fell back to just over 70 percent for the next two years—a decline much larger than that experienced by other sectors of the economy in the 1937–1938 recession. The New Deal programs had not succeeded in completely stabilizing agricultural prices.

The progress which had been made was threatened in 1936, when the Supreme Court ruled that the 1933 act was unconstitutional because of the manner in which the subsidies were financed. Spurred on by the slump in farm incomes after 1937, Congress passed a new Agricultural Adjustment Act in 1938 which expanded the commitment of the government to protecting farm prices. The concept of parity prices was made the foundation of agricultural policy. Few people at the time realized the extent of government intervention that would be required to maintain the commitment to keeping relative farm prices at the levels of 1909–1914 (which, after all, had been very favorable years for farm prices). By the mid-1950s the government price support system in agriculture was costing between $2 billion and $4 billion annually. Nevertheless, these payments had become so ingrained as part of agricultural policy that even the Republican victory of 1952 did not appreciably diminish the scale of the program.

Labor and Social Security

Of all the grim evidences of hard times in the 1930s, none more graphically portrayed the impact of the Depression than the long lines of unemployed laborers seeking jobs. Roosevelt continually emphasized this problem as he campaigned in 1932:

> What do the people of America want more than anything else? In my mind two things: Work; work, with all the moral and spiritual values that go with work. And with work, a reasonable measure of security—for themselves and for their wives and children.[29]

Once elected, Roosevelt and his advisers worked to developed a comprehensive approach to the question of unemployment. In May of 1933 Congress approved the result of this brainstorming: the National Industrial Recovery Act (NIRA). This bill included the two main approaches that shaped the direction of the New Deal policy towards unemployment for the balance of the decade:

1. The NIRA appropriated approximately $3 billion dollars for public works expenditures and established the Works Project Administration to oversee the expenditure of funds. The New Deal intended to fight unemployment through the creation of government-funded jobs.

2. The NIRA, in effect, suspended the antitrust laws. Not only were the sanctions against collusive behavior on the part of firms dropped; collusive behavior was actually encouraged. In place of the marketplace's invisible hand, the act established the National Recovery Administration (NRA), a board charged with the task of setting up codes of behavior which would create a more stable environment by eliminating the destabilizing effects of competition. Embedded in these industrywide codes were guidelines for labor-employer relations, which were to form the basis of Roosevelt's policy towards collective bargaining.

The NIRA was not a great success. Though the WPA and other public works programs did eventually make some headway against unemployment, the small amount budgeted and the lack of organization meant that the impact of increasing government expenditures on public works projects was still very small as late as 1937. To appreciate the magnitude of the problem, recall that over 20 percent of the labor force—or more than 12 million workers—was unemployed in 1933. An expenditure of $3 billion, even if it was spent at once and even if none of it was offset by collection of taxes, would represent less than a 5 percent boost in aggregate expenditures in the economy. The slump of 1937–1938 spurred new efforts at

---

[29] "Roosevelt Accepting the Democratic Party Nomination for President, July 2, 1932," in Hunt, ed., *Public Addresses of Franklin Roosevelt.*

public employment, but even at the peak of the WPA employment effort, fewer than 5 million people were working on public works programs.[30]

The section of the NIRA which created the National Recovery Administration was even less effective. The codes which were developed under the NRA's jurisdiction had the effect of suspending competition, which did as much harm as good. It soon became apparent that the cooperation imposed by the government resulted in little more than an uneasy truce between competitors and between labor and employers. When the Supreme Court declared the NRA unconstitutional in the spring of 1935, the administration made little effort to resurrect it. The blue eagle which symbolized cooperation (and a promised lack of competition) under the NRA code was already being asphyxiated by the time the court pronounced the death sentence.[31]

By that time other approaches were beginning to seem more fruitful anyway. In August of 1935 the president signed a bill which, he claimed,

> . . . gives at least some protection to 30 millions of our citizens who will reap direct benefits through unemployment compensation, through old age pensions, and through increased services for the protection of children and the prevention of ill health.
>
> We can never insure 100 percent of the population against 100 percent of the hazards and vicissitudes of life, but we have tried to frame a law which will give some measure of protection to the average citizen and to his family against the loss of a job and against poverty-ridden old age.[32]

The Social Security Act which Roosevelt signed into law represented a significant change in the economic environment of the United States. The act, as FDR conceded, fell short of covering all of the people against all risks. Indeed, only about half the labor force was covered by the terms of the act, and the unemployment benefits were minimal at best. But it was a start; "a cornerstone," the president noted, "in a structure which is being built." Gradually that structure would grow into the comprehensive system of social security, workman's compensation, and unemployment insurance we have today. The effects of those changes would be seen in the patterns of consumption, saving, and investment exhibited in the economy after 1935.

As is so often the case, the initial step was the hardest. The opposition which social security evoked when it was introduced came with par-

---

[30] See Chandler, *America's Greatest Depression*, Chapter 11, for a discussion of the public works program. We shall return to the implications of a systematic policy using public works to fight the business cycle later.

[31] For a discussion of the growing disenchantment of the administration with the NRA, see Rosenhof, *Dogma, Depression, and the New Deal*, pp. 83-91.

[32] Address by Roosevelt, August 14, 1935. Cited in Leuchtenburg, *The New Deal*, p. 18.

ticular force from employers. Social Security, they claimed, was nothing more than a compulsory insurance scheme whose costs were imposed on employers as well as workers. The social security tax represented an added burden to beleaguered employers, just when they were struggling to recover from the effects of the last three years. Together with those who opposed social insurance programs on the ideological grounds that such programs were an unwarranted infringement on individual liberty, the opposition to social security and unemployment insurance represented a formidable lobby.[33] But despite this opposition, the bill passed. Though the stipends were low and the coverage incomplete, the principle was established that in a modern industrial society, the state had a responsibility to see that some minimal level of economic security is provided.

The problem of economic security was not confined to the aged and the unemployed. As the industrial labor force grew, the position of the laborer became more precarious in other ways. How could a single worker effectively bargain with a firm employing hundreds—or perhaps even thousands—of people? The answer, of course, was that they could not; they must act collectively on matters of wages, hours, and working conditions. But collective bargaining, which was difficult in the best of times, was rendered still more tenuous by the declining economic situation of the early 1930s. Who in their right mind would threaten to walk out on their employer when one out of four persons had no job at all? The costs of organizing to obtain better wages and working conditions in the labor market of 1932 seemed very high indeed to those fortunate enough to be holding one of the available jobs.

The architects of the New Deal recognized this difficulty, and they included in the NIRA a section dealing with the rights of labor to bargain collectively with their employers. Section 7a of the act stated:

> Employees shall have the right to organize and to bargain collectively through representatives of their own choosing, and shall be free from interference, restraint, or coercion of employers—in the designation of such representatives.

The protection afforded labor for bargaining with employers did not disappear with the demise of the NRA at the hands of the Supreme Court. In July of 1935 Congress passed the National Labor Relations Act—more commonly referred to as the Wagner Act. The Wagner Act reiterated

---

[33] A synopsis of the events leading to the passage of the act in 1935 is in Daniel S. Sanders, *The Impact of Reform Movements on Social Policy Change: The Case of Social Insurance,* (Fair Lawn, N.J.: R.E. Burdick, Inc., 1973), Chapter 2. For an analysis sympathetic to the employer's plight, see Conklin, *FDR and the Origins of the Welfare State,* pp. 60-61. Lubove points out that there was also criticism from those who insisted that the Act did too little in the way of redistributing benefits and income to the elderly and the unemployed (in *The Struggle for Social Security*).

the intent of Congress to encourage and protect "the practice and procedure of collective bargaining," including "the exercise by workers of full freedom of association, self-organization, and designation of representatives of their own choosing" in the bargaining process. In addition to reaffirming the rights of labor, the Wagner Act empowered the newly created National Labor Relations Board to "prevent any person from engaging in an unfair labor practice" as defined in the legislation.

The true significance of the Wagner Act lies in the impetus it provided for the organization of labor. It has been referred to as "labor's Bill of Rights," with some justification. Union membership, which had declined substantially in the 1920s and early 1930s, suddenly grew by leaps and bounds. In 1935 total union membership was 3.7 million, or about 7 percent of the labor force. In five years the number had doubled; during the 1940s it doubled again. By 1950 organized labor claimed 17 million members, representing about 35 percent of the labor force.[34]

Labor constituted one of the major coalitions backing the New Deal. The Wagner Act represented a response to the pressure from that group to provide some means of equalizing the economic power between labor and employers. The act did this by considerably reducing the costs of organizing workers in the industrial labor force. Prior to 1935, organizers had difficulty in bringing employers to the table. The Wagner Act stipulated that employers must deal with authorized representatives, and provided a board of appeal to adjudicate instances in which employers had engaged in unfair labor practices. The relations between labor and employer were fundamentally altered from that time on.

The statistics on the fraction of the labor force that is unionized understate the full effect of the union movement on the economic position of labor in the economy. The role of unions tends to be much larger in the manufacturing and mining sectors than elsewhere in the economy, and the impact of a settlement in these sectors spreads beyond the confines of the industry involved. Union wages provide a scale which is then reflected in nonunion sectors of the economy as well. Furthermore, union pressures to bring about legislation on minimum wage laws, working conditions, and other aspects of the labor force have produced increased security for workers throughout the economy.

The passage of the Wagner Act was one of the few instances in which Roosevelt tackled head on the threat posed by the concentration of economic power. Under the NIRA, the administration had placed the antitrust laws in a sort of limbo, hoping that management and labor would be able to reach agreement on codes which would establish fair prices and wages.

---

[34] See *Historical Statistics*, Chapter D. The trend did not continue into the 1950s, as we shall discuss below.

But, as we noted, the cooperative spirit did not prove equal to the task. To supporters of the New Deal, it appeared as though labor was at a distinct disadvantage in the marketplace. The support for collective bargaining was therefore a conscious effort to alter the balance of economic power in the labor market. There seems little doubt, moreover, that the effort was successful, at least in the manufacturing and transportation sectors of the economy. By the end of the 1930s organized labor had become both a political and an economic force to be reckoned with.

THE LEGACY
OF THE GREAT DEPRESSION

The reform measures of the New Deal were passed in the face of a crisis of the economic system—a crisis which had paralyzed the economy for more than two years. Drastic action seemed necessary to deal with the situations in banking, farming, and labor. The measures we have discussed involved changes in specific institutional arrangements associated with the problem at hand. However, the impact of the New Deal did not end there. As the Depression wore on and the government achieved only modest success in getting people back to work, Roosevelt turned increasingly towards a very direct method to combat unemployment: spending on public works. The potential for the government to provide jobs had been recognized by New Dealers and opponents alike for some time; President Hoover had encouraged the states to implement such employment programs as early as November 1929.

While common sense might suggest that the government should provide jobs to those out of work, the prevailing economic theory of the time did not. The economic system, according to the conventional wisdom of the early 1930s, should correct itself. The invisible hand of Adam Smith which had produced the miracle of industrial production would develop the corrective forces to restore employment and output to prosperous levels. Wages and prices would adjust to reflect the current glut in markets, thus promoting the stimulus for the needed jobs and output. Government spending on public works, far from making the situation better, would further confuse markets by bidding resources away from potential uses in the private sector.

An added problem for those who did argue for government intervention in the job market was the fact that both economists' theories and business logic dictated that the government must pay for the public works. This meant that increased government spending must be accompanied by increased taxes—a policy Roosevelt himself stoutly defended in his 1932 campaign. As long as this was the principle of government finance to be followed, attempts to increase employment through public works projects such as the WPA and other "alphabet agencies" were destined to have only a minor impact on the number of jobs. The stimulus of the expenditure on public works was offset by the collection of taxes, which lowers private expenditures. In retrospect, it appears as though the inability of the New Deal to significantly reduce unemployment through public works stemmed not so much from a reluctance to spend as from an insistence that government budgets be balanced. At the local level, of course, there was no choice. As tax revenues declined, local expenditures followed suit. Whatever mild stimulus *did* result from the small deficits run by the federal government was thus offset by a decline in other government spending.[35]

In 1936, a British economist named John Maynard Keynes published a book which questioned both of these tenets of economic thinking. Keynes proposed the heretical notions that:

1. The capitalist economy would *not* necessarily automatically maintain a level of full employment.
2. The government should intervene with increased expenditures to boost aggregate spending *without* worrying about whether or not the government budget was balanced.

John Maynard Keynes was no crank; he was one of the most eminent economists of his day when he wrote *The General Theory of Employment, Interest, and Money*.[36] The theoretical framework which he outlined in *The General Theory* formed the basis for a major revision in economic theory which has come to be known as the "New Economics."

The New Economics turned the existing paradigm—which insisted that supply would always eventually create its own demand—on its head. Keynes and his followers insisted that it was the level of expenditures (aggregate demand) which would determine the level of employment (aggregate supply). There were not, according to this argument, any powerful forces operating to ensure that this equilibrium level of spending and production would provide jobs for all. On the contrary, it seemed probable that a situation of considerable unemployment could persist for some time. In Keynes' view it was folly to sit and wait for whatever corrective forces might be present to work; he advocated vigorous intervention on the part of the government. As for the problem of balancing the budget, Keynes asked in *The General Theory,* how much would it cost society to employ someone who is not presently employed? The answer, he insisted, was that

---

[35] Evidence that Roosevelt's early spending on public works had only a minimal effect on jobs is presented by E. Carey Brown, "Fiscal Policy in the Thirties: A Reappraisal," *American Economic Review*, 46 (December 1956), 857-79.

[36] John Maynard Keynes, *The General Theory of Employment, Interest, and Money* (New York: Harcourt Brace Jovanovich, Inc., 1936).

sought to protect workers from losing their jobs through discrimination or any arbitrary decision of an employer. "Fair Employment Practices Commissions" were empowered to hear any grievance by workers who felt that their employers had violated fair labor practices. Of particular importance in this regard was the basis on which an employee could be dismissed. By the 1970s it had become a legal presumption that persons were entitled to hold on to their jobs unless employers were able to show legitimate cause for dismissal. The establishment of impartial groups to hear appeals of unfair labor practices provided employees with an accessible means of protesting unwarranted dismissals.

The rulings (both actual and potential) of such commissions also had a more subtle effect on job security; they reinforced the rights of seniority on the job. Once seniority on the job became recognized as a basis for receiving preferential treatment in decisions involving layoffs, promotions, and hiring, a worker was able to gain a considerable degree of job security simply by remaining with the same employer for some period of time. Employers—especially in the public sector—granted security of employment as a reward for years of service. Recognition of seniority privileges was an important objective in labor's effort to win job security against fluctuations in the job market. Seniority, of course, had always provided an important means for obtaining job security. What had changed in the postwar years was that job security of senior workers became an institutionalized feature of the labor market which was increasingly independent of any agreements between workers and management. All workers had some seniority rights (though not all of them felt they had sufficient job security to insist on their rights).

Improved job security and the other gains to labor in the postwar years did not come about simply because of a generous attitude on the part of employers or the pressures of a benevolent government. The New Deal had greatly facilitated collective action by private groups in the labor market. The union movement, as we noted in the last chapter, grew rapidly between the passage of the Wagner Act and the middle of the 1950s. By that time, about one-third of the nonagricultural labor force was unionized; the fraction of union employees in the manufacturing sector was much higher. In many of the basic manufacturing industries the unions had managed to unite large segments of the work force into industrywide bargaining units, thus providing them with enormous leverage that could be used against any individual companies with whom they bargained. Once organized, unions did not limit their demands to higher wages; they also sought job guarantees, control over working conditions, and employer-financed "fringe benefits."

Such demands reflected the concern labor had about the threat of instability in the job market. Just how deep these concerns were can be it would cost *nothing,* and therefore the government need not concern itself about collecting revenues to pay for the public works. Deficit spending, Keynes insisted, was the obvious cure for the unemployment of the 1930s.[37]

That the Keynesian cure for unemployment was in fact what got the country out of the Depression is evident enough. Only three years after Keynes published his book, World War II touched off a spree of government spending that eventually pushed all of the western economies to the limits of their productive capacities. The war provided an excuse for government to engage in Keynesian public finance to a degree which would hardly have been possible in peacetime. It is also evident to the contemporary reader that the qualms which inhibited government expansion in the 1930s have been pushed aside; deficit budgets are no longer viewed with great alarm. The New Economics provided a rationale for creating jobs, but beyond that it also provided a rationale for an enormous expansion of government activity on all fronts.

The pressure for government expenditures which developed from the Keynesian framework of analysis developed from more than just a need to bolster expenditures in the face of a short-term crisis. The economists who used Keynesian analysis to develop policy recommendations for the United States in the late 1930s adapted the model to their own view of capitalism and the prospects for growth in this country. That view—best illustrated by Harvard Professor Alvin Hansen's presidential address to the American Economic Association in 1939—was profoundly pessimistic. Reflecting upon the economic situation, Hansen argued that the free enterprise system in the United States had failed. It had developed forces, he contended:

> . . . which tend to make business recoveries weak and anemic and which tend to prolong and deepen the course of depressions. This is the essence of secular stagnation—sick recoveries which die in their infancy and depressions which feed on themselves and leave a hard and seemingly unmovable core of unemployment.[38]

At the time of this speech Hansen was considered to be an influential adviser of the Roosevelt administration.

---

[37] The proposals which Keynes put forth in *The General Theory* touched off a debate that carried on for several decades, and we shall not concern ourselves with the details here. On the intellectual development of the New Economics in the United States, see William Breit and Roger Ransom, *The Academic Scribblers: American Economists in Collision* (New York: Holt, Rinehart & Winston, 1970), Chapters 7-10. A sympathetic account of the emergence of economic policy since Keynes is in Robert Lekachman, *The Age of Keynes* (New York: Random House, 1966); also see Herbert Stein, *The Fiscal Revolution in America* (Chicago: University of Chicago Press, 1969).

[38] Alvin Hansen, "Economic Progress and Declining Population Growth," *American Economic Review,* 29 (March 1939), p. 4.

The "stagnation thesis" was a symptom of both the disillusionment of economists with the performance of the market system during the previous decade and the inability of their own theories to explain the Great Depression.[39] The philosophy of individualism and laissez faire which had been accepted without question only a decade earlier was being challenged as inadequate to deal with the problems at hand. Instead of assuring us that the economic system would correct itself and once again provide our needs, the new explanations of market systems stressed the extent to which markets exposed us to unparalleled fluctuations in prices, jobs, and incomes. Others—particularly the Marxists—had argued that this was so for many years. But the Marxist analysis of class struggle and its recurring predictions of collapse due to the internal contradictions of capitalism provided little assistance to those seeking remedies in the United States of the late 1930s. Neither Roosevelt nor his critics were anxious to embrace the collectivist cures proposed by either the Marxists or more moderate socialists such as Norman Thomas.

One of the most appealing facets of the New Economics of Hansen and his students was that it remained rooted in the traditional view of the market society. The invisible hand was not rejected; they simply pointed to a number of features of modern economies which made it very unlikely that the corrective measures of the marketplace would restore full employment very quickly. Indeed, in the minds of economists such as Hansen, it was unlikely that the forces of growth would ever be powerful enough to guarantee full employment.

The pessimism of the stagnationist view was, therefore, a combination of theoretical and empirical views. The theoretical basis was provided by Keynes' demonstration that it was possible to construct a plausible economic model in which full employment was an elusive goal never attained without some government intervention. Though Keynes' original model was naive in its assumptions and the simplicity of the relationships it postulated, subsequent refinements of the Keynesian model were still able to show that underemployment could persist over long periods of time. The empirical support came from many directions, as the quotation from Hansen's 1939 address to the American Economic Association indicates. Faltering investment, monopolies of both output and labor, and a pessimistic view of technological change all painted a gloomy picture of the future. Added to all this was a strong conviction that the American economy was simply not able to make the adjustments required to maintain both stability and full employment.

The New Deal mixture of theory and empirical observations did not produce a simple bag of cures for the Depression. This put the New Deal-

---

[39] The "stagnation thesis" and its influence on Keynesian thought in the United States is examined in Breit and Ransom, *The Academic Scribblers*, Chapter 8.

ers at something of a disadvantage in arguments with their critics, who, as Theodore Rosenhof notes, had:

> . . . [a] single coherent underlying philosophy which shaped, ordered, and lent consistency to their particular views. They had . . . an inclusive theory of how the economy worked.[40]

That theory, relatively unchanged since the time of Adam Smith, asserted that the market *would* recover if left to its own devices, and that interferences by governments would do more harm than good. Neither side was impressed by the evidence offered by the other. It is hardly surprising to discover, then, that ideological views as well as economic theories influenced the proposals which formed the legislation of the New Deal. Writers who have searched for some consistent theme or plan behind the New Deal have met with only limited success. The adjective most often used to described Roosevelt's ideological approach is "pragmatic." Certainly the emphasis he placed on experimenting with whatever could work fits one connotation of a pragmatic leader. But, as Rosenhof has pointed out, the New Dealers were not as flexible as the pragmatic label would suggest. They tended to be dogmatic once their course was charted. Their flexibility stemmed not from a pragmatic philosophy, but rather from an uncertainty over what caused the Depression—and therefore an uncertainty over how to cure it.[41] The more they looked at the problem, the more convinced they became that the problem was one which was ingrained in the system. The Great Depression was not a random event; it had occurred —and might occur again—because of major flaws in the American economy.

The legacy of the Great Depression, therefore, included more than just some programs of reform which began with what we call the New Deal, and which gradually grew into a "New Frontier" and a "Great Society." The Depression left a generation of Americans deeply troubled over the ability of their economic system—a system dominated by private interests—to provide an acceptable solution to the economic problem. Just when it had seemed that the industrial system was on the threshold of removing any concern about want through the abundance of its productive capacity, the system short-circuited. The uncertainties of the 1930s would be somewhat allayed by the performance of the economic system in the 1950s, but the underlying fear remained—and was passed on.

---

40 Rosenhof, *Dogma, Depression, and the New Deal*, p. 119.

41 Rosenhof provides an excellent analysis of the ideological debates which went on both within the New Deal camp and with critics outside the administration *(Dogma, Depression, and the New Deal)*. Conklin, approaching the New Deal from a different perspective than Rosenhof, also insists that Roosevelt was not pragmatic *(FDR and the Origins of the Welfare State*, pp. 11-13).

Table A The New York Times Stock Index; Average Closing Value

MONTH/YEAR	AVERAGE VALUE	INDEX (1929 = 100)
OCT 1929	311.0	100.0
NOV 1929	200.2	64.4
DEC 1929	204.7	65.8
JAN 1930	206.4	66.4
FEB 1930	221.4	71.2
MAR 1930	226.0	72.7
APR 1930	240.0	77.2
MAY 1930	224.3	72.1
JUN 1930	208.1	66.9
JUL 1930	195.5	62.8
AUG 1930	196.9	63.3
SEP 1930	198.2	63.7
OCT 1930	170.5	54.8
NOV 1930	160.0	51.4
DEC 1930	147.8	47.5
JAN 1931	149.7	48.1
FEB 1931	158.8	51.0
MAR 1931	163.9	52.7
APR 1931	150.1	48.3
MAY 1931	132.8	42.7
JUN 1931	127.6	41.0
JUL 1931	134.4	43.2
AUG 1931	124.4	40.0
SEP 1931	109.3	35.1
OCT 1931	92.3	29.7
NOV 1931	92.7	29.8
DEC 1931	76.3	24.5
JAN 1932	73.9	23.8
FEB 1932	73.6	23.7
MAR 1932	73.7	23.7
APR 1932	57.5	18.5
MAY 1932	47.8	15.4
JUN 1932	40.7	13.1
JUL 1932	38.4	12.3
AUG 1932	57.9	18.6
SEP 1932	65.9	21.2
OCT 1932	58.9	18.9
NOV 1932	57.1	18.3
DEC 1932	55.2	17.7
JAN 1933	57.6	18.5
FEB 1933	54.0	17.3
MAR 1933	55.3	17.1
APR 1933	56.7	18.2
MAY 1933	73.4	23.6
JUN 1933	84.4	27.1

MONTH/YEAR	AVERAGE VALUE	INDEX (1929 = 100)
JUL 1933	89.9	28.9
AUG 1933	85.8	27.6
SEP 1933	89.4	28.7
OCT 1933	80.6	25.9
NOV 1933	81.6	26.2
DEC 1933	84.4	27.1

The index of stock prices in this table is an average of the "high" and "low" index of stock prices reported weekly in *The New York Times*. The monthly figures are an average of the weekly closings in that month.

6

THE STRUGGLE for ECONOMIC SECURITY

Few periods in history have produced more profound changes than the two decades that followed the Great Crash of 1929. The Depression and World War II touched off political repercussions both at home and abroad which dramatically altered the directions of world history. The hegemony of the "western powers" was shattered, and within another twenty years the colonial empires they had fashioned throughout the world were dissolved. The defeat of the Axis powers brought peace to the world in the summer of 1945, but it soon became apparent that the other alliance that had been shaped during the war would not last. By the end of the 1940s the "Cold War" between the West and the Soviets had settled into a pattern which was to dominate world politics for the next two decades. The United States, which for more than a century had struggled (with only limited success) to remain free from Europe's affairs, found itself thrust into the position of leadership of the Free World—a role with which it was not at all comfortable. The structure of American politics was transformed in these years as the influences of the Cold War and other international events took on added domestic importance because of our position as the leading "superpower" in the postwar era.

Superficially, at least, these dramatic changes in the international political and economic structure produced little change in the economy of the United States. Since our economy had controlled nearly half the world's production before World War II, the initial economic impact from the wartime destruction was to produce a further increase in the dominance of American producers in the international marketplace. In many areas, the wartime effort had actually increased productive capacity, and the four years of shortages and forced savings created a surge in the demand for goods which had not been available during the war years. Unlike the situation following other major wars, when the economy had experienced a severe problem of readjustment to peacetime production, the demobilization after World War II was accomplished with only a slight ripple in the economic indicators. Fears that the economic patterns of the 1930s would reemerge in the 1950s did not materialize. Instead, the economy embarked on a period of economic expansion that was to continue, with only minor interruptions, for the next twenty-five years.

AMERICA IN THE INTERNATIONAL MARKETPLACE

A closer look at the postwar economy reveals some significant changes resulting from our new role in the international economy. Despite the fact that two decades of depression and war had left the international marketplace in ruins, the economies of Western Europe and Japan recovered from the chaos of 1945 with remarkable speed. The United States played an important role in that recovery both as a supplier of goods and services (part of which was given as foreign aid), and also as a market for exports from the recovering nations. Between 1950 and 1970, U.S. exports expanded by a factor of almost three and a half, while the value of goods imported into the U.S. grew by a factor of four. The growth in imports was particularly dramatic. By the end of the 1960s American consumers were buying an increasing number of goods which were not "made in U.S.A." At the time, the influence was still small; imports as a fraction of domestic GNP totaled only 4.1 percent in 1970. Still, it was a portent of things to come; in the next decade, the trickle would grow into a good sized stream.[1]

A more immediate indication of changing times in the eyes of most observers was the role of the dollar in international currency markets. By the 1950s the dollar had replaced the pound sterling as the currency most commonly held by other nations as reserves for international exchange. The dollar, in effect, had become the money used in international exchange. In the years immediately following the war, this proved to be a great advantage to Americans; New York was able to extend its economic influence to the point that it had now become the center of international finance. Americans, who had previously shown very little inclination to make investments abroad, now did so in large amounts. American private

---

[1] Statistics on the foreign trade of the United States are from U.S. Bureau of the Census, *Historical Statistics of the United States: Colonial Times to 1970*, (Washington: G.P.O., 1976), Chapter U.

investment in foreign countries rose tenfold between 1950 and 1970. Foreign investors, for their part, found dollars an attractive investment. Among other things, this caused holdings of U.S. government securities to more than double over the same period. The position of the dollar in foreign exchange markets facilitated these developments because of the confidence in the stability of the currency, and, in some cases, because it gave Americans favorable rates at which to exchange goods and services.

Americans soon learned, however, that being the world's banker carried responsibilities as well as benefits. With large holdings of dollars being held as reserves by foreign banks (including central banks), our domestic monetary policy could no longer ignore international repercussions of changes in the United States money markets or in our balance of payments. In the 1950s the dominant position of the United States meant that the dollar was in great demand by other nations seeking to buy our exports—a situation which came to be known as the "dollar shortage." Unfortunately, the shortage proved to be only temporary, and by the mid-1960s the dollar shortage had turned into a dollar glut. The foreign appetite for dollars became satiated, and as the competitive positions of other nations in the international marketplace improved with the postwar recovery, the problem of maintaining the stability of the dollar became more and more troublesome. International trade was still a small fraction of total economic activity, yet it was a dominant consideration in the formulation of domestic economic policy. The tail was wagging the dog, and nothing could be done about this annoying situation, since the United States was committed to maintaining international monetary stability. The full implications of these changes were just beginning to become evident at the end of the 1960s; just how much autonomy our domestic economic policy had surrendered because of economic pressures in the international marketplace would not be evident for another decade.

To most Americans, the new international situation made its biggest economic impact through the taxes required to maintain national security because of the Cold War. In 1950, when the demobilization following World War II was largely completed, and before the new mobilization for Korea had really begun, the U.S. devoted about 7.5 percent of its GNP to national security needs. In twenty years of postwar "peace" the fraction had increased to just over 10 percent, and it did not appreciably diminish during the 1970s. Put another way, between one-fourth and one-third of all government spending in the United States went for defense-related activities.[2] Of course, the impact of the defense budget went far beyond the direct expenditures for military weapons and manpower. The arms

---

[2] The figures for government spending are taken from *Historical Statistics,* Chapter Y, pp. 1120-21. The fractions cited in the text include all those expenditures labeled "National Security," plus those payments to veterans which are not elsewhere classified.

race, and later the competition to reach and control outer space, created powerful pressures for increased expenditures in areas such as education, basic research, and those parts of the industrial sector involved with national defense production. So pervasive were these influences that a new term—the "military-industrial complex"—was coined to describe the economic activity relating to our national security.

While the United States' economy was adjusting to its new role as world leader, it was also responding to internal pressures for economic change. These pressures stemmed in part from the continuing number of economic and technological changes which, although small themselves, resulted in major shifts in the economic structure, and in part from the fact that the reforms of the New Deal had been left unfinished when the nation turned its attention to war in the early 1940s.

Although the period between 1945 and 1970 did not witness institutional changes on the scale of the preceding two decades, the unrelenting pace of progress continued to necessitate numerous adjustments within the economic system. Probably the most visible changes occurred as a consequence of the continued acceleration of technological change. New ideas and techniques appeared in virtually every area of the economy, and it seemed as though they were no sooner introduced than they were being pressed by still newer ideas. "Technological obsolescence" posed a continual challenge to producers seeking the most efficient means of production. The most dramatic technological improvements were those connected with the development of a computer technology which has allowed us to do things which were far beyond the imagination of even the most visionary men only a few decades earlier. Improvements in telecommunications and transportation further reduced the costs of travel and information. A journey which before World War II took five days took only five. hours in 1970; a message from one coast to another which took several minutes to complete in 1945 could be completed in a few seconds—or even milliseconds. By the 1960s a completely new phenomenon—television—had become a prominent part of every household. (In fact, the census of 1970 showed that more homes had television than had indoor plumbing). "Mass media" had revolutionized the way in which information was transmitted in the United States. Millions of people could be reached at home with a single message, and the message could be delivered with a speed and visual impact which could not be approached by either radio or the printed page.

Technological change and our increased involvement in the international economy brought to the forefront another familiar problem: the concentration of economic power. The boom following World War II created an economic climate which encouraged corporate mergers and the expansion of control by large firms. As was the case sixty years earlier, the pressures for increased size of firms were complex, and the apparent increase in the power of giant corporations continued to pose some uncomfortable choices for those concerned about the abuse of economic power in a market society.

As it had for many years, technology favored the creation of large units of production and distribution. In the past, however, these pressures had been greatest in agriculture, manufacturing, and transportation. In the 1950s, technological advances in telecommunications and data processing opened up a vast potential for scale advantages in other sectors as well. Financial institutions found that computers opened up markets for consumer credit on a scale never before feasible. By the 1970s, banking chains could offer "bank cards" not only throughout the United States, but throughout the world. The potential for storing and transmitting large amounts of information on market conditions, inventories, and the distribution of goods or services sold and purchased provided an edge to those firms able to utilize the technology of the computer age.

Initially, the advantage to large firms stemmed from the cost of installing and making good use of the computer equipment. But even as costs of the new technology fell dramatically, there remained substantial advantages to larger firms. The fact that small business computers were available at a reasonable cost could not offset the fact that large firms not only had larger computers, they had larger scales of operation as well. Without computer advances, that scale would have been far more expensive; with computers, the savings possible from large scale marketing were possible.

One of the most important of these advantages was the protection large size afforded against risk. As both the international and domestic markets expanded, the risks involved in competing in these markets increased as well. This was not a new phenomenon; we noted earlier that the advantages of large scale hedging against risks were an important factor encouraging the trust movement of the late nineteenth century. The mergers which created the trusts had tended to remain within a single market (such as oil, sugar, steel, tobacco). In the 1950s and 1960s the pressures towards larger scale produced a new twist: the "financial conglomerate." Rather than seeking control of a given market, these firms emphasized diversification to lessen the risks of doing business in a single market. Financial conglomerates acquired firms of varying size in wholly unrelated product lines and markets. The result was the formation of huge corporations which controlled a vast array of assets scattered over many areas of the economy. Because of their size and ability to transfer resources—whether in the form of cash, people, or products—from one "wholly owned subsidiary" to another, these conglomerates were in a position to concentrate their market power in a single market. The exercise of this power is far more subtle than was the case of the trusts years ago. Today the power of the giant is masked by the appearance of an average sized firm actually doing business. The appearance is deceiving, since the subsidiary can call for help from its parent firm—a luxury not available to the independent firms competing in the same market.[3]

In its most extreme form, this concentration of power in the hands of huge corporations spanned not only many different markets, but many different countries as well. The "multinational corporation"—a firm with offices and sizable holdings of assets in more than one country—has emerged as a significant force in the international economy and many domestic economies as well. In the first twenty years of the postwar era, Americans took little notice of this development. Most of the multi-nationals were, after all, still "American" firms. By the mid-1970s, however, foreign firms had begun to take an interest in American firms and the markets they served. There were some who viewed this interest with alarm.

Two actions particularly underscored the point. In 1969 British Petroleum reached an agreement with SOHIO—the company eventually fashioned from John D. Rockefeller's Standard Oil Trust—which resulted in BP owning a majority of SOHIO stock by the end of the 1970s. The agreement caused little fuss when it took place, but in 1979, when BP and SOHIO pulled out of a proposed oil pipeline from California to the East, Governor Jerry Brown darkly hinted of the dangers posed by decisions "made in London" which vitally affected American interests. At about the same time BP entered the U.S. oil market, Volkswagen of Germany announced plans to open a facility to produce VW Rabbits in Westmoreland County, Pennsylvania. While the creation of jobs was viewed with some joy (particularly in Westmoreland County), the sobering thought occurred to some that the nation's fourth largest auto producer was now a foreign firm. Volkswagen was not the only foreign car maker to enter the U.S.; the 1970s saw a merger between American Motors and Renault, as well as negotiations for a proposed merger between Chrysler and Peugeot. What was unusual about these partnerships is that the *foreign* firm was bailing out the American company. By the end of the 1970s the once dominant American auto industry was reduced to only two firms free from substantial foreign ownership: Ford and General Motors. And they were being challenged on their home ground. In addition to industrial investments such as these examples, foreign interests also moved into banking, real estate, and farming. The fraction of our wealth owned outside the U.S. remains tiny; but the presence in such key areas causes the same sorts of concerns in the United States that other countries have been wrestling with for some time.

The concentration of power in the hands of those who owned capital

---

[3] For a picture of the role of conglomerates in the American economy at the outset of the 1970s, see the essays in Arthur Johnson, ed., *The American Economy: An Historical Introduction to the Problems of the 1970s*, (New York: Free Press, 1974), Chapter 4.

was complicated at this time by an even more dramatic increase in the concentration of power in the labor market. By the 1950s organized labor had succeeded in unionizing between one-fourth and one-third of the labor force. These union members were not spread evenly throughout the economy. They were, in fact, concentrated in precisely those industries dominated by huge firms. This produced an alteration in the behavior of workers and management alike. As we shall note, the new arrangements to determine prices, output, and wages did not necessarily work to the advantage of those outside the industry in question.

The pressures for incremental change were manifested in major changes in the pattern of employment in the United States after the war—both the technological changes and the shifting tastes of consumers and workers in a more affluent society. Manufacturing, long the dominant factor in creating jobs for the economic system, had been declining in importance for some time, and that trend continued after 1945. In 1929 about one third of the labor force was employed in manufacturing industries; in the 1970s the fraction had dropped to less than one fourth. Partially balancing this shift of employment away from manufacturing was a rapid increase the number of people employed by the "service" sector, which grew from just over 11 percent in 1929 and 1946, to 16 percent in 1970. Only government employment had a higher rate of growth than services.[4]

One other change in the composition of the labor force is worthy of particular note. Since the turn of the century, when women constituted about one-fifth of the total labor force, their participation in the labor market had been increasing with each decade. By 1940 women accounted for just over 25 percent of the labor force; at the end of the war that fraction had increased to 30 percent. In the postwar years, participation by female workers accelerated still more, proceeding at a rate almost twice that for the labor force as a whole, and more than three times as fast as the growth in male participants. By 1970 four out of ten workers were women.[5]

The increased participation of women reflected, among other things, an increase in the fraction of the total population which entered the labor force. Up to 1940, the participation ratio stayed right around 52 percent to 54 percent; by 1970 it had jumped to over 58 percent. It is not entirely clear how one should interpret this shift in participation by women in the

---

[4] Between 1946 and 1970, the annual growth rates in employment for these major sectors of the economy are: Services: 3.67 percent; Manufacturing: 0.88 percent; Government: 4.67 percent. The figures are from Harry Scheiber, Harold Vatter, and Harold Faulkner, *American Economic History* (9th ed.) (New York: Harper & Row, Pub., 1976), 448-49.

[5] The statistics on the labor force are from *Historical Statistics*, Chapter D. Between 1950 and 1970 the annual rate of increase for the labor force as a whole was 1.57 percent; for men it was 0.93 percent; for women it was 3.15 percent.

labor force. Was it a reflection of increased opportunities in the labor market (and therefore a reflection of increased economic welfare)? Or was it a response to the pressures of the marketplace forcing many people (particularly married women) to seek employment as a hedge against economic insecurity (and therefore a reflection of a less secure economic position)? What is clear is that the employment patterns in the economy underwent some rather drastic changes in the 1950s and 1960s, and those changes involved both the nature of employment and the type of person who filled the jobs.

WORKING TOWARDS
A GREAT SOCIETY

There was a third group to emerge from the Depression and World War II with greatly expanded economic power: the government. The government—or, more accurately, the people who worked in the government—were committed to using their power to press for a continuation of the institutional reforms begun under the New Deal. The changes introduced by the New Deal had not yet been completed, and to these people the challenge of economic reform in the 1950s and 1960s was to make the ideas of the 1930s (and earlier) a reality. One aspect of reform in this period which stands in marked contrast to other periods we have examined is the manner in which a steady flow of legislation was enacted into law—laws which gradually expanded the beginnings of FDR's New Deal into the "Great Society" of LBJ. The passage of social legislation in the 1930s had demonstrated the impact government—particularly the federal government—could have when the clamor for change became loud enough. Moreover, Roosevelt had brought in many groups who saw for the first time that the government could be an effective mechanism for reform. This mechanism generated a steady pressure for government action. "Creeping Socialism," as its critics liked to call it, scored few dramatic victories comparable to the New Deal, but by consistently pressing for new forms of protection against economic insecurity, the coalition of interests that carried on the New Deal tradition was able eventually to bring about major institutional change.

The New Deal had laid a foundation for change; what was needed were the structures to complete the concept. That concept, in the minds of most New Dealers, had centered on the creation of some institutional arrangements which could protect the individual from the uncertainties and insecurities of the marketplace in an industrial society. This was the legacy of the Great Depression, and it played a major role in shaping the programs which formed the initial efforts at reform in the early postwar years.

The change in economic philosophy which emerged from the Depression and World War II was also a signicant factor in shaping the economic changes of the 1950s and 1960s. However powerful the intellectual logic dictating laissez faire economic policy might have been before 1929, it was swept aside by the force of events in the 1930s. Government intervention to maintain economic stability was not only accepted, it was mandated. People were no longer willing to let the economic problem be solved by the invisible hand of the marketplace.

The greatest fear in 1946 was the spectre of unemployment, as the war industries phased out their military orders and the men in the military rejoined the labor force. In 1946 Congress passed an Employment Act which unequivocally committed the federal government to "promote maximum employment, production, and purchasing power." The act did not go so far as to specifically endorse the New Economics; however, it did create two groups to monitor the economic health of the nation. The Joint Economic Committee was formed to provide Congress with a forum on economic policy, and the Council of Economic Advisers was created to assist the executive with the formulation of economic policy. The Employment Act of 1946 was largely symbolic. But it was a symbol which marked a very real change in philosophy. Henceforth, the government—and more specifically, the people who ran the government bureaucracy—was committed to an activist economic policy to combat economic fluctuations. The debate was no longer whether or not the government should intervene; it was now focused on what form the intervention would take. The experience of the 1930s had not been forgotten, and the change in attitude produced by the Depression was evident in the new law.

The effect this change in attitude and the passage of the Employment Act had on government policy was, according to the author(s) of the 1971 *Economic Report of the President,* quite significant. Taking notice of the twenty-fifth anniversary of the Act, the report noted:

> This much seems clear: The Employment Act of 1946, and the concerns that gave rise to its passage, moved the quality of our economic performance to a higher place on the Nation's agenda. The Act provided a flexible and general statement of what our economic activity ought to do for us.[6]

The commitment to full employment was not the only change in the role of government which had become evident by the outset of the postwar period. In 1927, on the eve of the Depression, the total expenditures at all levels of government in the United States were $11.2 billion—or about 12 percent of the GNP. In 1940, on the eve of our entry into World War II, this fraction had just about doubled; the government was spending $20.42 billion. By 1950 the level of expenditures had risen more than

---

[6] Quoted in Johnson, *The American Economy,* p. 79.

threefold to $70.5 billion, and the share of GNP taken by government spending was now one-fourth. During the decades of the 1950s and 1960s government expenditures continued to grow and by 1970 government was spending $333 billion, or three times the total GNP in 1929! [7] The increased role of government in the economy is reflected by statistics on employment as well as those on expenditure patterns. In 1929 less than 10 percent of the labor force was employed by all levels of government; by the 1980s that fraction had increased to almost 20 percent.[8] The forces which created this enormous expansion of public expenditures were not confined to a single area; the growth of government touched every region and affected every sector of the economy.

The unemployment of the 1930s had revealed just how fragile the economic security of wage earners could be in a market society. The New Deal had made considerable progress in providing greater security to people. Legislation such as social security, unemployment insurance, and the Wagner Act offered help to those who previously had virtually no assurances of security. The changed ideological atmosphere which emerged from the 1930s allowed for a far more active role not only for government, but for other organizations as well. Institutional arrangements were developed to ensure the labor market was no longer left to the whims of supply and demand. For the most part, these pressures for institutional change sought to mitigate the harshness of adjustments necessitated by market forces. Given an impetus to organize by the conditions of the Depression and the legal support of New Deal legislation, people redoubled their efforts to increase economic security after 1946. They acted to improve their economic security directly through government expenditures; through legislation or regulation by the government; and finally, through private collective action.

In 1946 about 400,000—or just more than a quarter of the population over 65 years of age—were covered by social security. By 1970 10.5 million people, or 90 percent of the elderly, were covered. In addition to the more comprehensive coverage, the benefits were greatly increased: In 1946 the average monthly benefit was $23.50; by 1970 it had risen to $114.00.[9] Though the effect was less spectacular, the coverage and level of benefits

---

[7] Measured in 1929 dollars, total government expenditures in 1970 would be about $125 billion, or not quite one and a quarter times the total GNP in 1929. Government expenditures as a percentage of GNP had risen to 30.4 percent by 1970. The figures are from *Historical Statistics,* Chapters F and Y.

[8] These figures understate the importance of government employment, since they count only people directly employed by government units. If the employment in government-related work were included, the fraction would almost surely be as high as one-fourth.

[9] The figures do not include payments connected with the introduction of Medicare and Medicaid in 1965. Even allowing for a substantial rise in the Consumer Price Index during that interval, the increase in real benefits was substantial. Expressed in 1946 dollars, the average benefit paid in 1970 was $57.34, or about 2½ times the earlier level. The statistics are from *Historical Statistics,* Chapter H.

offered under unemployment insurance also increased as states stepped up their efforts to provide greater economic security to the unemployed.

The effect of this enormous expansion in benefits was evident in the level of government expenditures. Between 1946 and 1970 the total direct expenditures on social security and unemployment benefits rose from $1.3 billion to $38.6 billion—or by a factor of thirty! By 1980 the federal government was spending more than $100 billion on social security payments to individuals. Whereas these programs had accounted for only about 5 percent of total expenditures by state and federal governments at the end of World War II, they accounted for over 20 percent during the decade of the 1970s.

The full impact of social security goes far beyond the payments made each year to those who have retired or are eligible for other benefits under the program. Millions of people contribute each year to social security, and to them the program represents their most important form of savings. Just how important this accumulation has been is evidenced by the fact that, according to one estimate, the value of those savings in 1971 totaled almost one-third the value of all personal wealth—more than $1 trillion. Moreover, the same study concluded that social security payments accounted for virtually *all* savings by low income groups.[10] The New Deal commitment to provide at least minimal economic security for older Americans had finally been kept—after thirty-five years of steady expansion from the small foundation announced by President Roosevelt in 1935.

When Roosevelt launched social security, he also pledged protection from another threat to individual economic security: the threat of illness and poor health. The rate of expansion in social security benefits seemed like a speeding train compared to the pace with which a program to deliver widespread health care to Americans was implemented. Despite the spectacular advances medical technology held out as a promise of better health care for everyone, that promise was marred by the possibility of financial ruin from medical bills for all but the well-to-do. Private insurance plans emerged to provide protection against such disasters, and employee pressures—especially in unionized industries—succeeded in having group health plans offered and partially paid for by employers. Yet the coverage was still inadequate; many people could afford neither the cost of insurance nor the cost of basic health care services.

By the mid-1960s, the pressure for expansion of public health programs had reached the point at which some major changes in government programs could be successfully introduced. Traditionally, the effort in public health had always concentrated on the provision of health facilities,

---

[10] Martin Feldstein, "Social Security, Induced Retirement, and Aggregate Capital Accumulation," *Journal of Political Economy*, 82 (September/October 1974), 916.

primarily through government subsidies for hospitals. But this changed dramatically in July of 1966, with the passage of a bill which provided Medicare—medical insurance for the elderly paid for by the federal government. Medicare was soon supplemented by Medicaid, which offered medical services to the indigent. The commitment of the federal government to provide medical assistance for the elderly and the poor marked a major shift in the direction of public health in the United States.

The effects of these new commitments in health were evident in the budgets—as well as the staffing—of public agencies. In 1946 governments were spending $700 million on health-related projects; by 1970 this had grown to $8.8 billion. Federal expenditures on the Medicare program totaled $28 billion by 1975, and an equivalent sum was spent on the Medicaid program. The trend has accelerated since that time; by the 1980s the federal government alone will be spending more than $50 billion annually, and spending on health-related programs by all levels of government will exceed $100 billion.[11]

Another area where direct government expenditures have had a major impact on economic security is the provision of educational services. Education does not by itself guarantee economic security. However, the more educated individuals are, the more likely it is that they will be able to adjust to changes in the economic environment. Because the marketplace insists that people be responsive to change, education can act as a means of increasing flexibility in the labor force. This flexibility is, in a sense, a form of security to the individual worker. Educated people can be more confident that they are capable of learning new skills on the job—which improves their chances of staying on the job. There is also, of course, a more tangible benefit from education which increases security: The educated worker will have a higher productivity—and therefore a higher salary—than a less educated person.

One of the problems with the supply of education provided by the marketplace is that—like medical services—if it is made available on the basis of ability to pay, then many people will be unable to choose to be educated because of the cost. The cost of education includes not only the explicit expenses such as tuition (or some other means) to pay for facilities and staff plus out-of-pocket expenses for books, living costs, and such, but also the implicit costs associated with foregoing a full-time job while still a student. This has proven to be a particularly difficult obstacle for the poor, who are least likely to have accumulated savings with which to finance the time spent as a student. The capital market might have been able

---

[11] It should be pointed out that the statistics for spending on health programs exaggerate the expansion of services provided. Throughout the 1960s and 1970s the costs of medical services rose substantially faster than prices in general. Thus a portion of the increase expenditures went to cover higher costs rather than to buy more services.

to solve this problem by providing loans to aspiring students. But, as we noted in connection with the provision of credit for poor southern farmers in the postbellum South, the costs and the risks associated with loans to low income students are considerable. Though borrowing from financial institutions has provided an important source of funds for middle and high income families, that option has not been readily available to many poor people.

Unlike public health, the commitment by the government to supporting education dates back to the beginning of our nation. Compulsory education had been enacted in every state of the Union within a decade of the end of the Civil War, and public school systems had been created to reduce the burden of education on the individual family. At the time of the Depression, the average American adult had completed 8.6 years of school; by the end of World War II almost half of all persons over the age of 17 had completed high school. Expenditures on public education totaled $4.1 billion in 1946—more than twice the amount budgeted for social insurance and health services combined!

Impressive though these statistics were (and they were quite impressive for the time), the United States in 1946 was on the threshold of an educational revolution. By the 1970s the average American had completed 12.2 grades—or more than a high school education—and the level of expenditures on public education had increased to almost $60 billion, fourteen times the amount in 1946. The fraction of youngsters finishing high school had risen to over 80 percent, and more than half of all high school graduates continued their education in some form. One out of four people aged 20 to 29 had completed four years of college by the end of the 1970s.

Much of this increased effort was simply a reflection of the deeply rooted belief on the part of Americans that public education was an important part of the "American Dream," together with the rising level of income which made education accessible to a larger fraction of the population. The availability of public schools did not, however, reduce the costs of education—particularly education beyond high school—to zero. The higher educational aspirations of young people after 1945 required private as well as public expenditures. (We should note in this regard that private spending on education grew as rapidly as public spending over this period.) One piece of legislation had a particularly pronounced impact on the pattern of education in the United States after World War II. Spurred on by concerns about the return of 12 million servicemen to civilian life at the end of the war, Congress passed the Serviceman's Adjustment Act of 1944—commonly known as the "G.I. Bill." The most significant provision of this bill offered any veteran money to attend school after leaving the armed forces. Between 1947 and 1952 nearly 8 million veterans of World War II received benefits from the original G.I. Bill, at a cost to the government of $14.5 billion. Subsequent renewals of the bill meant that a total of $21.6 billion had been spent on education benefits for veterans by the end of the 1970s.

The effect of this massive aid to education on college enrollment was dramatic. Whereas in the 1930s an average of just over 160,000 degrees had been awarded each year by colleges and universities in the United States; between 1948 and 1952 over 400,000 degrees were awarded annually. In 1950, the peak year, almost half a million degrees were given, a figure not reached again until 1962. Just how important this education was to those who received it can be seen in the difference it made in their incomes; one study estimates that between 1947 and 1959 the incomes of veterans eligible for benefits from the G.I. Bill were increased by about 20 percent due to the education they received.[12]

The long-run impact of the G.I. Bill went well beyond the effects on the veterans themselves. The surge of entrants to colleges created a demand for facilities which resulted in the construction of many new buildings on college campuses across the nation. The new facilities were then waiting when the next generation of students arrived. And, since the G.I. Bill had enabled many of their fathers to attend college, they sought to see that their children would get college degrees as well. By providing a subsidy that induced one generation of young males to go to college, the G.I. Bill altered the educational aspirations of future generations. The fraction of young people continuing beyond high school has continued to rise to the present. Moreover, this increase in the educational level of the population has been shared by both men and women; at the end of the 1970s female students outnumbered their male counterparts on many campuses throughout the United States.

There were other stimuli to education as well. One of the more spectacular was the launching of Sputnik by the Soviet Union in 1957. The Soviet space success jolted the confidence Americans had in their technological superiority and touched off one of the most dramatic races in history: the race to the moon. In the process of winning that race, Americans spent billions of dollars on education and research. The effects were particularly pronounced in higher education, where expenditures almost quadrupled during the 1960s—a marked increase even over the expanded pace of the 1950s.[13]

The enormous expansion of public programs to provide income

---

[12] For an analysis of the impact of the G.I. Bill on veterans of World War II, see Herman Miller, "Annual Lifetime Income in Relation to Education: 1939-1959," *American Economic Review*, 50 (December 1960), 976-80. The statistics for degrees awarded are from *Historical Statistics*, Chapter H.

[13] In 1950 total expenditures on institutions of higher learning were $2.25 billion; in 1960 they totaled $5.6 billion; and in 1970 they totaled $21.0 billion. This means they rose by a factor of 2.42 in the 1950s and by 3.75 in the 1960s.

security, better health, and free education greatly changed the situation of wage earners in the United States. What is particularly noteworthy about these efforts is that, with the possible exception of education, the primary impetus for increased government involvement came from the federal level. In 1980 the federal government budgeted $180 billion for programs related to income security; $53 billion for health programs; and $30 billion for support of education. Together these programs comprised almost one-half (48.9 percent) of all federal government outlays budgeted for that fiscal year.[14] Even when state or local governments were heavily involved, the federal funds played a pivotal role in shaping the direction of change and the level of activity. Fifty years after the onslaught of the Depression, the provision of guarantees for individual economic security occupied a significant fraction of the activity of Americans, and that activity was directed, by and large, from Washington.

That, as we shall see, proved to be both a blessing and a curse. To the extent that federal action provided a stimulus—and the necessary resources—for needed action, the centralization of action was a boon to the reform movement. But to the extent that the control remained with a federal bureaucracy, which was not always responsive to the conditions, the reform of welfare and educational programs elicited resistance from those who objected to the degree of control the federal projects introduced into the local decisions on these programs.

The effort to provide greater security involved more than just government expenditures. At both the federal and state levels, legislation was passed which sought to improve the position of the wage earner in an industrial society. The Fair Labor Standards Act of 1938 instituted a 40 hour work week and a minimum wage nationwide. Like social security, the initial efforts at the federal level were hardly earth shattering; the minimum wage was set at 25 cents in 1938, and had risen only to $1 by 1955. However, the establishment of a floor to wages, together with a ceiling on the number of hours worked, provided a protection to those workers who lacked the economic means to bargain reasonable terms from their employers. This attempt to assist workers at the lower end of the income scale was not an unmixed blessing. The enforcement of a minimum wage inevitably discouraged employers from hiring unskilled labor. To some, therefore, the guarantee of a minimum wage rate offered little comfort, since it eliminated jobs which might have been available if employers were allowed to pay a lower wage.

The rights of workers were further bolstered in the 1960s and 1970s by the expansion of agencies at both the federal and state levels which

---

[14] The figures are from Joseph Peckman, ed., *Setting National Priorities: The 1980 Budget*, (Washington: The Brookings Institution, 1979), p. 229.

judged by the lengths to which organized labor was willing to go in order to secure job security for their members. Disputes between labor and management over issues of economic security contributed to major strikes in important industries such as automobiles, steel, mines and transportation—strikes in which labor won substantial concessions from management on these issues. The gains were not easily won; the labor wars took their toll on both sides. Gradually, both organized labor and corporate management came to recognize and to respect the economic power of the other. In industries where labor was well organized and firms large, labor and management reached an uneasy "understanding" that it was better for both sides to settle their differences at the bargaining table rather than on the picket line.

How much progress has been made by labor in gaining some economic security? Even allowing for the variation in different jobs and different regions of the country, it is clear that labor has succeeded in substantially improving both wages and economic security over the past four decades. The exact degree to which the labor force has been protected by the factors discussed above is difficult to estimate because of the overlapping benefits enjoyed by some workers and the extent to which many workers benefit indirectly from the rules and contracts applying to others. Thus, for example, employees who belong to private pension plans (provided as a fringe benefit in addition to wages) still remain eligible for social security. Union wages and working conditions have an effect upon nonunion workers in many areas, so the impact of a union victory in securing higher wages and/or benefits for their members often spills over into other labor markets. The wages and fringe benefits to white-collar workers (who by the 1960s comprised nearly half the labor force) are tied to the level of benefits given to union workers—even though many of the white-collar workers are not themselves unionized.

Unions, in other words, create a standard by which the benefits for other workers are measured. This is why wage settlements between large unions such as the United Auto Workers, the Teamsters, the United Steel Workers, and the United Mine Workers and their management counterparts are watched with such great interest. These industries have set the pattern followed by other employers and their employees throughout the economy. In a sense, union gains such as pension plans, health benefits, and paid vacations became institutionalized into the labor market. This, as we shall see, has posed a serious problem for unions in their quest for increased membership.

At the other end of the scale, we can identify two groups that remain largely unprotected by any of the guarantees of economic security discussed thus far: agricultural workers and people employed in the service sector of the economy. Until very recently, most of these workers were not even covered by social security, unemployment insurance, or the minimum wage. These people, accounting for perhaps 15 percent of the labor force, remain at the mercy of the market forces in the labor market. For them, the promise of the New Deal put forward four decades ago remains to be fulfilled.

PROBLEMS
ON THE NEW FRONTIER

The changes we have just described affected virtually every American in one way or another. Not surprisingly, some people did not greet new arrangements with great enthusiasm. The growth in the power of labor unions has not gone unnoticed by those outside the labor movement, and measures designed to thwart some of the impetus to organization provided by the New Deal were introduced soon after the war. The growth in government has similarly met with disfavor among various groups—most noticeably taxpayers, who saw their tax bill more than quadruple between 1940 and 1970. Finally, concerns gradually surfaced that the effort to provide security from market forces may have created a drag on the economic system that threatened to take away the gains of economic growth in subsequent years. Each of these concerns merits some attention.

The success of organized labor in making the power to strike an effective economic weapon pointed out the enormous costs and dislocations labor stoppages could impose on others in the economy. In 1947 Congress reacted to this by passing the Taft-Hartley Act. The act amended the 1935 National Labor Relations Act by placing restrictions on some union practices (such as the "closed shop" and the use of secondary boycotts), and giving the president authority to declare an eighty day cooling off period when, in his judgment, a strike threatened to create a national emergency. The threat of a presidential injunction was considered an advantage for management, since they, in effect, were given time to prepare for a strike, while the union was enjoined from any strike activity. In addition to the Taft-Hartley Act, individual states passed legislation—generally termed "right to work" laws—which imposed limits on the extent to which unions could enforce membership requirements on all employees of a company that has already recognized a union. One effect of right to work laws is to weaken the incentive to join unions by making it possible for employees to enjoy full benefits of the union negotiated contract without incurring the full costs of being a union member.

These legislative actions, together with other changes in the structure of the labor market, had a sizable impact on union activity. After winning substantial gains for their members and experiencing increased membership in the 1930s and '40s, union membership peaked around 1955 and has not kept pace with the growth of the labor force thereafter. The appeal of collective action through unionization has seemingly diminished. Some slowing in the growth of union membership could be expected simply because those areas of the labor force in which workers saw the greatest benefits to unionization were the areas organized first in response to the Wagner Act. Those segments of the labor force that were still outside unions by the mid-1950s included many areas where the costs of organizing was quite high—much higher than had been the case in manufacturing and transportation. Union activity among government employees had always been hampered by the restrictions on public employee strikes in most cities and localities—restrictions which limited the options of public employee unions. Organizing low skilled workers in areas such as agriculture and services also proved difficult. Employers were able to resist union pressures by offering mild concessions to workers, and the small size of firms often provided a paternalistic atmosphere in which the union was depicted as an outside (and very sinister) force. The higher degree of job insecurity in agriculture and services also provided employers with an important weapon in their effort to deter would-be union organizers. Finally, organized labor had difficulty penetrating that large group of workers in white-collar occupations who traditionally have identified more with the professional and management groups rather than with labor unions.[15]

Even in those areas where labor retained a sizable fraction of the work force as members and therefore had a great deal of economic power, problems arose over the manner in which that power should be used. The practice of negotiating industrywide contracts brought about situations in which the contract terms were hammered out by negotiators who were sometimes far removed from the production sites themselves. The challenge of representing the individual interests of several hundred thousand members proved at times to be too much. Local dissatisfaction over details of the larger contract made it difficult to sell the contract to the rank and file, and sometimes produced wildcat strikes by locals who defied the union leaders at the top. Such defiance reduced the strength of the union in negotiations, by increasing the probability that the rank and file might reject the negotiated settlement.

In a larger sense, unions became the victim of their own success. For, as the wages, fringe benefits, and prerogatives won by unions for their members became institutionalized and therefore applied to an ever expanding portion of the labor force, the need to join unions became less

15 For an excellent discussion of the problems of unions since the 1950s, see Scheiber, Vatter, and Faulkner, *American Economic History*, pp. 479-82.

pressing. The practice of tying public sector wages to comparable jobs in the private sector meant that government employees were able to benefit from the wage and fringe benefit packages won by unions. Employees found that many firms paid very nearly union scale without insisting that one pay union dues. With the expanding economy of the 1950s and 1960s, unions held their own in absolute numbers, but they did not maintain their relative position in the labor market. Unlike the situation of the 1930s, when workers sought the security offered by collective bargaining, those who entered the labor force in the postwar years discovered that the changed environment of the labor market offered them sufficient security without collective action. Ironically, the unions, which had done so much to bring about that security, were now viewed with disfavor by many of the people who had benefitted most directly from the changes brought about with the help of union pressure. The change in attitude was apparent not only in the rank and file, but in the intellectual climate as well. As a recent article on the role of unions today points out:

> In the 1930s and 1940s, unions were at the center of attention among intellectuals, with most social scientists viewing them as an important positive force in society. In recent years, unionism has become a more peripheral topic and unions have come to be viewed less positively. . . . Economists today generally treat unions as monopolies whose sole function is to raise wages. Since monopolistic wage increases are socially deleterious—in that they can be expected to induce both inefficiency and inequality—most economic studies implicitly or explicitly judge unions as having a negative impact on the economy.[16]

The reaction to the effects of collective action by the unions is not the only instance of resistance to the changes since 1945; government programs to provide economic security have come under fire as well. There seems little question that programs such as social security, improved health care through Medicare and Medicaid, and the educational opportunities offered by increased government funding of schools had widespread support. In some cases (such as education) that commitment antedates the Depression years and reflects a long-standing commitment to public programs.

Nevertheless, some stirrings of discontent appeared almost as soon as the New Deal effort to gain economic security was launched. As the programs expanded, as the total costs rose with the expansion, and as the control of the day to day operation of the programs was shifted away from the local or state government and placed under the influence of the fed-

---

[16] Richard Freeman and James Medoff, "The Two Faces of Unionism," *The Public Interest,* 57 (Fall 1979), 69-70. Interestingly, the disaffection of economists with unions is not confined simply to the conservative or middle-of-the-road viewpoints. Note the comments by radical economists Michael Best and William Connolly, in *The Politicized Economy* (Lexington, Mass.: Heath, 1976), pp. 94-95.

eral government, support for projects viewed as being out of touch with local conditions began to fade. It is interesting to note that in each of the areas we have discussed—social security and welfare, public health care, and public education—one could find signs that public confidence in the government's handling of these programs had diminished markedly by the mid-1970s. This disaffection did not, for the most part, stem from a disagreement over the basic commitments established by earlier reforms; rather, it centered on how those commitments might best be met.

Finally, the reaction to the New Deal reforms centered on fears that the market mechanism had been short-circuited so thoroughly that the economic system was no longer capable of responding to the pressures of economic change. To the extent that labor had succeeded in protecting its economic security by preventing adjustments in the labor market, one of the great benefits of competitive markets—the competitive pressure to employ all inputs as efficiently as possible—had been relaxed. By itself, this relaxation of competitive pressures did not pose a serious problem. Studies of the postwar labor market have tended to show that industries with a highly unionized work force have been able to maintain productivity in all but a few cases. Potential gains in productivity which were lost because of a more rigid structure in the labor market have apparently been offset by the higher productivity gained through the performance of workers more secure in their economic position.[17]

The difficulties of adjustment are compounded, however, in the case in which the efforts of labor to protect itself is complemented by efforts on the part of large firms to similarly seek protection from market changes. Large firms which have substantial market power can afford to offer their workers generous wages and a high level of economic security by using their market position to pass the costs of such security on to consumers. Fluctuations in the demand for their products are met with rigid prices and wages; the adjustment comes in the form of variations in the quantities of goods on the market, and in temporary layoffs of workers—particularly nonunion labor. In the aggregate, such behavior will produce a wider fluctuation in employment and a floor on wages and prices in these industries.

The need for protection from market fluctuations has always been a major inducement for capitalists to seek control over their markets. We saw one manifestation of this in the efforts of railroads to use the Interstate Commerce Commission as a protective shield against competition. In the years following World War II, both organized labor and the manage-

---

[17] See the discussion by Freeman and Medoff, "The Two Faces of Unionism", pp. 76-82.

ment of large firms found that they had a common interest: Neither was anxious to have competitive market forces determine the levels of production or the use of inputs. Both sought institutional arrangements that would offer protection against the uncertainties and costs of market adjustment. Negotiations carried on by representatives of all unions and employers in an industry provided just such a mechanism. Although the antitrust laws (and the rewards from an increased market share) caused most firms to stop short of outright collusion on prices, the wage levels (and therefore the most important determinant of operating costs) were set for each firm by the union contract. Such an arrangement clearly reduced the incentive for firms to engage in either vigorous price competition, or in spirited bidding for labor in the factor markets. The needs of labor for economic security suited the needs of capitalists as well.

It is clear that the efforts by both groups to gain protection have borne fruit; wages and prices in the American economy became increasingly less flexible after 1945. Economists—particularly those economists who admire the efficiency of market decisions—have expressed great concern over this development. It has, they point out, made it more difficult for the economic system to absorb the shocks that inevitably create imbalances in the productive process. Workers thrown out of work in an industry experiencing a slump in demand will not find ready jobs in a stagnant economy, a situation which will make them more anxious than ever to hang on to their present employment and resist any change.

The solution to this problem in the postwar era was to advocate a policy of vigorous economic growth. Growth, economic advisers argued, produces a "social dividend" in the form of an expanding job market that can absorb the costs of adjustments required to maintain efficiency without threatening the economic security of labor or the profit margins of capital. In the growing economy of the 1950s and 1960s, workers moved to more efficient jobs in the expanding sectors, and the rising demand accommodated the output of not only the most efficient, but some of the less efficient firms as well. Stimulating the expansion of GNP was a cornerstone of economic policy in the Kennedy and Johnson years.[18] For a time, the prescription seemed successful. The American economy did grow, and that expansion was accompanied, as we have seen, by an unprecedented

---

[18] For an overview of economic policy in the Kennedy years, see E. Ray Canterbury, *Economics on a New Frontier* (New York: Wadsworth, 1968), especially chapters 4-8. The emphasis on "growth and prosperity" as essential ingredients for economic policy can be seen in the views of two former chairmen of the Council of Economic Advisers: Walter Heller (under Kennedy) and Arthur Okun (under Johnson). See Walter Heller, *New Dimensions of Political Economy* (Cambridge, Mass.: Harvard University Press, 1966); and Arthur Okun, *The Political Economy of Prosperity* (New York: W.W. Norton & Co., Inc., 1970).

effort to secure increased economic security for many groups in the economy. In 1965 President Lyndon Johnson could proudly boast of the progress we were making toward the "Great Society."

But appearances were deceiving. Behind the prosperity of the 1960s lay a nagging problem that could not be suppressed indefinitely. The gains in personal income and added output which were so proudly reported by administration spokesmen were accompanied by far less impressive (and therefore far less publicized) tables of statistics which revealed that the growth of labor productivity was lagging behind the growth in GNP. Indeed, by the late 1960s, the annual increase in labor productivity in the economy as a whole had shrunk to the point at which, in several years, they were negligible. It is a truism that an economy can not sustain a rise in real incomes if comparable increases in productivity are not also recorded; eventually the day of reckoning must arrive. And arrive it did. By the beginning of the 1970s the pressures of an expanding demand for goods and services on a lagging supply had created a new threat to the economic security of Americans: inflation. Ironically, the very safeguards which had been instituted with so much difficulty over the past forty years seemed now to feed the inflationary pressures that eroded away the economic position of the population in the 1970s.

A BACKWARD GLANCE

It seems appropriate to pause at this point and ask: What can we make of our study of economic change to this point? It is more apparent than ever that no single model of institutional change will fit all situations. Yet we should not despair; the themes we stressed at the outset of our inquiry have appeared with some regularity, and we are hopefully better equipped to deal with their complexities having examined a few specific periods of reform.

One of the more obvious points to emerge from our study is the extent to which economic reform in the United States has tended to involve a significant fraction of the population. The groups that have effectively lobbied for change in each of our episodes have represented a fairly broad cross section of interests, and the major reforms have been introduced with a strong consensus. (Ironically, the reform that would probably be judged the greatest success by most observers—the Constitution of the United States—probably had the least degree of consensus to support its introduction.) More often than not, it appears that this consensus was attained through a pooling of individual interests rather than through an appeal to class interest. The individualist ethic that was so prominent in the United States appears as a dominant factor in the process of economic change as well.

The individualistic nature of groups seeking reform brings forward a second observation: In each of our episodes, some real or perceived crisis served as a rallying point around which the reforms could be gathered. On those occasions when an economic or political crisis produced the pressures for change, the nature of the crisis shaped the reforms eventually adopted. In addition to creating a need for immediate action, the crisis served to bring some specific issues into sharper focus, and to define more starkly the manner in which the costs and benefits of various alternatives could be measured.[19]

The presence of a crisis enters into the dynamics of institutional change in a more subtle way as well. In "normal" times the problem confronting those seeking reform is mobilizing collective support to change a system which is, in most respects, functioning well enough. We have emphasized that the appearance of a crisis provides an opportunity not normally available. Once the process of reform is under way, the response to the crisis can be extended (or redirected) to other areas viewed as outside the initial proposals for institutional change. The possibility that opportunity for substantial revisions of the institutional framework appears only at particular points in history may account for the extent to which, at least up to 1929, major changes occurred in clusters. By the same token, the emphasis on a crisis as the initial force promoting reform may also account for the loss of enthusiasm as the movement progresses. Once the crisis passes and the initial responses are completed, the institutional framework is allowed to settle into the new pattern until another challenge comes along to require substantial revisions.

In none of the periods we examined could those pressing for change claim that every item on the original agenda had been adopted. Moreover, after a period of considerable activity, the pressures for additional action tended to subside as the impetus for reform slowed. The success of the reform groups inevitably provided the basis for a reaction by groups that opposed the changes. This was particularly evident in the Reconstruction reforms in the South; in the response to the antimonopoly pressures of the late nineteenth century; and, in more recent times, in the objections to some of the New Deal reforms. Those groups which felt threatened by the changes enacted sought to counter the reform movement with pressures of their own. To the extent that they were able to muster suffi-

---

19 I have cast the discussion of this section in the framework of Davis and North's approach to group action. The argument could also be cast in Marxist terms. In a Marxist approach we would say that the crisis brings out the class interest in a way that allows more effective mobilization of class action.

cient strength, the impact of the reform movement was lessened or even reversed. What emerged as a new arrangement was sufficiently different to satisfy those who wanted some change, yet it was also sufficiently similar to the past to mollify those opposed to such "radical" reforms.[20]

The opposition to each of the reform movements we have investigated in this book brings us back to the question of *economic power*. It does not take a very detailed review of our chapters to note that those reforms that threatened the greatest redistribution of power were the measures that sparked the greatest protest, while those that could be accommodated to the existing power structure were adopted with the least resistance. The politics of reform involve the formation of some base of political and economic power that can not only initiate change, but carry it through as well.

The emphasis on *both* economic and political power is worth repeating, for the absence of either can cripple reform efforts. Thus, for example, we noted that the efforts to provide free blacks with equal status in postbellum southern society failed in part because the economic power remained in the hands of the white landowning class. By the same token, the political pressures generated by the farm protest in the late nineteenth century failed to realize all of their objectives because the reformers lacked the economic power with which to counter the monopoly position of the trusts and railroads. The New Deal, by contrast, provides an example in which economic and political power were transferred to many workers— and the result was a substantial alteration in the way wages and working conditions were determined in the American economy.

Neither the politics nor the economics of institutional change, however, tells the whole story. In each of the periods we examined, the ideological implications of the proposed changes proved to be as important to their ultimate success as was the jockeying for power by various groups seeking to garner benefits or to avoid paying the costs of a particular proposal. Those reforms seen as inconsistent with the prevailing ideological views made far less of an impact than those which went along with the conventional wisdom. Opposition to reforms of the Reconstruction period in the South, and the attempts by large corporations to neutralize the impact of antimonopoly legislation stemmed from ideological convictions as well as economic or class interest. The Thirteenth Amendment may have freed the slaves, but in neither the North nor the South of 1865 was there very strong sentiment favoring genuine equality for blacks. As a conse-

---

[20] Again, the argument cast in terms of the neoclassical reasoning can be adapted to the Marxist framework. In Marxist terminology, the "synthesis" pointed out in the text would have been produced by the conflict between the "thesis" (the initial pressure for reform) and the "antithesis" (the countermovement which developed as a consequence of the reform). This, (in, admittedly, very rough terms) reflects the "solution" of reform and reaction discussed in the text.

quence, the opportunities for freedmen remained far more constrained than those for whites. The reforms of the Progressive Era fell short of achieving control of monopoly power in part because of the reluctance to tread on the prerogatives of private property—a reluctance shared by enough people to frustrate any steps that might actually place direct limits on the accumulation and use of economic power. Even the New Deal, which could appeal to the ideological disillusionment with laissez faire economics following the great collapse, began as a program firmly rooted in the precepts of private ownership of the means of production. It was not until the New Economics and the ideology of the welfare state had been accepted by a broad spectrum of people that the truly significant reforms of the New Deal were able to make substantial headway—more than three decades after Roosevelt's inauguration in 1932.

There is a final lesson taught by the reform movements since the Civil War. As industrialization has proceeded and the influence of markets become more pervasive, a new dilemma has presented itself. Markets stress *individual* decision making, an emphasis very much in keeping with the American ideological support for individual freedom. Yet markets also link us closer and closer together in a system in which the result of individual market decisions produces the need for *collective* action. Nowhere is this dilemma illustrated more clearly than in the search for economic security on the part of the individual in an industrial society. The attempts of people to gain a greater degree of security in an economic environment that seems increasingly beyond their control has been the single most powerful force producing pressures for introducing significant changes in our economic institutions today.

And so we come to the present—the 1980s. Two hundred years of economic progress have not yet solved the economic problem in America. The Full Employment Act of 1946 has not eliminated unemployment any more than the Sherman Antitrust Act eliminated monopoly. And while the vast increase in productive capacity has undeniably improved the standard of living for most Americans, it has not been able to provide us with the economic security which was the dream of the New Deal. Inflation, unemployment, discrimination, inequality . . . the list of contemporary problems is familiar.

We turn now to the problem of coping with capitalism today.

7

COPING
with CAPITALISM
TODAY

Half a century has passed since *Variety* ran its famous banner:

WALL STREET LAYS AN EGG

The egg, like poor Humpty-Dumpty, was broken, and all the king's horses and all the king's men couldn't put things together again. As we have seen, they tried. Although the administrations of eight presidents have struggled to provide a stable economic environment for Americans, the results have not been impressive. In spite of a variety of schemes designed to guarantee greater economic security for Americans, the past five decades of American history have been characterized by depression, war, unemployment and inflation. Apart from a brief interval in the late 1950s and the early 1960s, the American economy has been anything but stable.[1] This is not to ignore the substantial increases in output and real income which characterized the postwar decades. Clearly, Americans today enjoy a material standard of living which is far above that of 1929. Yet, despite our great affluence, our sophisticated technology, and all the lessons we have (we hope) learned since 1929—despite all this, Americans as they enter the 1980s seem insecure about their future—just as they were in 1930.

The fact that, after fifty years of progress, economic security remains an elusive goal is both frustrating and perplexing. Indeed, in some respects,

---

[1] For a summary of the performance of the American economy in the twentieth century, see Robert A. Gordon, *Economic Stability and Growth: The American Record* (New York: Harper & Row, Pub., 1974).

the present situation is even more frustrating than that of the 1930s. The forces that produce economic insecurity today seem to be more subtle than those that produced anxiety during the depression. We have experienced no sudden jolt comparable to the Great Crash. Our incomes are at historically high levels, and most Americans can barely remember a situation in which large numbers of people were unable to find any kind of work. Nevertheless, there is widespread concern about our economic future. Many Americans are apparently convinced that our economic system suffers from some sort of malaise that will prevent it from meeting the challenge of the 1980s.

For most of us, the malaise itself is something of an enigma. Like the doctors who diagnose a number of possible diseases which might account for a patient's symptoms of ill health, economists have detected many potential causes for the relatively poor performance of the American economy in the 1970s. The term most often used to describe the problem—"stagflation"—itself conveys the contradictory nature of the economic illness with which we are dealing. Inflation is universally regarded as a problem of a demand for goods and services which is *too large*. Stagnation, by contrast, is most often associated with a demand for goods and services *too small* to promote either economic growth or inflation. Combining these two disparate phenomena into a single diagnosis may allow us to describe the symptoms, but it reveals some confusions in our explanations of what lies at the root of our present predicament.

Whatever problems the doctor-economists may have in diagnosing the causes of the illness, the patients seeking a cure have no difficulty in identifying the *symptom* which is the source of their discomfort. The problem of which they complain is *inflation*. On the face of it, this is puzzling. Inflation is not a new phenomenon, and virtually any economist knows what causes it. Put very simply, inflation occurs whenever there is too much money chasing too few goods. We may have some difficulties controlling the supply of goods available, but we know who controls the amount of money available in the economy: the government! Accordingly, an obvious way to check inflation would be to have the government reduce the money available for purchasing goods and services. Economists have known this for years, and have suggested a variety of government policies that might accomplish this. Most of the proposals have been tried at one time or another, and several have proven quite effective. Yet we are reluctant to impose these well-known remedies. In other words, we tolerate inflation when we could stop it. Why?

One easy answer is to argue that the cures seem worse than the symptoms of the disease. But as the symptoms become more and more irritating, this argument becomes less and less useful. A second approach claims that our difficulty stems from the fact that we are fighting inflation in much the same way we fight the common cold—searching for relief from the cough and nasal congestion rather than trying to cure the cold itself. This argument suggests that our efforts are directed towards the wrong objective. That raises an interesting question: is inflation the disease—or only a symptom of some much more serious ailment? In trying to find a cure for the effects of the symptom, are we ignoring—perhaps even reinforcing—some much deeper problems within the economic system?

The deeper problems—the malaise that seems to have afflicted our economy in the 1970s—are the focus of this chapter. We will take a closer look at inflation and the rising cost of living in contemporary America. Our interest is in those institutional features of our economic system that contribute to the problems underlying the inflationary spiral, rather than on the policy options that might slow inflation in the short run. Specifically, we shall examine three broad theses which seek to explain the roots of inflation:

1. *The cost of living really is going up.* The United States has always been a land of abundance. We have had plenty of land, natural resources, and raw materials, and our institutional arrangements for the use of natural resources reflects this abundance. That situation may be changing. The current increase in the cost of living may be a warning that our dwindling resource base can no longer support the rate of expansion of activity that has characterized the last century, and that some institutional changes are needed to encourage better use of our resources.

2. *The United States suffers from "institutional sclerosis."* According to this thesis, our economic institutions are unable to adjust to changes in the economic environment. The problem of inflation stems from the inability (or unwillingness) of firms and labor organizations to respond to the pressures of changing market conditions. This approach stresses the extent to which our market institutions are unable to ensure a full employment of resources without encouraging a significant rate of inflation—the dilemma posed by stagflation.

3. *The public sector is too large.* In its simplest form, this view places the blame for inflation on a single culprit: the government and its propensity to spend. On a more complex level, the argument explores the pressures behind the expansion of government programs noted in the last chapter.

None of these theories is wrong. Each includes some arguments which help explain both the perplexing persistence of inflation over the past three decades and the sluggish performance of the economy in the last few years.[2] By exploring each approach we hope to shed light on the

---

[2] A considerable literature on inflation has developed over the past three decades. For the most part, economists have tended to examine the economic relationships which

final question of our study: What do we see in terms of the pressures for institutional change in the economy of the United States today?

THE HIGH COST OF LIVING

What has happened to the cost of living in recent years? Let's look at the facts about prices. Figure 7.1 summarizes the movements in the

Figure 7–1

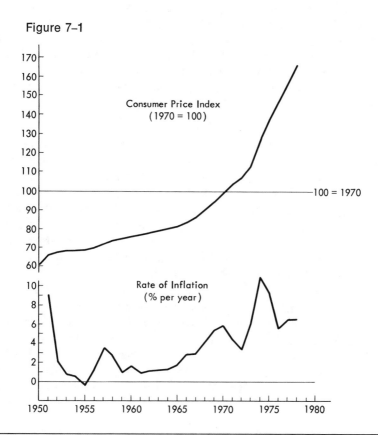

produce increases in the price level without giving a great deal of attention to the political problems involved. An excellent review of the contemporary views on inflation is Samuel Morely, *Inflation and Unemployment* (Englewood-Cliffs, N.J.: Prentice-Hall, 1979); a less technical presentation that highlights some of the difficulties of economic policy is provided by Raburn Williams, *Inflation!: Money, Jobs, and Politicians* (Arlington Heights, Ill.: AHM Publishing Co., 1980). The discussion of inflation in this chapter has drawn on the arguments and data in Joseph Peckman, *Setting National Priorities: The 1980 Budget* (Washington: The Brookings Institution, 1979), especially Chapters 1 and 3, as well as the essays by George Perry and Charles Schultze in *Setting National Priorities: The Next Ten Years*, eds. Henry Owen and Charles Schultze (Washington: The Brookings Institution, 1976).

Consumer Price Index from 1950 to 1978.[3] Examining the figure reveals three important facts about inflation over the past twenty-eight years:

1. Rising prices have characterized the entire postwar period. Out of twenty-eight observations, only a single year—1955—exhibited falling prices (that is, a negative rate of inflation).

2. The tendency has clearly been for the rate of inflation to increase since 1955, and it appears that there was a distinct shift in the rate of inflation during the mid-1960s. From 1950 to 1965, the rate of inflation was 1.9 percent per year. From 1965 to 1978—a period of approximately the same duration—the rate was 5.7 percent. In the last five years of the period (1973–1978) the rate was 7.7 percent! [4]

3. The rate of inflation has shown a tendency to become quite variable, particularly after 1970. During the 1970s, the rate fluctuated from a low of 3.3 percent in 1972 to a high of 11 percent only two years later! Thus, while we might confidently expect that there will be some inflation each year, it has become increasingly difficult to predict just how much inflation there will be in a given year.

There is one additional aspect of inflation which is not evident in the graph. Although prices generally have risen markedly, they have not all risen together. Ideally, a rate of inflation should tell us that *all* prices have gone up by the same proportion. This would mean not only the prices of goods and services consumers purchase, but the prices paid to consumers as well—their wages and salaries, together with all the components which go to make up their income. Of course, that is not the way things really work at all. Some prices (of both products and factors of production) go up much more than others. This poses a problem in our analysis of inflation, for it means that the effects of inflation are not uniform. When prices do not all move together (for example, when wages lag behind the increase in consumer prices), some people may suffer very real losses as a consequence of the shifts in prices, while others may actually gain. The people who lose will eventually seek protection from such losses, and their efforts may be directed towards some institutional arrangement (such as a cost of living allowance) which will protect their income position as prices rise.

---

[3] There are many indices which could be used to measure inflation. The two most common are the Consumer Price Index, which shows the relative cost of a typical "market basket" of consumer goods; and the GNP Deflator, which shows the relative level of prices weighted according to their importance in the composition of GNP. Though the two indices differ slightly in their values from year to year, the general trend over the period we are examining is virtually identical. Unless otherwise noted, references to inflation rates in the text are based on the CPI.

[4] These rates have been computed as the compound rate between the end points of the interval. The simple average of rates shown in Figure 7.1 would be: 1950-65: 1.7 percent; 1965-78: 5.7 percent; 1973-78: 7.5 percent.

Inflation does erode the purchasing power of the dollar, and it is hard to deny the legitimacy of those who seek protection from that effect. A real problem arises here, however. How are we to distinguish between those changes in prices caused by inflationary pressures (too much money chasing the available goods and services), and those price increases that reflect a real scarcity in the marketplace? Let us state the dilemma more concretely by contrasting two hypothetical situations. In the first, we have a rise in all consumer prices of exactly 5 percent. This is tantamount to saying that everyone's income has declined by 5 percent, since we must pay more for anything we buy. Now consider a second case, where the price of one item rises by 50 percent, and the prices of all other items remain unchanged. Suppose we spend 10 percent of our income on that one item whose price has gone up. In this example our index of consumer prices would also rise by 5 percent, even though only one price had changed! [5] Do the two examples have the same implications with regard to consumer decisions and welfare?

Clearly, they do not. In the first case, the general increase in prices created a situation where, if incomes rose by no more than the rate of inflation, consumers would still purchase roughly the same "basket of goods" with their income. (Economists would say that real income had not changed at all.) In this case the effects of inflation might be very slight. In the second case, by contrast, consumers would try to rearrange their purchases to reflect the fact that one commodity is now much more expensive. They will presumably try to shift their purchases to other goods. And, in fact, this is exactly what the market is signaling people to do. For some reason that good has become more scarce, and the increase in price is intended to discourage its consumption. (Economists would note that in this case real income has fallen.) In this situation, giving people an increase in income of 5 percent would tend to offset the market's attempt to ration a scarce commodity. Obviously, we need to know the source of the inflationary pressure before we determine the need for any correction of real income for consumers. We might also note that, in both of our hypothetical situations, providing people with a cost of living allowance will invariably add fuel to the inflationary fires by placing more money in their pockets.

Enough of this idle theorizing (for which economists are so famous). What does all this say about the real world? Allow us one more flight of fancy. Suppose we call the commodity in our second example "energy." Now does the example seem more familiar?

---

[5] The price index is computed by weighting the various prices we pay for commodities. In the example in the text, we are implicitly weighting prices by the proportion of income spent on each item. The overall index of prices would rise by 5 percent, since the one price with a weight of .10 rose by 50 percent; all other prices had no change.

The costs of energy in the United States during the 1970s rose much more rapidly than prices in general.[6] Energy costs figure into virtually every area of both production and consumption, so this sharp increase has been felt throughout the economy. The cost of living in general rose substantially between 1970 and 1978 because something we all need very much had become more scarce. Put bluntly, America is running out of readily available sources of energy, and the deficit between the energy demands of our economy and the ability of the domestic economy to produce enough to meet those demands has been lagging further and further behind for the past decade and a half. The energy crisis—and particularly the problem of locating sufficient supplies of petroleum products in the near future—has been building for a long time. Both the problem and our reaction to it are a reflection of the extent to which America has always taken for granted an abundant supply of natural resources.[7]

Until the early twentieth century there was virtually no attempt in the United States at regulating the use of our resource base. Rights to land—and to the resources on or under the land—were quite literally given away for the first century and a quarter of our nation's existence. The self-interest of the owner of the resources would, according to the view that prevailed until quite recently, regulate the utilization of those resources over time, just as it regulated the production of any other commodity. The possibility that natural resources were exhaustible was not a serious enough threat to worry about seventy-five years ago. The idea that resources might properly be considered a "social good" whose use should be determined by a collective, rather than private, decision, was considered equally farfetched. Some feeble conservation measures were introduced on public lands—particularly the timber and mining lands of the West—early in this century. One could hardly maintain, however, that these efforts represented a major commitment to lowering the rate at which Americans were using up their natural resources. Conservation efforts during the Progressive Era were a mere drop in the bucket when measured against the rapid expansion in resource utilization throughout the economic system in general.

The efforts to preserve forests and protect public lands from exploitation for private use did little to lessen the eventual problem of finding sufficient energy sources for our use in the last quarter of the twentieth

---

6 Energy prices have risen at a rate which is between 1.5 and 2.2 times the rate of inflation for commodities as a whole since 1967. For current data on the rise in consumer prices, see: U.S. Department of Labor, Bureau of Labor Statistics, *CPI Detailed Report,* (Washington: G.P.O., 1979). This bulletin is issued monthly by the bureau.

7 For an excellent background to the oil situation both in the United States and abroad, see the essays by Raymond Vernon, Joel Darmstadter and Hans Landsburg, and Nancy Penrose, in *The Oil Crisis,* ed. Raymond Vernon (New York: W.W. Norton, & Co., Inc., 1976).

century. Our present difficulties stem from a series of decisions made almost a century ago with regard to the sources of energy that could best supply the economic system with its needs. These decisions were not made by a small group with sinister motives; they were made by millions of people seeking the most efficient source of energy. As we entered the twentieth century, the United States seemed to have an almost unlimited supply of crude oil and natural gas. Despite a rapidly growing demand, producers were able to extract enough gas and oil at a very low cost and provide it to those in need of cheap energy. There was little incentive to develop alternative forms of energy to supply our needs. On the contrary, we found an almost endless list of uses for oil and gas: to run our cars, buses, and trains; to heat our homes; to generate a sizable portion of our electricity; and to provide a multitude of synthetic materials. All of that not only greatly altered our lifestyle, but gradually made oil and naural gas an indispensible part of our lives. By 1979, oil and natural gas together accounted for about 70 percent of all energy consumed in the United States.[8]

Given the low price of oil and natural gas over the past fifty years, this dependence on oil was perfectly rational from the standpoint of both producers and consumers seeking to minimize their energy costs. Nor can the producers of oil and gas be viewed as irrational. After all, once the reservoirs of oil and gas were discovered, the costs of extracting the resources from the ground were almost trivial. Why expect a single producer to refrain from marketing his valuable resource while others did not? Although the costs mounted as producers were forced to tap less easily accessible reserves, oil remained a very cheap source of energy. Moreover, through the 1960s, discoveries of new petroleum and gas reserves within the United States kept pace with the depletion of resources from existing known reserves, so reserves remained at a stable level.

In the 1970s that ceased to be the case. The United States began to deplete its known reservoirs of natural gas and oil. As these sources of energy became less and less available, their price rose. It did not, however, rise by an amount that reflected the extent to which the resource base of the United States was being depleted. There was, after all, plenty of oil still available elsewhere in the world. Rather than cut back consumption, the U.S. chose to continue the historical pattern of maintaining a low price of oil by importing it from abroad. For a time, this worked well enough. Between 1950 and 1969 the price of energy actually rose *less* than the Consumer Price Index. But we were living on borrowed time. Industrial economies other than the United States were also experiencing ex-

---

[8] These estimates on energy use are taken from U.S. Senate, Committee on Energy and Natural Resources, *Energy: An Uncertain Future*, 95th Congress, 2nd Session, Publication No. 95-157 (Washington: G.P.O., 1978), p. 326.

panding demands for energy, and they too wished to buy in the international marketplace.[9]

In the 1970s the nations that held the bulk of available oil reserves joined together into a group called the Organization of Petroleum Exporting Countries—*OPEC*. Oil reserves in the OPEC countries are owned by the state, not private producers, and these governments decided to insist on higher prices for their nations' valuable resource. They succeeded to a degree that no one would have thought likely only a few years earlier. Since 1973, when the OPEC producers really began to exercise control over oil exports, the price of crude oil on the international market has risen by a factor of more than three. The United States has tried to hold down the impact of this increase in prices by placing price ceilings on oil products sold in the U.S. But as prices bumped against the ceiling and shortages developed, the costs of oil products rose substantially at home as well as abroad.

Because petroleum products are used throughout the economic system, the rise in the price of crude oil initiated by the OPEC producers had an impact on virtually every price in the United States. (The impact on transportation of goods and people was alone a significant item in the increased costs between 1973 and 1979.) To wage earners, this increase in prices was inflation, and they rather naturally sought to protect themselves by asking for higher wages to cover the higher cost of living. If, however, the increased costs were real (and from the United States' standpoint the OPEC price increases were very real), then increasing consumers' purchasing power through cost of living allowances simply exacerbated the situation. We have both inflation and an energy crisis.

Energy is not the only area in which the real cost of living has gone up in recent years. As our industrial system expands, it not only devours huge quantities of raw materials; it also requires an ever expanding means of disposing of the wastes of production and consumption. The costs of pollution have not, however, been included in the statistics on output, which we use to measure our economic growth. In a few instances, these costs were visible enough and large enough to require government action. But the few examples of such intervention underscore just how great the environmental damage had to be to spur action. Huge areas of forest land were denuded of timber by the practices of lumber companies before any attempt was made to ban the wasteful lumbering techniques which left the land in an unusable state after the trees were harvested. American farmers, after all, had been doing roughly the same thing when they abandoned

---

[9] Over that period of time, the CPI rose 52.3 percent. The price index for fuel oil and coal rose 45.3 percent; the price index for gas and electricity rose by only 26.6 percent. See U.S. Bureau of the Census, *Statistical Abstract of the United States: 1978* (Washington: G.P.O, 1979), p. 490.

soil worn out from intensive farming and moved to new land. The devastation from placer mining for gold in California and mining techniques such as the open pit and strip mining practices in other states is equally vivid testimony to both the disregard of private interests for social costs and the tenacity with which Americans clung to the belief that there was plenty of land. Why worry about a few spoiled acres?

Eventually, of course, the environmental degradation reached a point at which neither the public nor the producers could ignore it any longer. For centuries, two of the most economical methods of disposing of waste have been to dump them into the air or into the nearest body of water. This time honored procedure was practiced to the extent that, in many of our cities, it was no longer healthy to breathe the air or drink the water. At this point people realized that the environment was *not* a limitless dumping ground. Pressures gradually developed for a more accurate reckoning of the costs of production. During the 1960s, government intervention began to exert a steady pressure on producers to consider not only the direct costs of production, but also the impact of their actions on others. If there were additional costs involved in cleaning up production, producers were asked to shoulder the burden. The result was a cleaner environment—but also higher costs of production. And higher production costs meant higher prices to consumers. Environmental protection is not free. Here, again, we have inflation, this time as a consequence of a more comprehensive accounting of the cost of living.

In large measure, these difficulties are a consequence of the extent to which our institutional arrangements rely on a system of property rights which was not well suited to handle either situation. Private owners have not taken the larger implications of their actions into account in allocating energy sources over time, nor have they included the costs of environmental destruction into their production costs. Unfortunately, some of the costs compounded themselves. By delaying collective action of any kind for so long, the magnitude of the problem was allowed to grow to the point at which even the most miminal corrective measures would now create serious readjustments in the economic system.[10]

One might argue that this is all just a problem of adjustment—that by correcting the low price of fuel or insisting that the costs of environmental damage be charged to producers, we can bring the system back into a stable path of economic expansion. There are, after all, a number of alternative energy sources available, and though it may be expensive at first, technologies can be developed to exploit these alternatives. By the

---

[10] Economists have recently devoted a great deal of energy to examining the way in which the economic system interacts with the environment. An excellent collection of essays covering this very broad area are in Robert and Nancy Dorfman, eds., *Economics of the Environment* (New York: W.W. Norton, & Co., Inc., 1977).

same token, once environmental costs are recognized and included in the production decisions, producers will be encouraged to seek cleaner methods of production.

Such an argument points out the important fact that we *do* have options. But it overlooks the extent to which cheap resources have always been an essential part of the American economic system. Americans for the past seventy years have predicated their choice of energy sources on cheap fossil fuels. To be confronted suddenly with a massive increase in the costs of those fuels is a blow that threatens our entire lifestyle. To take one of the most obvious examples, consider the spatial distribution of the population today. Americans have used their cheap energy to fashion a dispersed pattern of residential housing. We live in homes scattered ubiquitously over areas we call "suburbs"—areas which are usually a considerable distance from both our jobs and the places where we do our shopping. How reasonable is it to expect people to suddenly abandon such a lifestyle? Eventually, perhaps, changes in our institutional structure, together with a gradual process of market adjustments, might mitigate the impact of this shift in supply of energy. But in the short run, markets bear the entire brunt of adjustment. And the market system responds to scarcity by raising prices. Normally we do not become concerned over this, since that is what markets are for. In this case, however, the result is an inflation triggered by drastic increases in a few prices, and the effects of those increases are magnified by the inability of people to adjust in the short run. This inflation is not a result of profligate spending by the government or consumers; the cost of living has gone up and our real income has diminished.

THE PROBLEM OF INSTITUTIONAL SCLEROSIS

A market economy should be able to adjust to changes in the relative scarcity of some resources and the recognition of the need for a cleaner environment. Higher prices in one area of the economy should not necessarily lead to higher prices throughout the system. Our dwindling resource base only partly explains the inflationary tendencies of the American economy. To understand why the impact of the energy crunch was so large, we must look at the manner in which prices are determined in our modern economy.

An increase in the general level of prices occurs as a result of the efforts of consumers to purchase more than the system can produce. For inflation to persist over a prolonged period of time, two conditions must be present:

1. Something must be restraining the expansion of supply. Normally, we would expect that the pressures of excess demand in various markets

would encourage producers to expand their output, and in so doing satisfy the demands of consumers. One obvious obstacle to expanded output would be a situation in which all of the resources of the economy are fully employed. Further increases in output would then be impossible. This is why inflation is most often associated with a situation of full employment—such as wartime mobilization of production.

2. Something must be sustaining the ability of consumers to maintain their level of expenditures. In other words, the incomes of consumers must be augmented in some way. If this were not happening, the rise in prices would choke off the excess demand as people found that their money income bought fewer and fewer goods in the marketplace.

The puzzle confronting those studying the American economy over the past decade centers on the first of these two conditions. For the American economy most certainly has not been operating at a full employment level; between 1969 and 1979 the percentage of the labor force unable to find work averaged just over 6 percent. While this might look impressive next to the decade of the 1930s (when unemployment *averaged* 18 percent per year), the 1970s is the only other decade in the twentieth century to exhibit a rate of unemployment above 6 percent. In every other decade, the average level of unemployment has been between 4.4 percent and 5 percent.[11] In recent years the problem of stagflation has been particularly acute. Since 1973, prices have increased by an average of 7.7 percent each year, unemployment has averaged 6.6 percent of the labor force, and the level of gross national product per worker (adjusted for inflation) has not perceptibly increased at all.

There have been other periods when the performance of the American economy has faltered for a few years. Maybe the 1970s are just another interruption of the long term growth trend. As economist Edward Dennison, who was unable to discern any major causes for the problems of the late 1970s in his extensive study of the data on productivity, notes: "It is possible, perhaps probable, that everything went wrong at once." [12] Perhaps. But that should still leave us uneasy over the inability of the American economy to make some adjustment which might reduce the impact of our misfortune. One possible answer with which economists have been flirting for many years is that prices in the American economy have become too insulated from market pressures by institutional arrangements

---

[11] The average rates of unemployment, by decade, are: 1900-1909, 4.39; 1910-1919, 5.04; 1920-1929, 4.67; 1930-1939, 18.23; 1940-1949, 5.17; 1950-1959, 4.51; 1960-1969, 4.78; 1970-1978, 6.23. The figures are computed as a simple average of the annual data. For data before 1970 see: U.S. Bureau of the Census, *Historical Statistics of the United States, Colonial Times to 1970,* (Washington: G.P.O., 1976), p. 135; the figures for 1970-1978 are from U.S. Department of Labor, Bureau of Labor Statistics, *Employment and Earnings,* 26 (September 1979), 21.

[12] Edward F. Dennison, "Explanations of Declining Productivity Growth," in *Survey of Current Business,* U.S. Department of Commerce, 59 (August 1979), Part II, 21.

which have emerged over the past several decades. We have stressed at several points in this book that price changes have both positive and harmful effects on the economic system. On the one hand, they provide an important means for producers to adjust to changing market conditions. At the same time, they create uncertainty for consumers and producers alike. For this reason, many groups have sought protection from the effects of price variation. While these efforts did not always succeed, we can look back on several developments which together have had a significant effect on the price mechanism in the United States.

One of the most obvious ways of protecting oneself from market forces was to create a monopoly situation. Reducing uncertainty in the marketplace has always been a major reason for firms to collude, or for a single firm to seek domination of its market. Having control of supply removes the uncertainty of potential threats from competitors and allows the firm more options in reacting to changes in demand than would be the case under competition. Monopolistic firms do not allow the forces of supply and demand free reign in determining prices; as some economists put it, firms "administer" prices to suit their situations. If the situation calls for keeping prices rigid rather than lowering them, the monopolistic firm can choose to do this.[13] The result is well known: Strongly monopolistic elements in the markets for goods or services tend to produce a resistance to price cuts. They do not, however, exhibit a similar reluctance to increase their prices should demand permit it.

A single monopolist controls only one market, and by himself cannot cause inflation. Widespread monopoly power can, however, impart a very definite inflationary bias to the price system, for two reasons. First, the monopolist will resist lowering prices even in the face of slack demand. Second, monopolists may seek to take advantage of increased demand to increase prices. The manner in which monopoly power affects responses to changes in aggregate demand are sometimes subtle, but the general tendency of monopolists is reasonably clear. As economist Richard Caves puts it:

> . . . [C]oncentrated industries sometimes push up prices when they have not realized all of the monopoly profits potentially available and they see a chance to do so. It apears that during the 1950s powerful oligopolies, with a boost from their equally powerful trade unions, took the lead in pushing up the price level. . . .
> When the economy first swings into a phase of prosperity the prices of concentrated industries actually rise less, but increase when the eco-

---

[13] There are many theories of pricing that account (more or less) for the unwillingness of firms to lower prices even in the face of declining demand. For example, see William Leonard, *Business Size, Market Power, and Public Policy* (New York: Harper & Row, Pub., 1969), Chapter 6; or Richard Caves, *American Industry: Structure, Conduct, and Performance* (Englewood Cliffs, N.J.: Prentice-Hall, 1977) Chapters 4 and 5.

nomic boom tops out. They continue to rise as it slides toward recession, worsening the policy-makers' dilemma of inflation with unemployment.[14]

Such behavior not only has the effect of making the system sensitive to inflation; it also creates fluctuations in the level of employment. Though they can elect to absorb fluctuations in demand by adjusting the level of output offered for sale at a given price rather than lowering that price, monopolists can not eliminate the need for some adjustment. Their price rigidity therefore has the effect of channeling the need for adjustment into the factor markets—and particularly the labor market. Workers are let go when the market for output slackens, and hired back when business picks up again. This means that, although the concentration of monopoly power documented in Chapter 4 unquestionably reduced the degree to which output responded to prices, there was still a good deal of room for flexibility and adjustment in the system as a whole, as long as wages could (and did) fluctuate to accommodate the need for cost saving adjustments on the part of the monopolistic firms.

As one might expect, this situation was not popular with workers. For a long time there was little they could do about it. As we noted in Chapters 5 and 6, industrial workers found themselves increasingly exposed to the vicissitudes of the marketplace. Not until the 1930s did an effective means of countering the economic power of the employer—union organization and collective bargaining—become widespread with the passage of the Wagner Act.

While the development of effective unions enabled workers to gain some economic security, it did not bring about an increase in the price responsiveness of the economic system. In fact, it almost certainly added to the rigidity of prices. In cases in which large firms with monopoly power negotiated with large groups of workers, the interests of employer and laborer to a considerable extent coincided with each other. Labor had a strong interest in maintaining its wage level—particularly when there was a slackening of demand. The main obstacle to doing this was the variation in employment that caused the number of jobs to fluctuate. This problem was solved by labor and management both agreeing on a formalized system of layoffs which permitted the firm to furlough workers on a regular basis in order to create flexibility in the number of hours worked. Everyone was happy. Employers retained some flexibility in the level of employment. Workers maintained a guaranteed wage and retained their job security. Workers who were laid off were assured of being recalled later, and in times of excess demand for labor, employers might ask currently

---

[14] Caves, *American Industry*, p. 79.

employed workers to work overtime rather than bring in new workers. Both employees and employers benefit from the guarantee of a stable work force.

The monopoly position of the firm is crucial to this convenient harmony of interests. The firm and the union must, in effect, agree to maintain the profits from the monopoly of production in the interests of both parties. (Exactly how they split these profits depends on the relative power of the two adversaries; the point here is that *each* has an interest in maintaining the monopoly position of the firm.) Who pays the costs of this arrangement? In the short run it is the consumer who pays the monopoly price. Eventually, we all incur some additional costs because of the rigidities this arrangement introduces into the economic system. Those costs show up in the form of inflation and greater fluctuations in the level of employment.

One of the effects of monopolistic rigidities is to force an increasing burden of adjustment onto those areas of the economy which are neither monopolized nor unionized. Firms and workers in these industries do not have the luxury of a sufficiently strong market position to control their price or wage. Therefore, to the extent that there are fluctuations in the aggregate level of economic activity, and to the extent that the protected industries avoid the costs of adjustment, those costs must be borne by employers and workers who are exposed to more competitive pressures. Firms in these areas are typically small scale enterprises which are "price takers," and which have no choice but to adjust both the price and the output to changed market conditions. Though they represent a relatively small fraction of total production, they play a pivotal role in absorbing any fluctuations in demand. Without such a buffer, monopolistic industries would have a more difficult time avoiding adjustments in the labor market.

Wage rigidity has been introduced into the labor market in more subtle ways than employee organization. There is a tendency for wages to be institutionalized by the manner in which jobs are categorized by employers and employees. Uniform job descriptions are adopted by employers using a common set of criteria to evaluate whether workers are qualified (or, on occasion, even overqualified) for a position. The definition of the specific job describes in some detail both the tasks that worker must perform, and a number of specific qualifications that must be met by workers seeking jobs with that description. Wage rates are attached to job descriptions, not to individuals. If most employers follow these procedures, the result will be a standardization of both jobs and wage rates offered to various groups of workers. The labor market becomes a complex matrix of many little boxes; each little box carries with it a wage and a job description. Employers put the workers into the appropriate box; workers strive to get to the box of their choice, if possible.

What is important to emphasize is that *both* employers and employees find that this institutional arrangement has convenient properties. The advantages to employers are a much more impersonal means of searching for and hiring labor. People are fitted to the job classification—which has been designed to optimize production—rather than the job being matched to the person. Workers find such a system to their advantage because, within each box, there is little competition among workers. The job description and the wage are both fixed, eliminating a major cause of tension among workers. Advancement is made possible in this system by acquiring the necessary characteristics to qualify for a job in a better box. The choice of whether to do so is left up to the worker; with job security from seniority or a union contract, workers are able to resist attempts to arbitrarily move them to different boxes. Like the firm which is willing to raise its price but reluctant to lower its price, the worker introduces elements of rigidity into the labor market which hinder the adjustment of prices throughout the economy.

These institutional arrangements in the labor market not only provide economic security for workers; they also are an important protection against the presence of economic power in the hands of a large employer or strong union. Because the wage rate and accepted working conditions are broadly defined by institutional considerations in many occupations, the exercise of economic power is curtailed. Even though there is little explicit policing of such arrangements, their acceptance by both employees and employers constrains the actions of particular groups which try to obtain substantially different terms. The obvious beneficiaries of this tendency are the small firms and unorganized workers who would be unable to resist the market power of adversaries who are much stronger. The costs of such a policy are much more subtle (and probably also much smaller); they are spread throughout the economy in the form of a lower degree of flexibility in the labor market.

There is, of course, one major sector of the economy that is largely insulated from any impact of changes in the prices of goods or services. Government today accounts for about one-fifth of all goods and services purchased in the economy, and one out of every five employees works in the public sector. Governments do not price their outputs according to the market demand; the price of a public service is its dollar cost to the taxpayer. Government salaries are, for the most part, fixed by rather cumbersome regulations—regulations which do not change as the economic indicators move up or down. Unless the government unit is one whose revenue fluctuates with changes in the economy, employment and wages are not likely to change. To the extent that changes in revenues force some adjustment on the government units, the reaction is similar to that of any other monopolist. Governments economize by offering fewer services.

Public agencies also affect pricing decisions in more subtle ways. Producers—both large and small—seek government aid in stabilizing their prices. And the government has willingly obliged. Probably the most time-honored method of honoring such a request is the enactment of a tariff. Tariffs reduce competitive pressures from abroad and lessen the need for domestic industries to respond to such pressures. It is interesting to note that pressures to enact strong tariff laws come not only from producers threatened by foreign competition, but from their workers as well. Tariffs save jobs. (More accurately, tariffs reduce the need for workers to change jobs.) And there are other, more direct ways of getting protection. In Chapter 4 we examined the way in which the first major government regulatory agency—the Interstate Commerce Commission—evolved from an agency whose purpose was to protect the consumer with government enforced pricing to eliminate competition within the rail industry. Since that time there has been a huge proliferation of regulatory bodies and statutes that fix prices, for the convenience of producers more often than for the protection of consumers. Whatever the merits of such regulation from the standpoint of those who thought it necessary, the effect of government price regulation has invariably been to *reduce* the sensitivity of producers in the regulated industry to changes in prices.

Producers are not the only group seeking protection. The efforts of laborers to gain economic security, which we discussed in Chapters 5 and 6, in most cases involved protection against fluctuations of prices and wages. Minimum wage laws, which serve to establish a floor for wages in virtually every sector of the economy today, are the most obvious manifestation of the demands for some minimal compensation, regardless of skill or performance. The overall effect of these developments—many of which are a direct result of the institutional changes discussed in earlier chapters—is to make the economic system less responsive to changes in market conditions. The American economy, according to economist Mancur Olson, is suffering from "institutional sclerosis"—an inability to generate the economic flexibility so essential to the process of economic adjustment.[15]

There is, it seems, only one means of adjustment left: inflation. Inflation allows adjustment to occur by varying the relative rates at which prices rise. Thus, we noted earlier that energy prices rose far more than other prices, a situation that will eventually discourage consumption of energy. Inflation can create similar adjustments in the labor market. Consider the following example with respect to the salaries of teachers:

---

[15] Professor Olson used the expression in a paper presented to the Cliometric Society in May of 1977 entitled "The Political Economy of Comparative Growth Rates." See his comments in *The Market and the State: Essays in Honour of Adam Smith*, eds. Thomas Wilson and Andrew Skinner (New York: Oxford University Press, 1976), pp. 105-112.

Real wages for secondary school teachers fell about 6 percent from 1972 (the peak for real earnings) to 1977, despite a 36 percent increase in nominal wages. Had the rate of price inflation been zero during this period, a 6 percent wage cut might have been more difficult to accomplish and, indeed, might not have occurred at all.[16]

While it may be effective in some cases, inflation is neither an efficient nor an equitable way to bring about changes in relative prices in the economy. Although it allows for some adjustment in prices that otherwise might be too rigid, inflation also brings forth substantial distortions in the pricing system. Those with greater economic or institutional power will be better able to protect themselves, while the weaker groups will suffer. Inflation—particularly unexpected inflation—produces a pressure to shorten one's time horizon. Long-term plans and investments are disrupted and discouraged in favor of quick returns. As the expectations of inflation become more and more ingrained in the marketplace, these distortions become increasingly pronounced. Inflation is, at best, a very poor way of solving the adjustment problem.

Our emphasis has been on the difficulties of getting units in the economy to adjust supply in response to the inflationary situation. Such difficulties would account for the presence—and the persistence—of unemployment with rising prices. But it does not explain how consumers are able to keep buying goods and services in the face of increasing costs. Why don't rising prices choke off demand? For most of us it would. As our purchasing power dwindled our purchases would decline. But there is one group which has no such budget constraint: the government. We turn now to the third and final aspect of inflation—the growth of the public sector.

A GROWING PROBLEM WITH GOVERNMENT

If you were to ask someone on the street, "What causes inflation?", chances are they would answer "government spending." And they would be right. We have mentioned several times that inflation is a result of excess demand—people trying to buy more than the economic system can produce. In the United States today governments account for one-fifth of all direct purchases, and if we add to that total the transfer payments made to individuals for programs such as social security, Medicare, unem-employment insurance and welfare payments, then public expenditures would total more than one-third the value of GNP. Obviously, the determinants of spending in the public sector have a significant impact on total

---

[16] Peckman, *Setting National Priorities*, p. 62.

spending—and therefore on the rate of inflation. What sets these expenditures apart from those in the private sector of the economy is that the budget constraints that limit government spending are very different from those that confront private individuals or groups. Governments have the power to tax, and in the case of the federal government, simply to print money.

We must not, however, jump to conclusions. The fact that government is directly involved in such a large fraction of our economic activity does not, by itself, mean that the public sector causes inflation. If the government chooses to raise enough tax revenue to pay for the expenditures, then the purchase of goods and services by the government would be offset by a fall in the purchasing power of consumers. Resources would be transferred to the government, but there is no reason to expect that this transfer would generate inflation. In fact, the emergence of a large public sector should greatly increase the potential for stopping inflation by cutting back on existing expenditures, or by raising taxes. In other words, the very size of the government budget should allow it to wield a great deal of influence through the use of monetary or fiscal policy. Yet the historical record shows that government has not done this, despite the commitment that was part of the Full Employment Act of 1946. Why?

The reason most often given is that attempts by the government to reduce expenditures will generate unemployment—and that low rates of unemployment are also an important objective of government stabilization policy. The inability of the government to fight inflation, according to this argument, results from the unfortunate trade off between price stability and low levels of unemployment. The price rigidities identified in the previous section hinder any attempt to apply fiscal or monetary policy as a weapon against inflation. Effective use of these tools requires a situation in which prices are responsive enough to ensure that a reduction in aggregate demand will not cause people to lose their jobs or be temporarily laid off.

Does this mean that we have no option other than to suffer with inflation while trying to create enough jobs to maintain full employment? Not necessarily. While many people would concede that rigidities in the labor market complicate the use of fiscal policy, there remains a nagging suspicion that it is not the dilemma of trading inflation for unemployment that hinders stabilization policy.

An argument can be made that governments are ineffective inflation fighters because they are probably not hurt a great deal by the effects of the inflationary spiral. Indeed, far from suffering from inflation, many government agencies appear actually to be prospering in these inflationary times. Their revenues seem to rise by more than enough to keep up with the rising costs. And, in this case, appearances are not deceiving; government—particularly the federal government—*does* gain from inflation. To see how this is so, think of inflation as a *tax*—a tax levied on all of us to pay for government expenses not covered by revenues collected from various sources. How does government collect this "inflation tax"? By bidding up the prices of the resources they need. Because the federal government has the power to create money, it will be able to outbid private buyers who have only limited sources of funds. Inflation is a very efficient tax, in the sense that it costs the government virtually nothing to collect it, and it is impossible to evade—*someone* must eventually pay the "tax" of higher prices. Using inflation in this fashion is hardly a new idea. Governments in the United States, faced with wartime expenditures, have invariably resorted to deficit spending and increased prices to acquire the resources needed for the war effort. In fact, most of the inflation that occurred prior to the 1970s was a direct result of wartime spending.

Unfortunately, this line of reasoning does not take us very far. For, if government expansion is the cause of rising prices, then we have demonstrated once more that inflation is merely a symptom of some larger disease—in this case our inability to control government spending.

The problem of controlling government spending has been with us for approximately as long as governments themselves have been with us. Traditionally, government spending has been controlled by limiting the revenues available from taxes. For the first century or so of our nation's economic life, this check seemed to work rather well. Though we do not have very accurate estimates of the magnitude of government spending during the nineteenth century, it is a reasonably safe guess that, with the exception of the Civil War years, direct government spending as a fraction of total economic activity seldom exceeded 10 percent of total GNP. Over the last twenty-five years of the nineteenth century, the importance of government spending was almost certainly declining. In 1902, the first year for which we have comprehensive data comparable to our present accounts, the spending on all levels of government totaled $1.7 billion, or just under 8 percent of GNP.[17]

The massive increase in government spending represents one of the most significant structural changes to occur in the past 100 years. And, while it is true that the largest increases occurred during the 1930s and 1940s, it is interesting to note that government spending grew at a more rapid pace than GNP in *every* decade following 1900. The stimulus for government expansion may have been accelerated by the New Deal and World War II, but the growth of government spending was well under way even before the 1930s. We have already examined the changes which produced the increased need for government intervention after 1930. Three

---

[17] The best quantitative estimates of government spending in the nineteenth century are those of Lance Davis and John Legler, "The Government in the American Economy, 1815-1902: A Quantitative Study," *Journal of Economic History,* 26 (December 1966). The statistics on government spending in the twentieth century are from U.S. Census Bureau, *Historical Statistics of the United States, Colonial Times to 1970,* Chapter Y.

aspects of this growth in spending seem particularly important with regard to the discussion of government spending and inflation in the economy today:

1. The economic insecurity of individuals in an industrial society produced government intervention to protect individuals from the risks and costs of market adjustments. This intervention involved the introduction of many payments to individuals, a development that represented a sharp break with the pattern of expenditures before 1930.

2. The emergence of the New Economics, based on John Maynard Keynes' analysis of aggregate spending, led to acceptance of the idea that the government should spend at least enough to ensure full employment, without regard to the possibility of operating with a budget deficit.

3. The importance of the federal government increased enormously between 1940 and 1980. In 1902 federal expenditures represented about one-third of all government payments; by 1940 that fraction had increased to one-half; by the end of the 1970s the federal government accounted for almost two-thirds of all government spending in the United States. Of particular interest for our discussion is the dramatic change in sources of revenue that accompanied this growing importance of the federal government.

The first point reflects changes we have been discussing throughout this book. As people have become exposed to greater risks with the extension of market activity, they have sought to mitigate the effects of these risks by seeking protection from the government. In Chapters 5 and 6 we discussed how the Great Depression accentuated these problems and eventually produced the impetus for institutional changes—changes which established a whole class of government programs we today call "income maintenance" expenditures. We noted how these programs were gradually expanded in the 1950s and 1960s to the point at which, by 1980, such payments account for about 40 percent of all nondefense expenditures by the federal government.

Programs enacted to provide income maintaince are seldom useful for countercyclical economic policy. Imagine the fuss if the government decided that social security checks would be reduced as an anti-inflation measure! Far more likely would be the announcement that they had been increased—even though this would add to the inflationary pressures. Inflationary periods are precisely the time when people seek even greater protection from government support programs. It is not, in other words, simply a fear of rising unemployment that causes the government to hesitate in its fight against inflation; it is a broad commitment to many programs which were instituted to protect people against fluctuations in their real income. These programs affect not only the unemployed, but the retired and those with jobs as well. To eliminate these programs would force a specific subset of the population—those who were involved with income maintenance programs of the government—to bear the major costs of adjusting to whatever was causing the inflationary pressures. The government's commitment to lessen insecurity complicates the options of those who try to act on economists' advice that the most effective cure for inflation is a reduction in government spending.

The second point is closely related to the first. The experience of the 1930s convinced people that the American economy contained elements of instability which might reappear in future years. As we noted in Chapter 5, many economists shared those fears—fears that the economic system of the United States could not recover the pattern of vigorous growth that had characterized the first three decades of the twentieth century. To forestall this possibility, these men advocated a very radical notion: The federal government should set its level of spending with the explicit intention of creating a sufficient volume of spending in the economy to assure full employment. One of the pivotal points in this new approach was that the government should, if necessary, engage in deficit finance to accommodate the level of spending necessary to maintain full employment in the economy. Government debt, according to the new doctrine, was not a burden; it was a debt we owed ourselves.

The view that government should abandon the practice of balancing its budget was not received well in most financial circles. Yet, resistance gradually weakened. The financing of World War II created a huge national debt which seemed to have little effect on the economy. In fact, the debt provided the financial community with highly liquid assets which had virtually no risk attached—something bankers who recalled the problems of the 1930s found particularly attractive. Resistance to government debt had subsided sufficiently by 1964 so that President Lyndon Johnson was able to get a substantial tax cut approved by Congress even though the federal government was running a hefty deficit at that time. The 1964 tax cut is generally regarded as indicating that the New Economics had come of age.[18]

Once they caught on to the idea, politicians pursued the notion with great vigor. Since 1964 there have been only two years (1965 and 1969) when the federal government generated a budget surplus. In the 1970s the federal government has operated with an annual deficit that averaged about $25 billion—or roughly 9 percent of the total outlays each year.[19]

Though it runs counter to most people's intuition on how to manage a budget, the Keynesian approach to deficit spending has one element that struck a responsive chord with politicians and lay people alike. Gov-

---

[18] On the politics of the tax cut and the role of Keynesian economics in bringing it to fruition, see E. Ray Canterbury, *Economics on a New Frontier* (New York: Wadsworth, 1968).

[19] Peckman, *Setting National Priorities*, p. 218.

ernment spending, argued the New Economics, created jobs, and that in itself was an important contribution to economic welfare—particularly when the private sector had been unable to find jobs for people. Beginning in the 1930s, projects were evaluated on the basis of the number of jobs created as well as on the need for the services produced.

Of course, the idea that governments should act to provide or protect the jobs of its citizens is hardly new. Mercantilist writers of the seventeenth and eighteenth centuries, wrestling with the problems created by the presence of unemployment in their times, advocated a variety of measures for governments to deal with unemployment. Even at the height of laissez faire policy in the United States, it was quite permissible to argue for tariffs on the grounds that such barriers to foreign competition protected domestic jobs. What was novel about the New Economics' approach to the problem was its directness: The government should simply put people to work.

As long as the unemployment rate is high, such a policy seems well-founded, since, in an economic sense, the cost of putting idle men to work is zero. But as the labor market begins to tighten, the costs do not remain negligible. As we near full employment and prices begin to rise from the pressures of demand (including government demand), the New Economics prescribes that expenditures be reduced. Maintaining full employment may even call for the government to take in more revenues than it spends. Unfortunately, the nice symmetry in the logic is not reflected in the realities of political economy. Once jobs have been created, they are not easily destroyed simply to fight inflation. Government officials are caught in an unfortunate bind. For while constituents may not like reductions in their government services, they recognize the extent to which it is government spending that drives the prices of everything higher—and threatens their economic security.

The last of our three points is also connected to the other two. As the demands for increased economic security emerged, the response was answered increasingly by the federal government rather than by state or local governments. And it was the federal government that undertook the task of maintaining economic stability under the Full Employment Act of 1946 and the doctrines of the New Economics.

One of the factors that produced this shift of economic activity to the federal government was the problem of finding funds for the new social programs. State and local governments, with their limited tax bases and without the power to create funds, found themselves pressed to meet the demands for expanding social services. Even the federal government could not meet the revenue demands without some additional taxes. The solution appeared during the World War II, when the public was willing to accept a far higher level of taxation due to the emergency situation.

The restructuring of the tax structure of the United States during the war did two things. First, it enormously expanded the revenue base, thus providing funding for the extension of New Deal programs after the war. Second, the shift to a reliance on income taxes rather than property taxes meant that tax revenues rose faster than incomes.

Though the Sixteenth Amendment to the Constitution had provided the federal government with the power to levy an income tax, the potential for gathering large sums from this base was not developed prior to 1940. In that year, the total revenues from taxes on both individual and corporate incomes was $2.5 billion—or about 14 percent of all government revenues. In 1950 income taxes raised just over $27 billion—or about 40 percent of all revenues (and over 50 percent of all taxes collected)! The increased burden of taxes introduced during World War II and only partially removed after 1945 enormously expanded the tax base. What is significant about the income tax is not only the discovery of a new tax base, but the creation of a tax rate structure that would ensure that as income rose, taxes would rise *more!*

The logic that produced this result had nothing to do with either inflation or the growth in government programs. Progressive income tax rates were defended on the grounds that equity considerations demanded that the rich pay a higher fraction than low income groups. But the result proved rather startling—particularly at the federal level—when the inflationary spiral of the 1970s developed. Almost 90 percent of the revenue to the federal government comes from three sources: individual income taxes, taxes on social security, and corporate income taxes. Each of these taxes is, in the economists' jargon, "elastic" with respect to the level of money income. That means that an increase in GNP will produce an even larger increase in federal revenues. Just how substantial this increase will be is a matter of some debate. One sudy suggests that, for every 1.0 percent increase in the price level, government tax revenues will rise by 1.2 percent—or 20 percent more than the rate of inflation! [20]

Ideally, such a tendency should produce the funds with which to fight inflation by producing a surplus for the full employment budget. But in the asymmetrical world of political economy such is not the case. Increased revenues have not encouraged parsimony on the part of the government; they have instead been used to fund the increased costs—and occasional expansion—of programs. For the most part, those programs have been in the areas of income security, which we discussed in previous chapters.

This brings us back to the initial point of this section: the pressures for government expansion are pervasive, and they are not likely to give

---

[20] U.S. Congress, Congressional Budget Office, "The Effects of Inflation on Federal Expenditures," *Background Paper No. 9, June 18, 1976*, (Washington: G.P.O., 1976), p. 21.

way simply to check an increase in the price level. This fact causes us to raise a more basic question: Is it possible that the real cause of inflation is that we want to have our cake and eat it too? Let us quickly review our discussion thus far.

To begin with, we pointed out that there were a number of areas in which it seems as though the increased cost of living was not merely a general rise in prices, but rather a reflection of some very real costs which must be taken into account if we are to maintain our standard of living. Rather than face up to those problems, we have preferred to keep the cost of energy artificially low (which encouraged people to continue squandering it), and we prefer to keep the costs to polluters artificially low (which encouraged them to continue polluting). And to the extent that we *have* forced some adjustments in the prices, we compensate people with a cost of living allowance (which encouraged them to bid up *all* prices rather than responding to the higher prices of scarce items).

Next we argued that the efforts of people to protect themselves from the vicissitudes of market adjustments had created rigidities in the economic system that hampered the process of adjustment to change. The result was an economy that suffered from institutional sclerosis—an inability to adjust to changes or to generate the economic growth which might permit adjustments to be easily absorbed by the labor market.

Finally, we argued that the agency responsible for stemming the inflationary pressures—the government—had very little incentive to do so. In fact, the federal government may have substantial incentives to allow inflation to persist—at least within limits. The common perception that government spending causes inflation is at least superficially correct.

There is a common thread running throughout this discussion of inflation: the tension between market and nonmarket institutions; between individual and collective choice. Capitalism is a system that relies on markets to allocate resources in accordance with the individual decisions of producers and consumers. We have found, in our discussion of economic change, that there are situations in which that combination simply does not work. The recent episode with inflation reveals that we have not yet worked out a means of resolving the conflict between individual and social choices. We "choose" to have inflation, it turns out, because it is viewed as the lesser, not the greater, of the evils confronting us.

But the greater evil still remains. We will someday be forced to make the hard choices we are avoiding today. Accepting inflation amounts to procrastinating—putting off the need to develop some institutional arrangements which can help us forge a consensus on issues such as income security, energy, economic growth, and environmental protection. Those problems will not be solved by inflation, and procrastination may—indeed almost certainly will—make the eventual adjustment that much more difficult.

The vacillation evident in our approach to the issue of inflation points up the extent to which the New Deal, while it pioneered a new era in economic policy and economic thinking, did not provide any political mechanism capable of dealing with the problems of economic policy in the 1980s. The programs discussed in Chapters 4 and 5 each involved the formation of a national coalition, forged in the years of the Great Depression. That coalition, with an emphasis on the need for greater equity in the economic system, was maintained through the 1950s and 1960s, when an expanding economy allowed us to have our cake and eat it, too. But by the 1980s it is becoming apparent that the cake is disappearing. We must make some choices—whether we like it or not.

THE TWILIGHT OF CAPITALISM?

> [Capitalism] has reformed itself and created new problems; it has been forced to make significant concessions to militant mass movements, and it has coopted them, but only in part. Inexorably, for well over a century, it has been collectivizing itself. . . .
> It is the twilight of the bourgeois epoch because this process of collectivization will eventually lead to a transformation of the system itself.[21]

Ever since Marx coined the phrase "capitalism," writers—including non-Marxist writers—have pointed out various tensions (or contradictions) which would ultimately spell the demise of the system of industrial capitalism. Yet, as Michael Harrington's epitaph to the "bourgeois epoch" suggests, capitalism in the United States has managed, one way or another, to adapt (or be adapted) to the changing economic situation.

For the most part we have depended upon a marketplace dominated by private interests to help us solve the economic problem. That is not surprising. For many—perhaps for most—economic activities, markets provide the most convenient means of converting individual actions into a consensus in the marketplace that resolves competing pressures for scarce resources and at the same time manages to reflect the desires of consumers. The success of market institutions is evident enough in the accomplishment of the American economy to date; we have fashioned an industrial system capable of overcoming the challenge of scarcity to a degree which only a few decades ago seemed impossible.

It is not just the observed efficiency of markets that endears capitalism to Americans. Capitalism is also a system that determines the distribution of economic power within our society. The essence of a capitalist economy is private ownership of the means of production, an arrangement nicely consistent with the highly individualistic nature of American culture.

---

[21] Michael Harrington, *The Twilight of Capitalism* (New York: Simon & Schuster, 1976), p. 339.

We have seen how several major reform movements have been stymied by the tenacity with which Americans cling to their individualism. As we noted in the opening chapter of this book, despite all the changes, ours is still very much a capitalist society, one in which ownership of property remains the basis of economic power. Successful though that arrangement has been over the past two centuries, the criticisms persist. And they come from many directions. It is clear that, within our capitalist economy, there are some severe tensions that surface from time to time. We can identify at least three such tensions which were evident in our study of institutional change:

1. The tension produced by the continual need to adjust to new market situations;
2. The tension resulting from the extreme inequality of economic power in the United States throughout our history;
3. The tension created because private and social interests do not always coincide.

The tension created by the problems of economic adjustment has played a prominent role throughout our study. We have found markets to be very efficient allocators of resources, and this makes them valuable in the struggle to overcome the constraints imposed by scarce resources. There are, however, some very real costs which must be incurred if the economic system is to remain efficient over time. Because things do not remain static, there will necessarily be periodic dislocation involving new or different uses for land, labor, and capital. As we have seen, the full extent of these costs—the "price of progress," so to speak—is not included in the market calculations of the cost of production.

Those who stood to gain from increased efficiency (often at little or no cost to themselves) could ignore the costs of adjustments borne by others. If the costs of adjustment were very small, or if the people who gained from greater efficiency were willing to use these gains to compensate those who bore the costs, then the problem was unimportant. This was not, however, the typical situation. The costs and risks associated with market activity were often not trivial, and there was very little pressure put on the winners to share their gains with the losers. In the "good old days" those in command of the system simply ignored such considerations and proceeded with their new (and more efficient) program. The doctrine of laissez faire endorsed such actions as necessary to maintain an efficient economic system, and the legal framework of private property protected the prerogatives of those owning the capital and land to dictate the options open to the third factor of production—labor.

Those who bore the brunt of such adjustments in the marketplace— the farmers, workers and small-businessmen—were not unaware of this situation, and they increasingly began to raise objections. Each of the major reform movements after the Civil War was involved to some extent with the issue of economic security. By the middle of the twentieth century the quest for economic security had become a major political issue in the United States. The reforms suggested by the populists, by the New Dealers, and, more recently, by the followers of the New Economics, have preoccupied two generations of Americans. The lack of economic security is very evident in the United States today.

Market forces have not, in general, acted to reduce another problem that has played a prominent role in our story: the inequality of economic power in the United States today. If anything, the presence of a market economy has reinforced the status quo. Ninety years of antitrust effort has only been able to keep the level of concentration in industry even, and the distribution of income and wealth has become only slightly less concentrated over the same period. The reforms discussed in Chapter 3, and several of the New Deal measures noted in Chapter 4, were deemed necessary (in the eyes of those who initiated them) precisely because of imbalances in economic power—imbalances *created* by markets and industrial capitalism. These reforms encountered strongest resistance in those instances in which the changes threatened to significantly redistribute economic power. Their lack of success in this area is a reminder of just how protected wealth and economic power are in a system of private property rights.

The fact that income remains very unevenly distributed in the United States today should not surprise anyone. Markets allocate goods and services on the basis of who can pay. It is the wealthy members of society who can afford to purchase not only the goods and services they desire, but protection from economic insecurity as well. As one recent report on wealth in the United States today pointed out, the slight lessening of inequality in wealth that has taken place in the last fifty years

> . . . all occurred during periods when the market system was functioning under distress or was in administrative abeyance, specifically the Great Depression and World War II.[22]

The third tension evident in a capitalist system exists because there are many instances in a modern society in which private and social interests are not in harmony with each other. By leaving the means of production exclusively in private hands, a capitalist economy will allow serious distortions to develop. An obvious example of such a case is the question of monopoly power in the marketplace. Firms seeking to maximize their profits will always try to monopolize a market whenever possi-

---

[22] James Smith and Stephen Franklin, "The Concentration of Personal Wealth, 1922-1969," *American Economic Review*, 64 (May 1974), 163. For a further discussion of the distribution of income and wealth in the United States today, and the manner in which the market system protects the wealthy, see Howard Tuckman, *The Economics of the Rich* (New York: Random House, 1975).

ble. Yet the public clearly loses when monopoly is present. It is easy to see that private and social interests diverge.

It is not, however, a simple matter to correct this distortion. The potential conflict between individual and collective interest is such a troublesome problem because, in a market society, virtually *any* economic decision affects *somebody* else! What is "private" and what is "public"? To illustrate the ambivalence people have on this matter, we need only recall how the public interest in keeping railroad rates reasonable was compromised because of the private interest of ensuring that the railroad made a reasonable return. Because the line is seldom starkly drawn, the division between private and public interest remains a subject of continuing controversy. About the only thing one can say for capitalism in this case is that *any* system of property rights will encounter some form of difficulty with the need for both collective and private decisions.

The tensions that exist in a market-capitalist system are neither new, nor are they unique to a capitalist system. There are many ways to solve the "Economic Problem." All of them involve *choice.* The tensions we have identified are difficult for the capitalist system to handle because they call for some of those choices to be made on a *collective,* rather than on an *individual* basis. The problem, as we also noted in the introduction, is that social scientists have not yet devised a process for making collective decisions which will produce solutions that are both unambiguous and consistent with complete freedom on the part of every individual.

There is a further complication. People view the institutional framework—and proposals to change that framework—through the perspective of their ideology. More than fifty years ago, John Maynard Keynes succinctly stated the difficulties which lie ahead, in a series of lectures entitled "The End of Laissez Faire." Keynes observed that:

> . . . [T]he fiercest contests and the most deeply felt divisions of opinion are likely to be waged in the coming years not round technical questions, where the arguments on either side are mainly economic, but round those which, for want of better words, may be called psychological or, perhaps, moral.
>
> Many people, who are really objecting to Capitalism as a way of life, argue as though they were objecting to it on the ground of its inefficiency in attaining its own objects. Contrariwise, devotees of Capitalism are often unduly conservative, and reject reforms . . . which might really strengthen and preserve it, for fear that they may prove to be the first steps away from Capitalism itself. . . . Our problem is to work out a social organisation which shall be as efficient as possible without offending our notions of a satisfactory way of life.[23]

Have we, then, come to the twilight of capitalism? Perhaps we have. Certainly capitalism as Marx saw it has long since faded into the sunset,

---

[23] John Maynard Keynes, *The End of Laissez Faire* (Edinburgh: Neill & Co., 1927).

and the vision of capitalism seen by its more ardent admirers has yet to see the light of day. Be it twilight or dawn, we cope as best we can. And for the most part, Americans have not found serious fault with their institutional arrangements. As Michael Harrington wryly observed, when things were going bad:

> "One simply cursed the accumulation of misfortunes and looked for ways to muddle through.[24]

Table B   Consumer Price Index and Inflation Rate; 1950–1978

DATE	PRICE INDEX	RATE OF INFLATION
1950	61.2	0.98
1951	66.9	9.26
1952	68.4	2.18
1953	68.9	0.75
1954	69.2	0.49
1955	69.0	−0.37
1956	70.0	1.49
1957	72.5	3.56
1958	74.5	2.72
1959	75.0	0.80
1960	76.4	1.71
1961	77.0	0.90
1962	77.9	1.11
1963	78.8	1.21
1964	79.8	1.30
1965	81.3	1.72
1966	83.6	2.85
1967	86.0	2.88
1968	89.6	4.20
1969	94.4	5.37
1970	100.0	5.91
1971	104.3	4.29
1972	107.7	3.29
1973	114.4	6.22
1974	127.0	10.96
1975	138.6	9.14
1976	146.6	5.76
1977	156.0	6.45
1978	166.1	6.44

Source: U.S. Bureau of the Census, *Statistical Abstract of the United States: 1978* (Washington: G.P.O., 1979), p. 490.

---

[24] Harrington, *Twilight of Capitalism,* p. 12.

BIBLIOGRAPHY

AITKEN, HUGH G., *Did Slavery Pay?* Boston: Houghton Mifflin, 1971.

ANDREANO, RALPH, ed., *The Economic Impact of the Civil War* (2nd ed.). Cambridge, Mass.: Schenkman, 1964.

ARROW, KENNETH, *Social Choice and Individual Values.* New Haven, Conn.: Yale University Press, 1951.

BEARD, CHARLES, *An "Economic" Interpretation of the Constitution of the United States.* New York: Macmillan, 1913.

———, and MARY BEARD, *The Rise of American Civilization.* New York: Macmillan, 1927.

BENSEN, LEE, *Merchants, Farmers, and Railroads.* Cambridge, Mass.: Harvard University Press, 1955.

BEST, MICHAEL, and WILLIAM CONNOLLY, *The Political Economy.* Lexington, Mass.: Heath, 1976.

BREIT, WILLIAM, and ROGER RANSOM, *The Academic Scribblers: American Economists in Collision.* New York: Holt, Rinehart & Winston, 1971.

BROWN, E. CAREY, "Fiscal Policy in the Thirties: A Reappraisal." *American Economic Review,* 46 (December 1956), 857–79.

BROWN, ROBERT, *Charles Beard and the Constitution.* Princeton, N.J.: Princeton University Press, 1956.

BROWN, WILLIAM and MORGAN REYNOLDS, "Debt Peonage Re-examined." *Journal of Economic History,* 33 (September 1973), 862–71.

BUCHANAN, JAMES and GORDON TULLOCK, *The Calculus of Consent.* Ann Arbor, Mich.: University of Michigan Press, 1962.

CANTERBURY, E. RAY, *Economics on a New Frontier.* New York: Wadsworth, 1968.

CARSTENSEN, VERNON L., ed., *The Public Lands.* Madison, Wis.: University of Wisconsin Press, 1963.

CAVES, RICHARD, *American Industry: Structure, Conduct, and Performance* (4th ed.). Englewood Cliffs, N.J.: Prentice-Hall, 1977.

CHANDLER, LESTER V., *America's Greatest Depression, 1929–1941.* New York: Harper & Row, Pub., 1970.

CLARK, THOMAS, *Pills, Petticoats, and Plows.* Norman, Okla.: University of Oklahoma Press, 1944.

CONKLIN, PAUL, *FDR and the Origins of the Welfare State.* New York: Harper & Row, Pub., 1967.

DAVID, PAUL A., HERBERT G. GUTMAN, RICHARD SUTCH, PETER TEMIN, and GAVIN WRIGHT, *Reckoning with Slavery: A Critical Study in the Quantitative History of American Negro Slavery.* New York: Oxford University Press, 1976.

DAVIES, WALLACE E., and WILLIAM GOETSMAN, eds., *The New Deal and Business Recovery.* New York: Holt, Rinehart & Winston, 1963.

DAVIS, LANCE, and JOHN LEGLER, "The Government in the American Economy, 1815–1902: A Quantitative Study." *Journal of Economic History,* 26 (December 1966): 514–52.

———, and DOUGLASS NORTH, *Institutional Change and American Economic Growth.* New York: Cambridge University Press, 1971.

DECANIO, STEPHEN, *Agriculture in the Postbellum South: The Economics of Production and Supply.* Cambridge, Mass.: MIT Press, 1974.

———, "Cotton 'Overproduction' in Late Nineteenth-Century Southern Agriculture." *Journal of Economic History,* 33 (September 1973): 608–33.

DEGLER, CARL, *Out of Our Past.* New York: Harper & Row, Pub., 1959.

DENNISON, EDWARD, "Explanations of Declining Productivity Growth," in *Survey of Current Business,* U.S. Department of Commerce. 59 (August 1979), Part II, 1–24.

DICKENSON, OLIVER, *The Navigation Acts and the American Revolution.* Philadelphia: University of Pennsylvania Press, 1951.

DOWNS, ANTHONY, *An Economic Theory of Democracy.* New York: Harper & Row, Pub., 1957.

DORFMAN, ROBERT, and NANCY DORFMAN, eds., *Economics and the Environment.* New York: W. W. Norton & Co., Inc., 1977.

FELDSTEIN, MARTIN, "Social Security, Induced Retirement, and Aggregate Accumulation." *Journal of Political Economy,* 82 (September/October 1974), 905–26.

FINE, SIDNEY, *Laissez Faire and the General Welfare State.* Ann Arbor, Mich.: University of Michigan Press, 1956.

FOGEL, ROBERT W., and STANLEY L. ENGERMAN, "The Economics of Slavery," in *The Reinterpretation of American Economic History,* Robert W. Fogel and Stanley L. Engerman. New York: Harper & Row, Pub., 1971.

———, *Time on the Cross.* Boston: Little, Brown, 1974.

FREEMAN, RICHARD, and JAMES MEDOFF, "The Two Faces of Unionism." *The Public Interest,* 57 (Fall 1979), 69–94.

FRIEDMAN, MILTON, *Capitalism and Freedom.* Chicago: University of Chicago Press, 1962.

———, and ANNA SCHWARTZ, *A Monetary History of the United States, 1867–1960.* Princeton, N.J.: Princeton University Press, 1963.

FROHLICH, NORMAN, and JOE OPPENHEIMER, *Modern Political Economy.* Englewood Cliffs, N.J.: Prentice-Hall, 1978.

FUSFELD, DANIEL, *The Age of the Economist* (3rd ed.). Glenview, Ill.: Scott, Foresman, 1977.

GALBRAITH, JOHN K., *The Great Crash.* Boston: Houghton Mifflin, 1955.

———, *The New Industrial State.* New York: Houghton Mifflin, 1967.

GENOVESE, EUGENE, *Roll, Jordan, Roll.* Boston: Pantheon, 1974.

GOLDIN, CLAUDIA, "The Economics of Emancipation," *Journal of Economic History,* 33 (March 1973), 66–85.

———, " 'N' Kinds of Freedom: An Introduction to the Issues." *Explorations in Economic History,* 16 (January 1979), 8–30.

GOODRICH, CARTER, *Government Promotion of American Canals and Railroads.* New York: Columbia University Press, 1960.

GORDON, ROBERT A., *Economic Stability and Growth: The American Record.* New York: Harper & Row, Pub., 1974.

GUNDERSON, GERALD, "The Origin of the American Civil War." *Journal of Economic History,* 34 (December 1974), 915–50.

HACKER, LOUIS, *The Course of American Growth and Development.* New York: John Wiley, 1971.

———, *The Triumph of American Capitalism.* New York: Columbia University Press, 1940.

HANSEN, ALVIN W., "Economic Progress and Declining Population Growth." *American Economic Review,* 29 (March 1939).

HARPER, LAWRENCE, "Mercantilism and the American Revolution." *Canadian Historical Review,* 23 (March 1942).

HARRINGTON, MICHAEL, *The Twilight of Capitalism.* New York: Simon & Schuster, 1976.

HEILBRONER, ROBERT, *The Worldly Philosophers* (3rd ed.). New York: Simon & Schuster, 1967.

HELLER, WALTER, *New Dimensions of Political Economy.* Cambridge, Mass.: Harvard University Press, 1966.

HERSH, BURTON, *The Mellon Family: A Fortune in History.* New York: Morrow, 1978.

HICKS, JOHN D., *The Populist Revolt.* Norman, Okla.: University of Oklahoma Press, 1961.

HIGGS, ROBERT, *Competition and Coercion: Blacks in the American Economy, 1865–1914.* New York: Cambridge University Press, 1977.

———, *The Transformation of the American Economy, 1865–1914.* New York: John Wiley, 1971.

HOLMES, GEORGE K., "Peons of the South." *Annals of the American Academy of Political and Social Science,* 4 (September 1893), 65–74.

HUGHES, JONATHAN R. T., *The Government Habit: Economic Controls from Colonial Times to the Present.* New York: Basic Books, 1977.

HUNT, E. K., *Class Conflict and Social Harmony*. New York: Wadsworth, 1978.

———, *Property and Prophets*. New York: Harper & Row, Pub., 1971.

HUNT, MERVIN, *The Public Addresses of Franklin Delano Roosevelt*. Los Angeles: De Vorss & Co., 1934.

JOHNSON, ARTHUR M., ed., *The American Economy: An Historical Introduction to the Problems of the 1970s*. New York: Free Press, 1974.

KEYNES, JOHN MAYNARD, *The End of Laissez Faire*. Edinburg: Neill & Co., 1927.

———, *The General Theory of Employment, Interest, and Money*. New York: Harcourt Brace Jovanovich, Inc., 1936.

KOLKO, GABRIEL, *Railroads and Regulation, 1877–1916*. Princeton, N.J.: Princeton University Press, 1965.

———, *The Triumph of Conservatism: A Reinterpretation of American History, 1900–1916*. New York: Free Press, 1963.

LAMPMAN, ROBERT, "Changes in the Share of Wealth Held by Top Wealth-holders, 1922–1956." *Review of Economic Statistics* (1956), pp. 379–92.

LEKACHMAN, ROBERT, *The Age of Keynes*. New York: Random House, 1966.

LEONARD, WILLIAM N., *Business Size, Market Power, and Public Policy*. New York: Harper & Row, Pub., 1969.

LEUCHTENBURG, WILLIAM E., ed., *The New Deal: A Documentary History*. New York: Harper & Row, Pub., 1968.

LUBOVE, ROY, *The Struggle for Social Security, 1900–1935*. Cambridge, Mass.: Harvard University Press, 1968.

MACAVOY, PAUL, *The Economic Effects of Regulation*. Cambridge, Mass.: MIT Press, 1965.

MARSHALL, ALFRED, *Principles of Political Economy* (1st ed.). London: 1890.

MARX, KARL, *Das Kapital*. London: 1867.

MAYHEW, ANNE, "A Reappraisal of the Causes of Farm Protest in the United States, 1870–1900." *Journal of Economic History*, 32 (June 1972), 464–75.

McKENZIE, RICHARD, and GORDON TULLOCK, *The New World of Economics* (revised edition). Homewood, Ill.: Richard D. Irwin, 1978.

MILLER, GEORGE, *Railroads and the Granger Laws*. Madison, Wis.: University of Wisconsin Press, 1971.

MILLER, HERMAN, "Annual Lifetime Income in Relation to Education: 1939–1959." *American Economic Review*, 50 (December 1960), 962–86.

MITCHELL, BROADUS, *Depression Decade: From New Era Through New Deal, 1929–1941*. New York: Holt, Rinehart & Winston, 1947.

MOODY, JOHN, *The Truth About the Trusts*. New York: Moody Publishing Company, 1904.

MORELY, SAMUEL, *Inflation and Unemployment*. Englewood Cliffs, N.J.: Prentice-Hall, 1979.

NORTH, DOUGLASS C., "A Framework for Analyzing the State in Economic History." *Explorations in Economic History*, 16 (July 1979), 249–60.

———, *The Economic Growth of the United States, 1790–1860*. Englewood Cliffs, N.J.: Prentice-Hall, 1960.

NUTTER, G. WARREN, and HENRY A. EINHORN, *Enterprise Monopoly in the United States: 1899–1958.* New York: Columbia University Press, 1969.

OKUN, ARTHUR, *The Political Economy of Prosperity.* New York: W. W. Norton & Co., Inc., 1970.

OLSON, MANCUR, *The Logic of Collective Action.* Cambridge, Mass.: Harvard University Press, 1964.

———, "The Political Economy of Comparative Growth Rates." Unpublished paper (May 1979).

OWEN, HENRY, and CHARLES SCHULTZE, eds., *Setting National Priorities: The Next Ten Years.* Washington: The Brookings Institution, 1976.

PECKMAN, JOSEPH, ed., *Setting National Priorities: The 1980 Budget.* Washington: The Brookings Institution, 1979.

POLLACK, NORMAN, *The Populist Mind.* Indianapolis: Bobbs-Merrill, 1967.

RANSOM, ROGER, "British Policy and Colonial Growth: Some Implications of the Burden from the Navigation Acts." *Journal of Economic History,* 28 (September 1968), 427–35.

———, "Was It Really All That Great To Be A Slave?" *Agricultural History,* 48 (October 1975), 578–85.

RANSOM, ROGER and RICHARD SUTCH, "Credit Merchandising in the Post-Emancipation South: Structure, Conduct, and Performance." *Explorations in Economic History,* 16 (January 1979), 64–89.

———, "Growth and Welfare in the American South of the Nineteenth Century." *Explorations in Economic History,* 16 (April 1979), 207–36.

———, *One Kind of Freedom: The Economic Consequence of Emancipation.* New York: Cambridge University Press, 1977.

REID, JOSEPH D., "White Land, Black Labor, and Agricultural Stagnation: The Causes and Effects of Sharecropping in the Postbellum South." *Explorations in Economic History,* 16 (January 1979), 31–55.

ROSENHOF, THEODORE, *Dogma, Depression, and the New Deal: The Debate of Political Leaders over Economic Recovery.* Port Washington, N.Y.: Kennikat Press, 1975.

SAMUELS, WARREN, "Technology vis a vis Institutions in the *Journal of Economic Issues:* A Suggested Interpretation." *Journal of Economic Issues,* 11 (December 1977), 867–95.

SANDERS, DANIEL S., *The Impact of Reform Movements on Social Policy Change: The Case of Social Insurance.* Fair Lawn, N.J.: R.E. Burdick, Inc., 1973.

SCHEIBER, HARRY N., HAROLD G. VATTER, and HAROLD U. FAULKNER, *American Economic History* (9th ed.). New York: Harper & Row, Pub., 1976.

SCHUMPETER, JOSEPH A., *Capitalism, Socialism, and Democracy.* New York: Harper & Row, Pub., 1947.

SHERMAN, HOWARD, *Radical Political Economy.* New York: Basic Books, 1972.

———, "Technology vis a vis Institutions: A Marxist Commentary." *Journal of Economic Issues,* 13 (March 1979), 175–91.

SILVERSMIT, ARTHUR, *The First Emancipation: The Abolition of Slavery in the North.* Chicago: University of Chicago Press, 1967.

SMITH, ADAM, *An Inquiry into the Nature and Causes of the Wealth of Nations.* New York: Modern Library Edition, 1937.

———, *An Inquiry into the Nature and Causes of the Wealth of Nations.* Chicago: Encyclopedia Britannica, 1952.

SMITH, JAMES, and STEPHEN FRANKLIN, "The Concentration of Personal Wealth, 1922–1969." *American Economic Review,* 64 (May 1974).

SOLTOW, LEE, "Evidence on Income Inequality in the United States, 1860–1913." *Journal of Economic History,* 29 (June 1969), 279–86.

———, *Men and Wealth in the United States, 1850–1860.* New Haven, Conn.: Yale University Press, 1975.

———, and DEAN MAY, "The Distribution of Mormon Wealth and Income in 1857." *Explorations in Economic History,* 16 (April 1979), 151–62.

STEIN, HERBERT, *The Fiscal Revolution in America.* Chicago: University of Chicago Press, 1969.

SUTCH, RICHARD C., "The Breeding of Slaves for Sale and the Western Expansion of Slavery, 1850–1860," in *Race and Slavery in the Western Hemisphere: Quantitative Studies,* eds. Stanley Engerman and Eugene Genovese. Princeton, N.J.: Princeton University Press, 1975, pp. 173–210.

SYLLA, RICHARD, "American Banking and Growth in the Nineteenth Century: A Partial View of the Terrain." *Explorations in Economic History,* 9 (Winter 1972), 197–228.

———, "Federal Policy, Banking Market Structure, and Capital Mobilization in the United States, 1863–1913." *Journal of Economic History,* 29 (December 1969), 657–86.

TAYLOR, GEORGE ROGERS, ed. *The Turner Thesis: Concerning The Role of The Frontier in American History.* Boston: D.C. Heath & Co., 1956.

TEMIN, PETER, *Did Monetary Forces Cause the Great Depression?* New York: W. W. Norton & Co., Inc., 1976.

———, "Freedom and Coercion: Notes on the Analysis of Debt Peonage in *One Kind of Freedom.*" *Explorations in Economic History,* 16 (January 1979), 56–63.

THOMAS, ROBERT, "A Quantitative Approach to the Study of the Effects of British Imperial Policy upon Colonial Welfare: Some Preliminary Findings." *Journal of Economic History,* 25 (December 1965), 615–38.

TUCKMAN, HOWARD P., *The Economics of the Rich.* New York: Random House, 1975.

U.S. Bureau of the Census, *Historical Statistics of the United States, Colonial Times to 1970.* Bicentennial Edition, 2 Parts. Washington: G.P.O., 1976.

———, *Statistical Abstract of the United States: 1978.* Washington: G.P.O., 1979.

U.S. Congress, Congressional Budget Office, "The Effects of Inflation on Federal Expenditures." *Background Paper No. 9, June 18, 1976.* Washington: G.P.O., 1976.

U.S. Department of Labor, Bureau of Labor Statistics, *CPI Detailed Report, September 1979.* Washington: G.P.O., 1979.

———, *Employment and Earnings,* 26 (September 1979). Washington: G.P.O., 1979.

U.S. Senate, Committee on Energy and Natural Resources, *Energy: An Uncertain Future.* 95th Congress, 2nd Session, Publication No. 95–157. Washington: G.P.O., 1978.

VERNON, RAYMOND, ed., *The Oil Crisis.* New York: W. W. Norton & Co., Inc., 1976

WHICHER, GEORGE F., ed. *William Jennings Bryan and the Campaign of 1896.* Boston: D.C. Heath & Co., 1953.

WIENER, JONATHAN, "Planter Persistence and Social Change: Alabama, 1850–1870." *Journal of Interdisciplinary History,* 3 (Autumn 1976), 235–60.

———, *Social Origins of the New South: Alabama 1865–1885.* Baton Rouge: Louisiana State University Press, 1978.

WILLIAMS, RABURN, *Inflation! Money, Jobs, and Politicians.* Arlington Heights, Ill.: AHM Publishing Co., 1980.

WILSON, THOMAS, and ANDREW SKINNER, eds., *The Market and the State: Essays in Honour of Adam Smith.* New York: Oxford University Press, 1976.

WOLF, CHARLES, "A Theory of Non-market Failures." *Public Interest,* 55 (Spring 1979), 114–33.

WOODMAN, HAROLD, *King Cotton and his Retainers.* Lexington, Ky.: University of Kentucky Press, 1967.

WRIGHT, GAVIN, " 'Economic Democracy' and the Concentration of Agricultural Wealth in the Cotton South, 1850–1860." *Agricultural History,* 44 (January 1970), 63–93.

———, "Freedom and the Southern Economy." *Explorations in Economic History,* 16 (January 1979): 90–108.

———, *The Political Economy of the Cotton South.* New York: W. W. Norton, & Co., Inc., 1978.

INDEX